THE SELECTED WRITINGS

OF SIR EDWARD COKE

EDWARD COKE

THE SELECTED WRITINGS

AND SPEECHES OF

Sir Edward Coke

Volume Three

EDITED BY

STEVE SHEPPARD

LIBERTY FUND

INDIANAPOLIS, INDIANA

© 2003 Liberty Fund, Inc.

Frontispiece and cover art:
volume I: Reproduced courtesy of the Right Honourable
the Earl of Leicester and the Holkham Estate.
volume II: Collection of the Editor.
volume III: Corbis-Bettmann.
Material from Robert Johnson, Mary Keeler, Mija Cole, William Bidwell,
Commons Debates, 1628, Yale University Press, 1977:
reprinted by permission of Yale University Press.

08   07   06   05   04   03   P   5   4   3   2   1

Library of Congress Cataloging-in-Publication Data

Coke, Edward, Sir, 1552–1634.
[Selections. 2003]
The selected writings and speeches of Sir Edward Coke
edited by Steve Sheppard.
p.   cm.
Includes bibliographical references and index.
ISBN 0-86597-313-X (pbk.: alk. paper)
1. Law—England.
I. Sheppard, Steve, 1963–
II. Title.
KD358.C65   2003
349.42′092—dc22   2003061935

ISBNs:
0-86597-313-X   volume I
0-86597-314-8   volume II
0-86597-441-1   volume III
0-86597-316-4   set

Liberty Fund, Inc.
8335 Allison Pointe Trail, Suite 300
Indianapolis, Indiana 46250-1684

Contents to Volume III

V

Speeches in Parliament

Coke's service in Parliament brackets his career both in time and in politics, from a devoted servant of the Crown to a leader of the opposition. There are, however, numerous constants among the issues he promoted in each sitting he attended; most important, he sought to secure the privilege of an independent Parliament, with members protected from sanction for their parliamentary speech. Throughout the parliaments of the 1620s, his concern deepened that the King could not be relied on either to allow Parliament its prerogatives of making laws for the subjects and of passing taxes or to protect subjects from arbitrary rule. Those concerns resulted in his support of increasingly powerful protests and petitions to the Crown. The capstone of these was the Petition of Right.—*Ed.*

A. 1593
Three Petitions—Liberty of Speech, Freedom from Arrest, and Free Access for Parliamentarians; Laws; Coke as Speaker

The Parliament of 1593 was a triumph for Coke. He navigated the conflict that arose regarding members' privileges in a series of incidents beginning when Thomas Fitzherbert was arrested for debt between his election to Parliament and the receipt of his election by the sheriff, deflecting his claim that, as a member, he was free from arrest. Coke was a loyal lieutenant to the Queen, burying a bill on reformation of the ecclesiastical courts, while promoting bills to more closely regulate both Puritans and Catholics, and helping to deliver large new subsidies, or taxes. He did much to protect Parliament's recently acquired "ancient" rights.—*Ed.*

February 22, 1593[1]

Speech to the Queen, in the House of Lords

The Speaker's Speech. The queen being come again to the Upper House, the Commons presented the famous Edward Coke, esq. solicitor-general, as their

---

1. [*Ed.:* Cobbett, *Parl. Hist.,* Vol. I. pp. 859–62.]

Speaker; who, being placed at the bar of the house, delivered himself as follows: "Your maj.'s most loving subjects, the knights, citizens, and burgesses, of the house of commons, have nominated me, your grace's poor servant and subject, to be their Speaker. Though their nomination hath hitherto proceeded, that they present me to speak before your maj.; yet this their nomination is, only as yet, a nomination and no election, until your maj. giveth allowance and approbation. For, as in the heavens, a star is but *opacum corpus*,[2] until it have received light from the sun; so stand I *corpus opacum,* a mute body, until your highness's bright-shining wisdom hath looked upon me, and allowed me. How great a charge this is, to be the mouth of such a body as your whole Commons represent, to utter what is spoken, *Grandia Regni,*[3] my small experience, being a poor professor of the law, can tell. But, how unable I am to do this office, my present speech doth tell, that of a number in this house, I am most unfit. For, amongst them are many grave, many learned, many deep wise men, and those of ripe judgments: but I am untimely fruit, not yet ripe, but a bud scarcely blossomed. So, as I fear me, your maj. will say, *Neglectâ frugi eliguntur folia:*[4] amongst so many fair fruit ye have plucked a shaken leaf.—If I may be so bold as to remember a speech (which I cannot forget) used the last parl. in your maj.'s own mouth, Many come hither *'ad consulendum qui nesciunt quid sit consulendum';*[5] a just reprehension to many as to myself also, an untimely fruit, my years and judgment ill befitting the gravity of this place. But, howsoever, I know myself the meanest, and inferior unto all that ever were before me in this place; yet, in faithfulness of service, and dutifulness of love, I think not myself inferior to any that ever were before me. And, amidst my many imperfections, yet this is my comfort; I never knew any in this place, but if your maj. gave them favour, God, who called them to the place, gave them also the blessing to discharge it."

The Lord Keeper's Answer. The *Lord Keeper* having received instructions from the queen, answered him: "Mr. Solicitor, her grace's most excellent maj. hath willed me to signify unto you, that she hath ever well conceived of you since

2. [*Ed.:* an obscure body.]
3. [*Ed.:* the great matters of the Kingdom.]
4. [*Ed.:* The fruit is neglected and the leaves are picked.]
5. [*Ed.:* to give advice who know not what is to be advised about.]

she first heard of you, which will appear, when her highness elected you from others to serve herself. But, by this your modest, wise, and well-composed speech, you give her maj. further occasion to conceive of you, above that which ever she thought was in you; by endeavouring to deject and abase yourself and your desert, you have discovered and made known your worthiness and sufficiency to discharge the place you are called to. And, whereas you account yourself *corpus opacum,* her maj. by the influence of her virtue and wisdom, doth enlighten you; and not only alloweth and approveth you, but much thanketh the lower house, and commendeth their discretion in making so good a choice, and electing so fit a man. Wherefore now, mr. Speaker, proceed in your office, and go forward, to your commendation, as you have begun."

The Speaker's Reply. The lord keeper's speech being ended, the speaker began a new speech: "Considering the great and wonderful blessings, besides the long peace we have enjoyed under your grace's most happy and victorious reign, and remembering with what wisdom and justice your grace hath reigned over us, we have cause daily to praise God that ever you were given us; and the hazard that your maj. hath adventured, and the charge that you have borne for us and our safety, ought to make us ready to lay down ourselves and all our living, at your feet, to do you service.—After this he related the great attempts of her maj.'s enemies against us, especially the Pope, and the king of Spain, who adhered unto him. How wonderfully we were delivered in 88, and what a favour God therein manifest unto her maj. His speech, after this, tended wholly to shew, out of the history of England and the old state, how the kings of England, ever since Hen. III.'s time, have maintained themselves to be the supreme head over all causes within their own dominions. And then reciting the laws that every one made in his time, for maintaining their own supremacy, and excluding the Pope, he drew down this proof by a statute of every king since Hen. III. to Edw. VI. This ended, he came to speak of laws, that they were so great, and so many already, that they were fit to be termed '*elephantinae leges.*'[6] Therefore to make more laws it might seem superfluous. And to him that might ask, *Quid causa ut crescant tot magna volumina legis?* It may be answered, *In promptu causa est, crescit in orbe malum.*[7] The malice

---

6. [*Ed.:* elephantine laws.]

7. [*Ed.:* What is the reason for the growth of such a large volume of law? . . . The immediate answer is, because evil is on the increase in present times.]

of our arch-enemy, the devil, though it were always great, yet never greater than now; and that '*dolus et malum*' being crept in so far amongst men, it was requisite that sharp ordinances should be provided to prevent them, and all care be used for her maj.'s preservation. Now am I to make unto your maj. 3 Petitions, in the name of the Commons; 1st, That Liberty of Speech, and Freedom from arrests, according to the ancient custom of parl. be granted to your subjects; 2d, That we may have access unto your royal person, to present those things that shall be considered amongst us; lastly, That your maj. will give your royal assent to the things that are agreed upon. And, for myself, I humbly beseech your maj. if any speech shall fall from me, or behaviour found in me, not decent and fit, it may not be imputed blame upon the house, but laid upon me, and pardoned in me."

The lord Keeper's further Answer. To this speech, the *Lord Keeper,* having received new instructions from the queen, made his reply. "In which he first commended the Speaker greatly for it; and then he added some examples of history for the king's supremacy in Hen. II. and other kings before the conquest. As to the deliverance we received from our enemies, and the peace we enjoyed, the queen would have the praise of all those attributed to God only. And, touching the commendations given to herself, she said, 'Well might we have a wiser prince, but never should they have one that more regarded them, and in justice would carry an evener stroke, without exception of persons; such a prince she wished they might always have.' To your 3 demands the Queen answereth; Liberty of Speech is granted you; but how far this is to be thought on, there be two things of most necessity, and those two do most harm, which are wit and speech: the one exercised in invention, and the other in uttering things invented. Privilege of speech is granted, but you must know what privilege you have; not to speak every one what he listeth, or what cometh in his brain to utter that; but your privilege is, *aye* or *no.* Wherefore, mr. Speaker, her maj.'s pleasure is, That if you perceive any idle heads, which will not stick to hazard their own estates; which will meddle with reforming the Church, and transforming the Common-wealth; and do exhibit any bills to such purpose, that you receive them not, until they be viewed and considered by those, who it is fitter should consider of such things, and can better judge of them. To your Persons all privileges is granted, with this caveat, that under colour of this privilege, no man's ill-doings, or not performing of duties, be covered and protected. The last; Free Access is granted to her maj.'s person, so that it be upon urgent and weighty causes, and at times convenient; and when her maj. may be at leisure from other important causes of the realm."

April 10, 1593.[8]

Speech to the Queen at the House of Lords

The Speaker's Speech to the Queen at the Close of the Session. April 10, the Queen came to the House of Lords; and the Commons being called up, the Speaker, on delivering the bills, made the following most elaborate Speech on the Dignity and Antiquity of Parliaments:—"The high court of parl. most high and mighty prince, is the greatest and most ancient court within this your realm. For before the Conquest in the high places of the West-Saxons, we read of a parl. holden; and since the Conquest they have been holden by all your noble predecessors kings of England.—In the time of the West-Saxons a parl. was holden by the noble king Ina, by these words: 'I, Ina, king of the West-Saxons, have caused all my Fatherhood, Aldermen and wisest Commons, with the godly men of my kingdom, to consult of weighty matters, &c.' Which words do plainly shew all the parts of this high court still observed to this day. For by king Ina is your maj.'s most royal person represented. The Fatherhood, in ancient time, were these which we call bps. and still we call them rev. Fathers, an ancient and chief part of our state.—By Aldermen were meant your noblemen. For so honourable was the word Alderman in ancient time, that the nobility only were called Aldermen.—By Wisest Commons is meant and signified knights and burgesses, and so is your maj.'s writ, *de discretioribus & magis sufficientibus.*[9]—By Godliest Men is meant your convocation-house. It consisteth of such as are devoted to religion. And as godliest men do consult of weightiest matters, so is your highness's writ at this day *pro quibusdam arduis & urgentibus negotiis, nos, statum & defensionem regni nostri & ecclesiae tangentibus.*[10] Your highness's wisdom and exceeding judgment with all-careful Providence needed not our councils: but yet so urgent causes there were of

---

8. [*Ed.:* Cobbett, *Parl. Hist.,* I, 889–91.]

9. [*Ed.:* of the more discreet and sufficient.]

10. [*Ed.:* for certain difficult and urgent business touching us, the estate and defence of our realm, and of the Church.]

this parl. so important considerations, as that we may say (for that we cannot judge) never parl. was so needful as now, nor any so honourable as this. If I may be bold to say it, I must presume to say that which hath been often said (but what is well said cannot be too often spoken) this sweet council of ours I would compare to that sweet Commonwealth of the little bees:

Sic enim parvis componere magna solebam.[11]

The little bees have but one governor whom they all serve, he is their king, *quia latera habet latiora;*[12] he is placed in the midst of their habitations, *ut in tutissima turri.*[13] They forage abroad, sucking honey from every flower to bring to their king. *Ignavum fucos pecus à praesepibus arcent.*[14] The drones they drive away out of their hives, *non habentes aculeos.*[15] And whoso assails their king, in him *immittunt aculeos, & tamen rex ipse est sine aculeo.*[16]—Your maj. is that princely governor and noble queen, whom we all serve; being protected under the shadow of your wings we live, and wish you may ever sit upon your throne over us. And whosoever shall not say Amen, for them we pray *ut convertantur ne pereant, & ut confundantur ne noceant.*[17] Under your happy govt. we live upon honey, we suck upon every sweet flower: but where the bee sucketh honey, there also the spider draweth poison. Some such venoms there be. But such drones and door bees we will expel the hive and serve your maj. and withstand any enemy that shall assault you. Our lands, our goods, our lives are prostrate at your feet to be commanded. Yea, and (thanked be God, and honour be to your maj. for it) such is the power and force of your subjects, that of their own strength they are able to encounter your greatest enemies. And though we be such, yet have we a prince that is *sine aculco;*[18] so full of that clemency is your maj. I fear I have been too long, and therefore to come now to your Laws.—The Laws we have conferred upon this session of so honourable a parl. are of two natures; the one such as have life but are ready

---

11. [*Ed.:* For thus great things are built by little things.]
12. [*Ed.:* because he has broader sides;]
13. [*Ed.:* as in the safest tower.]
14. [*Ed.:* They drive the drones out of their dwellings.]
15. [*Ed.:* having no stings.]
16. [*Ed.:* they insert their stings, and yet the king himself is without a sting.]
17. [*Ed.:* that they be converted lest they perish, and that they be confounded lest they cause harm.]
18. [*Ed.:* without sting.]

to die, except your maj. breathe life into them again; the other are laws that never had life, but, being void of life, do come to your maj. to seek life.— The first sort are those laws that had continuances until this parl. and are now to receive new life or are to die for ever. The other, that I term capable of life, are those which are newly made, but have no essence until your maj. giveth them life.—Two laws there are, but I must give the honour where it is due; for they come from the noble wise Lords of the upper house; the most hon. and beneficial laws that could be desired: the one a Confirmation of all Letters Patents, from your maj.'s most noble father, of all Ecclesiastical Livings, which that king took from those superstitious monasteries and priories, and translated them to the erecting and setting up of many foundations of Cathedral Churches and Colleges, greatly furthering the maintenance of learning and true religion.—The other law to suppress the obstinate Recusant and the dangerous sectary, both very pernicious to your govt.—Lastly, your loving and obedient subjects, the Commons of the lower house, humbly and with all dutiful thanks, stand bound unto your gracious goodness for your general and large Pardon granted unto them, wherein many great offences are pardoned. But it extendeth only to offences done before the parl. I have many ways, since the beginning of this parl. by ignorance and insufficiency to perform that which I should have done, offended your maj.; I therefore most humbly crave to be partaker of your maj.'s most gracious pardon."

B. 1621

Petition of Grievances; Privileges of Parliament; Impeachments

---

The parliament of 1621 was the first in which Coke was clearly in opposition to the legislative agenda of the King. Increasingly faced with evidence of the King's contempt for parliamentary responsibility and increasingly opposed to national policies pursued by Buckingham in the King's name, Coke worked to tie the passing of the Bill for Supply, or the King's request for Commons to grant him tax funds, to a petition for grievances against Parliament's privileges. Coke presented a defense of Parliament based on Magna Carta. The argument between King and Commons for the upper hand took several forms. James I suggested Parliament be suspended from May to November, which Coke opposed as an act against Parliament's privileges to decide its own adjournment (although the King could dismiss it). Coke succeeded in having a royal commission requiring adjournment of Commons from being read, after which a majority of the House voted to adjourn. Coke moved resolutions to the King advising him against a Spanish marriage and alliance with Spain, after which James ordered the House not to discuss such matters and denied the members any privileges by right. Coke authored a protestation arguing for the liberties of Parliament, including parliamentarians' freedom of speech as "the ancient and undoubted birthright and inheritance of the subjects of England."

Coke led or assisted in several impeachments, including one of a parliamentarian named Sheppard, who argued flippantly against a Puritan-sponsored bill to bar dancing on the Sabbath, which he held should be Saturday. More significantly, Coke assisted in impeachments of several officials for bribery, most notably, assisting in impeaching Francis Bacon on twenty-eight charges of misconduct as chancellor. Those changes consisted mainly of accepting gifts of money from litigants before him (although many of those donors lost their cases).

Coke supported bills for free trade and against monopolies. He also approved of the impeachment of two monopolists.

At the end of the 1621 parliament, James I sent Coke, John Selden, William Prynne, and other leaders of the opposition to the Tower. Coke's house, Holborne, was sealed and his legal papers were seized. See Coke's "Arrest after Parliament," pp. 1329–1331.—*Ed.*

February 5, 1621.[1]

Ed.: In a debate on the grant of a supply to the Kings the question was whether to tie the supply to conditions of parliamentary grievance.

Sir Edward Coke. "'*Virtus silere in convivio, vitium in consilio.*'[2] I joy that all are bent with alacrity against the enemies of God and us; Jesuits, Seminaries, and Popish Catholics: it was a grievance complained of the 8th of this reign, that the laws against Recusants were not executed; I would have all those Grievances, 8 Jac. reviewed, of which that was one; if any new increased to take special consideration of them. I and Popham were 30 days in examination of the Powder-Plot at the Tower. The root of it was out of all the countries belonging to the Pope, and Faux repented him that he had not done it. God then, and in 1588, delivered us for religion's sake.—The privileges of the house concern the whole kingdom; which, like a circle ends where it began. But take heed, we lose not our liberties, by petitioning for liberty to treat of Grievances, &c. No proclamation can be of force against an act of parl. In Edw. IIId.'s time, a parl. was holden every year, that the people might complain of Grievances. If a proclamation comes against this; the law is to be obeyed and not the proclamation. The 4th Hen. VIII. Strowde moved against the Stannary court: but was fined after the parl. and imprisoned by the steward of the Stannary. Thereupon, a law ensued, for freedom of speech in the house; but

1. [*Ed.:* Cobbett, *Parl. Hist.,* I, 1187–88.]
2. [*Ed.:* Virtue keeps silence in company, vice in counsel.]

it ought to be done in due and orderly manner. My motion is, that the Grievances may be set down; those that are nought *in radice, or tractu temporis,*[3] first. The king's ordinary Charge and Expences much about one; the extraordinary ever born by the subject; therefore the king can be no beggar. And, if all the corn be brought to the right mill, I will venture my whole estate, that the king's will defray his ordinary charges. Lastly, he moved for a committee of the whole house for Grievances; and said the remedying them would encourage the house, and enable them to increase the Supply."—After this the question was put, Whether a Petition to the king for Freedom of Speech, against Recusants, the business of the Supply, and for Grievances, should be referred to a committee of the whole house? And it was resolved to go upon them that afternoon.

February 7, 1621.[4]

> *Ed.:* In a debate on an alleged unlawful election of a member of the House, the question was whether the member should be allowed to speak on his own behalf.

Sir Edward Coke divides our laws into three parts: 1, common law; 2, custom; 3, statute law. A committee is a jury. The committee may examine for matter of fact and what they had done for the fact the House would not alter, but for matter in law or right the parliament might, after the committee, alter it.

February 13, 1621.[5]

> *Ed.:* In a debate on bills for limitations of suits, the question was whether the limitations should apply in the courts of equity.

3. [*Ed.:* at root, or by the lapse of time.]

4. [*Ed.:* A Journal or Diary of the Most Material Passages in the Lower House of the Parliament Summoned To Be Holden the Sixteenth Day of January Anno Domini 1620 but by Prorogation Adjourned Till the 23th and then again to 30th of the same month, *from* Notestein, Relf, and Simpson, *Commons Debates, 1621,* Vol. 2. [Hereinafter referred to as the "X Journal."], February 7, 1621, p. 35.]

5. [*Ed.:* X Journal, February 13, 1621, ff. 64–65.]

Sir Edward Coke. I have motions to have some bills preferred. We had a bill for limitation of suits in all the courts of England, both temporal and ecclesiastical. I love the courts, yet I would have the suits limited within some time. I will rehearse two examples to shew the inconveniencies which do arise for want hereof. 1, Doctor Julio that was but an experimental physician at length became the Queen's physician in ordinary. But his wife must be divorced after eighteen years (*causa precontractus*).[6] But by whom. By old Stapleton that would make love to any woman. And then he married the fair lady he had begotten with child. But mark the judgment, the lady and the child died within a month. If this divorce had been limited this had never been. 2, Another example, there was a legacy given; long after the party challenged it but the witnesses were dead, whereas had he brought his suit in reasonable time it would have easily been decided. Therefore to have these suits limited within a certain time is that which I desire may be committed to the committees of the former bills of limitation of suits. Now if this like you, *paulo maiora canamus.*[7] All courts are either temporal or ecclesiastical. Temporal are either of ordinary jurisdiction or extraordinary, of the common law or of equity. My meaning is not to limit the king, for *nullum tempus occurrit regi.*[8] But in the courts of equity I would have the parties limited. It is good to deal openly and plainly. My Lord Chancellor hath power to proceed according to the common law. According to the common law subjects be limited already but not in equity. There is a great reason they should be limited there also, for if the King's Bench which is *coram domino rege*[9] be limited, why should not the Chancery. If a fine and recovery be passed, if a deed be enrolled, these are of record and may be had at any time after; yet they are limited. How much more should suits in Chancery, which have no writing to prove but oath of witness, which may die. So that if one bring witnesses to outswear me, my land is gone and yet there is no fault in the judge. I think this will be both plausible to the subject and acceptable to the judges who for want of this limitation are many times perplexed with these things.

---

6. [*Ed.:* (by reason of precontract [of marriage]).]
7. [*Ed.:* let us sing of somewhat greater things.]
8. [*Ed.:* time does not run against the king.]
9. [*Ed.:* before the lord king [a court limited to royal causes].]

February 15, 1621.[10]

> *Ed.:* In a debate to impeach Sheppard from Parliament, Coke agrees to Mr. Thomas Sheppard's expulsion.

Sir Edward Coke. Whatsoever hindereth the observation of the sanctification of the Sabbath is against the scripture.

. . .

Sir Edward Coke. That it is in religion as in other things, if a man go too much on the right hand, he goes to superstition, if too much on the left, to profaneness and atheism. And, take away reverence, you shall never have obedience: *maxima charitas, facere justitiam.*[11] He wisheth to have such birds crushed in the shell: for, if it be permitted to speak against such as prefer bills, we should have none preferred.

February 17, 1621.[12]

> *Ed.:* In a debate on a bill for explanation of the statute 3 Jacobi, the question concerned the taking of recusant's land for payment of debt.

Sir Eward Coke. I agree with that which was spoken last but yet let us husband time. It is good for a man in these days to take sureties and if one die, to put in another, for there is no trusting to executors in these days. Sureties bound jointly and severally are all principals. I would have a bill drawn which should give the creditor his debt and damages and the sureties should be secured only of the lands of the heir.

---

10. [*Ed.:* Cobbett, *Parl. Hist.,* I, 1191–92.]
11. [*Ed.:* To do justice is the greatest charity.]
12. [*Ed.:* X Journal, February 17, 1621, f. 100.]

February 19, 1621.[13]

In the Committee of Grievances

> *Ed.:* In a debate on the patent for Inns, which would effectively allow local monopolies for inns to be granted by the crown, the question is whether the power to grant such patents is in the king's prerogative.

Sir Edward Coke. There is prerogative indisputable, and prerogative disputable. Prerogative indisputable, is that the king hath to make war: disputable prerogative is tied to the laws of England; wherein the king also hath divers prerogatives as *nullum tempus,*[14] &c. None of all these Monopolies but have fine examples. There are 3 sorts of patents. 1st. Directly against the law: 2d. good in law, but ill in execution: 3d. neither good in law nor execution. For the first, when the sword of justice, which the laws have trusted the king withal, is given to a subject; and the king saith in his Book, that all grants of Monopolies, and dispensations of penal laws are void in law: when the king granteth his power to a subject, the commonwealth rues for it; and of this kind are old debts. For remedy of this that a course be taken, that, if debts owing to the king are not called for within a time, then to be lost. Of the 2nd kind are Patents for Inns. A 3rd are those which are neither good in law nor execution; and these are concealments, which are dishonourable to the king, for no subject may do it; and indeed the king never knows of it, the sole fault whereof lies in the referrees; and for this a bill should be drawn, that if the king hath been out of possession 60 years, and not recovered any rent for it within that time, then not to be recovered by the king as a concealment. Monopolies are now grown like Hydras' heads: they grow up as fast as they are cut off. All new offices raise the prices of things. In 4 Hen. 7. a dispensation was granted, that some should not pay Subsidies: this was after repealed by act of parl. for otherwise it would have grown so common, that no man would have paid, seeing others freed. He shewed that all the kings, from Edw. III. to this king have granted Monopolies; and, even in queen Elizabeth's time, there were some granted. Sir Rd. Mompesson and one Rob. Alexander pro-

---

13. [*Ed.:* Cobbett, *Parl. Hist.,* I, 1193.]

14. [*Ed.:* no time [runs against the king].]

cured of queen Eliz. a Patent for the sole transporting of anise-seed. Monopolies have been granted heretofore *de vento & sole;*[15] that in Devonshire and
Cornwall a patent was granted, that none should dry pilchards but those pat-
entees.

February 26, 1621.[16]

> *Ed.:* In a debate on the scarcity of money, the question was the causes of
> the lack of gold and silver coins throughout the kingdom.

Sir Edward Coke sheweth, that there were two things that principally concern and encrease kingdoms and commonwealths, viz. soldiers and money.
That there was coined from the 1 Eliz. unto 16 Jac. nine millions and a half
of silver and gold. Sheweth further, that there are 7 Causes of want of Money
and Coin in this kingdom.—1. Money turned into plate.—2. Gold folia that
is employed in gilding of things.—3. Change of Money, or silver being much
undervalued by us here of that our gold is; which was raised; and so was not
our silver, and also all our money passeth at lower rates here, than it doth
beyond sea in other countries.—4. The East India Company, who had licence
to transport 100,000 l. at their first setting up; and albeit they do not, since
that time carry out of the kingdom any more English money, yet they intercept
the dollars and other money that would otherwise come into this kingdom,
and bring in for it nothing but toys and trifles.—5. The goods imported exceed
the goods exported, and therefore there must needs go forth of our coin to
pay for the surplusage.—6. The French merchants for wine carry forth
80,000 l. *per ann.* and bring in nothing but wines and lace, and such like
trifles.—7. The Patent for Gold and Silver lace, which not only wastes and
consumes our bullion and coin, but hindereth the bringing of any into the
kingdom; which was wont to be so much as would yield 20,000 l. *per ann.*
of good bullion.

15. [*Ed.:* of the wind and sun.]
16. [*Ed.:* Cobbett, *Parl. Hist.,* I, 1194–95.]

March 1, 1621.[17]

Ed.: In the proceedings against Sir Giles Mompesson, a Monopolist and Patentee, Coke made observations about men of six types of occupations.

Sir Edward Coke. There are in my observation 6 kinds of men, that never thrive or prosper. 1. Alchymist; for *omne vertitur in fumum*[18] with him. 2. Monopolizer; for he engrosseth to himself what should be free for all men. 3. Promoter, who for the most part lives upon the spoil of poor men. 4. Concealment-monger, or he that gets Concealments. 5. Depopular, who turns all out of doors, and keeps none but a shepherd and his dog. 6. New Projector, who is lately started up.

March 8, 1621.[19]

Conference with the Lords in the Painted Chamber

Ed.: In a debate concerning Sir Giles Mompesson and monopolies.

Sir Edward Coke. There is (you have heard) the public good pretended but a private intended. Then to have a proclamation to attend a private gain is a great grievance and a lamentable thing.

That which I shall say shall be distributed into four parts: 1, for clearing of, an adding to, the King's honor; 2, for remedies of these things in time to come; 3, to shew precedents how such like cases have been censured and punished in former times; 4, to add a conclusion. I will not meddle with the King's prerogative, which is twofold: 1, absolute, as to make war, coin money, etc.; 2, or in things that concern *meum et tuum*,[20] and this may be disputed of in courts of parliament.

The King was careful to have prevented the grievances, as appears by his

---

17. [*Ed.:* Cobbett, *Parl. Hist.,* I, 1198.]
18. [*Ed.:* everything is turned into smoke.]
19. [*Ed.:* X Journal, March 8, 1621 f. 170–76.]
20. [*Ed.:* mine and thine (i.e. property).]

proclamation *primo Jacobi* and his Declaration set forth 8 Jacobi. If these had been observed, we had not been troubled. The King never granted any but he referred it, as you have heard. Further, the 12 Jacobi *ex parte Regis,* in the Exchequer, he granted a seal wherein he expressed himself thus: *We, having a just care of our loving subjects, will not have our prerogative extended to private uses.* Overflowing will make rivers lose their proper channels. It may be said that these patents were granted as rewards of former services, and is not *prae-mium*[21] as necessary for good service as *poena*[22] for evil service. Yes, but yet kings will not have any men serve them for reward and therefore when any such patents were granted they went in this form: *ex mero motu et gratia speciali etc.*[23] 4 Hen. 4, there was a statute of bargain because many grants had passed without deliberation; it was ordained by the king that whosoever shall sue for any lands, he should be punished by the Council and disabled of the thing sued for; he was a wise and potent king and knew his revenue could not subsist if he gave way to such suits.

Now for remedies. 1, He that hath thus offended is in the king's mercy and that all such patents be called in again. 5 Edward 3 the Commons complain that many persons about the king had got a commission to inquire of all things that belong to the king's revenue. By the way, what persons were these to whom the king granted this? It is said it was granted to ribaulds. What are they? Ribaulds are such as always beg and never work. What do they with this commission? They by virtue hereof make writs, returns, inquisitions and get escheators to take possession and then the ribaulds sue to the king to have some of these things thus found granted unto them in the very same manner as Sir Giles Mompesson hath done. But the Commons desired that these commissions might be repealed and hereafter granted to men of account.

It's necessary that some law be made for the time to come that no monopoly be granted, and they that procure any such may incur some great punishment, and this will kill the serpent in the egg.

Now for precedents. I remember Phaeton's counsel to Icarus, *altius egressus etc.,*[24] and concludes *medio tutissimus ibis.*[25] So if we go too high we may wrong

---

21. [*Ed.:* a prize.]
22. [*Ed.:* a penalty.]
23. [*Ed.:* of our mere motion and especial grace, etc.]
24. [*Ed.:* the higher flight, etc.]
25. [*Ed.:* You will go most safely in the middle way.]

the king's prerogative; if too low, we betray our country. Therefore *medio tutissimus ibis.*[26] How is that to go by precedents. I find then that in parliaments (besides the way of acts and petitions) there is a power of judicature or judicial proceedings and that in 4 sorts: 1, *coram domino rege et magnatibus vel consilio suo; 2, coram magnatibus solis; 3, coram magnatibus et communitate; 4, coram communitate tantum.*[27] I will give several examples of these. First, *coram domino rege et magnatibus,* in Edw. 1 time the Bishop of Coventry *queritur de Hugone extraneo*[28] 10 Rich. 2, the Commons complained to the king and the Lords of a very great man called Michael de la Pole, then Lord Chancellor, for that he for his own private gain had suffered divers letters patents to pass in disherison of the crown and subverting courts of justice. 28 Hen. 6 (vel 8), there was a complaint against William, Duke of Suffolk, for that he procured from the king divers liberties in derogation of the common law; the justices in eyre did enquire of this.

Secondly *coram magnatibus* only, and there is a necessity in this because else justice will fall to the ground and the subject in some cases cannot be relieved. As, suppose a judgment be given for the king in the King's Bench, there is no help for this but a writ of error which must be brought before the Lords in the Upper House of parliament. Now the king cannot be judge in his own case, therefore it must be judged by the Lords alone or not at all. Alice Pearce, 1 Rich. 2, was complained of to the Lords for preferring many suits in derogation of the common law and against the commonwealth. The Lords awarded imprisonment and banishment. 42 Edw. 3, John de la Lee, steward of the king's house, kept a court in his chamber and sent pursuivants for men and imprisoned them. He was committed to the Tower there to remain till he had paid fine and ransom. 5 Edw. 3, William Ellis, a merchant of Yarmouth and farmer of the customs, under color hereof oppressed divers of the king's subjects by exactions.

The Commons complained, the Lords awarded him to prison until he had made fine and ransom. 5 Edward 3, Richard Lyons, a merchant of London, a notable projector (he was well acquainted with divers Lords and promised

26. [*Ed.:* You will go most safely in the middle way.]
27. [*Ed.:* 1. Before the lord king and his great men or council. 2. Before the great men alone. 3. Before the great men and commonalty. 4. Before the commonalty alone.]
28. [*Ed.:* complained against Hugh the stranger.]

great matters as all projectors do), was accused that by his solicitation he procured dispensations to carry staple commodities to other places than to the staple towns, contrary to the law; 2, that having taken the customs to enhance them, pretended the king's gain but intended his own lucre; 3, that he devised such a new kind of money as would have robbed and overthrown the kingdom. This was a merchant indeed but for the horribleness of his fact he was sentenced: 1, to be sent to the Tower there to remain till he had made fine and ransom; 2, never to bear office; 3, never to come near the king nor his Council; 4, to be disfranchised of his liberty of London. John Peache, *Anglice* John Sin (*conveniant rebus nomina saepe suis*),[29] was complained of for that he had gotten the sole selling of sweet wines. This sole selling sheweth it to be a plain monopoly; hereby the price was enhanced. He was committed to the Tower and paid fine and ransom. But some may say these be but poor fellows, shew an example of a great man. John, Lord Neville, who had a regiment in Britain, the Commons complained of him that under color of the king's authority he had oppressed and impoverished the people. He was sentenced to the Tower and paid fine and ransom. All these in Edward the Third time.

3, Thirdly, *coram magnatibus et communitate*. William Lord Latimer (hath his name because he was interpreter betwixt the Britons and us), who was Lord Chamberlain, was accused that he was partaker with Richard Lyons in all his projects and was sentenced deeply, but the king pardoned him. The tenor of which pardon was thus: *cum fidelis et dilectus noster etc., coram magnatibus et communitate regni indicatus fuit etc.*[30] I say the king pardoned him but it cost him six score thousand marks, 7 Rich. 2.

4, *Coram communitate tantum.* Arthur Hall wrote a book in derogation of the House of parliament. He was imprisoned in the Tower and fined, expelled the House and another chosen in his room, 23 Eliz. 28 Eliz., a simple and weak man (one somewhat frantic) gave v*li.* to a mayor to choose him burgess. The mayor was fined for it. 38 Hen. 8, in Brooke, if a burgess be made a mayor *sedente parliamento*,[31] presently a new must be chosen for he is tied to another charge. Adam de Berry, Mayor of Calais and a captain, had been such

---

29. [*Ed.:* Names are often suited to their subjects.]

30. [*Ed.:* whereas our faithful and beloved, etc. was indicted before the great men and commonalty of the realm, etc.]

31. [*Ed.:* while parliament was sitting.]

an oppressor as that he was complained of, whereupon he fled. It was awarded his goods should be seized. That's the parliamentary course. And thus I leave you to tread in the steps of your noble progenitors. Empson was hanged, but his offence was not so great as Sir Giles Mompesson's. He indeed got a grant to dispense with penal laws according to his discretion and caused men to be endicted for riots and to be imprisoned and caused divers to be outlawed, so that the subjects being thereby vexed and terrified murmured in their hearts and were alienated from the King. Mompesson hath exceeded him in the like, at least succeeded him. See the fortune of it, Empson made one Mompesson his heir for so I find it. Mompesson, son of Empson.

It's recorded in a book called the *Mirror of Justices* that King Allured called Alfred, *anno* 873, made an act to have 2 parliaments in one year. Edward the First made an ordinance to have one parliament in two years, and performed that. 4 Edward 3. for the redress of many mischiefs and grievances which daily encrease in the commonwealth, it was ordained that a parliament be held every year. In those days parliaments were accounted necessary every year. And is there not the same necessity still. The kingdom and commonwealth may be likened to a fair field and a pleasant garden, but if the field be not tilled and the garden often weeded, *infaelix lolium et steriles nascuntur avenae.*[32] And all ill humors increase in the body and hurt the body if they be not purged, *humores moti non remoti corpus laedunt.*[33] So likewise abuses and corruptions increase in the commonwealth. Therefore often parliaments are necessary that good laws may be made to prevent and punish them, *ut poena ad paucos metus ad omnes perveniat.*[34] And we by daily experience find that of diseases to be true, *quia non profertur cito contra mala sententia.*[35] Therefore the hearts of the sons of men is set on them to do them mischief.

March 14, 1621.[36]

Ed.: In a debate concerning a bill on monopolies and dispensations.

32. [*Ed.:* there rise up barren tares and wild oats.]
33. [*Ed.:* Humours hurt the body when they are disturbed, not when they are removed.]
34. [*Ed.:* that a penalty administered to a few may strike terror in everyone.]
35. [*Ed.:* because sentence is not executed quickly against evil actions.]
36. [*Ed.:* X Journal, March 14, 1621, f. 193.]

Sir Edward Coke. All the Judges of England are all *una voce,*[37] when the law gives the Crown a penalty he cannot grant the penalty to a private man, for it is inseparable and cannot be divided. We come to the Council Table where it is recorded by the Council, who confirmed it and liked it very well, that there should be no sole selling. No law can be equal to all countries and cannot be granted to a private man. The sole buying and selling of anything and sole importation and exportation is a monopoly. Sir Richard Mompesson, sole importation of   upon a *quo warranto*[38] was judged a monopoly. Another, for sole importation of stone pots was likewise judged a monopoly, and likewise exportation. And for the parliament, who denies that it is a court of record at Westminster.

March 15, 1621.[39]

> *Ed.:* Following a debate on whether a member of the House can protect a bankrupt, Coke reports his conference with the Lords in which he discussed the King's power over the penal laws.

Sir Edward Coke, according to an order being to go up to the Lords to carry the heads of the conference unto them, returning made this report. First, to prevent that this sending of the heads in writing might not be made a precedent against us to do the like hereafter, I told them then when the Commons sought conference with their Lordships it hath been always verbal and upon the Lords' report it was entered in their Journal. Yet because it was requested by them, whom we had found so ready and kind to us in the said conference and the rather for that it stood upon so many particulars as that the best memory could scarce carry them away, we have condescended unto them.

I proceeded to shew what good ground the King had for saying in his Book of Declaration of his royal pleasure that monopolies and dispensations of penal laws were against law. For the Judges 2° Jacobi took it into deliberation three days, looked into their books and precedents, whereupon having resolved they

---

37. [*Ed.:* of one voice.]

38. [*Ed.:* Writ to enforce the limits of an office, power, or franchise, or to bar someone from acting without legal authority.]

39. [*Ed.:* X Journal March 15, 1621, ff. 280–3.]

signified their resolutions in writing to the Lords of the Council that the taking of forfeitures of the penal laws was an inseparable prerogative of the Crown not to be imparted to any. Their reasons were: first, because those laws were made *pro bono publico*.[40] If a private person have the forfeiture it will be *pro privato*.[41] Secondly, the King is *pater patriae*.[42] Therefore the realm trusteth him when they will not trust a private man. Thirdly, because of the inconveniences of it. For when a subject is clothed with the King's prerogative he seldom keeps a measure. For I never saw an universal patent granted but it was disorderly executed. Fourthly, it's a scandal to justice. The Council Board approved and applauded this resolution of the Judges as one of the best that ever was given. The King then, having the opinion of the Judges in point of law and of his Council for point of state, had good and sufficient ground for making such a Declaration.

I shewed precedents likewise against monopolies. King Philip, coming over to marry Queen Mary, arrived at Southampton where, being royally received by the town, to gratify them granted them a monopoly that all sweet wines which were brought into this kingdom should be brought into Southampton. During Queen Mary's time none durst speak against it, but 2° Eliz. it was questioned and judged to be a monopoly, whereupon 5to Eliz. the subject by an act of parliament was freed from it, but the stranger remained bound, William Simpson had gotten a patent for the sole importation of stone pots and heath to make brushes withal. This was complained of to the Queen. Go (said she) to Burleigh, then Lord Treasurer, Popham and Coke, and cause a *quo warranto* to be brought against it. And it was adjudged a monopoly. Sir Thomas Wilkes his patent of sole making of salt in Norfolk, because he had made a new addition to it, yet it was adjudged to be a monopoly because a new button added to an old coat makes it not a new coat, and etc. Sir John Paggington his patent of sole importation of starch, his patent overthrown. Richard Mompesson and Robert Alexander for the sole importation of drugs and aniseeds, a monopoly. Elizabeth Martin, the sole buying of fish livers to make train oil. Sir Edward Darcy, the sole importation and exporting of cork prohibited and adjudged a monopoly.

40. [*Ed.:* for the public good.]
41. [*Ed.:* for private gain.]
42. [*Ed.:* father of the nation.]

Next, for concealments, a patent as bad or rather worse than any other. First, that no nobleman can grant land wherein he hath not actual possession. Therefore it cannot stand with the justice of the king to grant any land to the disherison of his subjects. Secondly, it robs the king of his tenures which is the tree of his revenue, with which goeth licence of alienation, wards, and marriage. Thirdly, it robs the church. Christ whipped the buyers and sellers out of the temple; he would much more whip the buyers and sellers of churches. Fourthly, it robs the poor, for Sir Giles Mompesson had passed twelve hospitals in one book. Therefore the King hath reserved these things justly to himself, commanding in his said Book that neither the Broad Seal nor his Privy Signet should be put to any of these.

I told them also that this parliament we had been careful to observe these three things diligently: first, that we would not deal with the King's absolute power, whereby he may make war, etc. *Cum canerem regis et proelia Cinthius aurem vellet et admonuit.*[43] When as I did begin to sing of kings and war, Apollo pulled me by the ear and said I went too far. Secondly, to preserve the King's honor. And to this end we have set down the King's guides, the referees. Thirdly, to provide for the wealth of the King. But the King cannot be rich if the subject be poor.

I then told them I had one thing more if they were not weary. The Prince desired to hear it. I said, in the Italian history there was mention made of a friar who had spent his time in holy devotion. He was sent to Rome to preach, and because he had never been at Rome before he went 10 or 12 days before the time. And when he came and observed so much ceremonies and pomp and so little devotion, what a lamentable thing (said he) is this, I will not preach here. Yet when his day came he went into the pulpit, and said this, *matto Sante Piero*, St. Peter was a fool. This he said three times and came down again; and being examined why he spake those words, answered, St. Peter said *non habeo aurum nec argentum,*[44] silver and gold have I none, but the Pope hath plenty. He spent his time in prayer, the Pope in pleasure and vanity; he in building the inward man, you in pampering the outward man. If any of you do go to heaven, St. Peter was a fool to undergo such pressures.

---

43. [*Ed.:* When I sang of Kings and wars, Cynthius (i.e. Apollo) seized me by the ear and rebuked me (a quote from Vergil's *Eclogues,* 6.1).]

44. [*Ed.:* Gold and silver have I none.]

So surely I may say *matto Signor Empsono, matto Signor Dudleio*. Our Mompesson hath gone beyond you, what fools were they to be hanged (for, as it were, a matter of nothing). Sir Giles Mompesson hath gone so far beyond them all as that a man had need of an astrolobe to take the height of it. And therefore I hoped they would give condign punishment. So I delivered them the heads.

March 16, 1621.[45]

> *Ed.:* In a debate concerning the propriety of serving a subpoena on judges to testify in a matter over which they are not presiding.

Sir Edward Coke said, that every one who sitteth here is as a judge, and hath a vote negative in the making of the laws of this kingdom: that the Judges of the Common Pleas, or of any court, are never sworn as witnesses in any case, albeit they know of something concerning it, and can testify in it; but, if their knowledge be asked, they answer it without an oath: that no Judge of the Star-Chamber can be served with a *subpoena ad testificandum* in that court; and therefore none of us are to be examined as witnesses in any thing whereof this House with the Lords are to be judges.

. . .

Sir Edward Coke. That for a member of this house to be examined on oath in a business sent from us to the Lords was never before desired: that we were best to answer, that we have no precedents that ever it was done, and that there is no necessity in it, because the greatest matters are sufficiently proved.

March 22, 1621.[46]

> *Ed.:* In a debate concerning a bill on the election of burgesses.

Sir Edward Coke. I had rather live under severe laws than under any man's discretion. *Misera servitas est ubi ius est vagum et incognitum.*[47]

---

45. [*Ed.:* Cobbett, *Parl. Hist.,* I, 1206–7.]

46. [*Ed.:* X Journal, March 22, 1621, f. 224.]

47. [*Ed.:* It is miserable slavery where the law is vague or unknown. (*Servitas* in the journal is a misprint for *servitus*)]

April 20, 1621.[48]

> *Ed.:* In a debate concerning the bribery of judges.

Sir Edward Coke. I love Sir John Bennet well but I hate bribery. First let it be set down in writing and then present it to the Lords. If it be found true, it will touch him near. If not, *beatus est,*[49] for blessed is he that keepeth his hand from bribery.

May 3, 1621.[50]

> *Ed.:* In a debate on a bill concerning unjust exaction of fees in courts of justice.

Sir Edward Coke. Courts of justice are like a circle, you cannot add anything unto it but you mar it. If you put new to old it will never agree. If the king will grant an office to two whereas anciently it appertained to one, it will never do well. 13 Hen. 4, there is a resolution that a fee cannot be set to a new office without an act of parliament. It's in the canvas case and the grant of an office without a fee is void. 27 Hen. 8, if I grant to one to be my steward without a fee, it's void. But in a court of justice if you bring in a new office it will never want fees. Therefore let there be none. If the King grant a new office and give him a fee, it's void.

May 4, 1621.[51]

> *Ed.:* In a debate regarding when the King can intervene in proceedings.

Sir Edward Coke. When any judgment is given in a case concerning the king (as all criminal cases do for they are *contra coronam et dignitatem suam,*[52])

---

48. [*Ed.:* X Journal, April 20, 1621, f. 267.]
49. [*Ed.:* he is blessed.]
50. [*Ed.:* X Journal, May 3, 1621, f. 304.]
51. [*Ed.:* X Journal, May 4, 1621, f. 308.]
52. [*Ed.:* against his crown and dignity.]

the king may stay judgment and execution. 2 Edw. 3; 20, it's enacted that no judgment shall be stayed for any message whatsoever. This is true for the late Queen hath sent and the Judges have answered they may not. Nay if the Great Seal come they may not stay judgment between party and party. But if the king be a party he may stop it, 1 Hen. 7. To question this judgment is strange; if a judgment be given when a judge is absent, if he come after into the court it shall be accounted his judgment. Nay, if a judge be present and give his voice against a judgment yet, being judged by the rest it shall be his judgment. If the king send to stop an indictment in an appeal I would not do it but in an indictment I would let the judgment entered stand, referring the execution to his Majesty, my great master.

May 5, 1621.[53]

Ed.: In a debate concerning a bill to confirm Magna Charta in chapter 29, to bar corporations from engaging in the imprisonment of individuals.

Sir Edward Coke. The Statute of Magna Charta hath ben 32 [times] Confirmed, and never hath it ben so infringed as of late yeears. Corporations have gotten by Lawes according to Law, and to imprison for breach, but that is against all Law. But this bill trenshes so deepe that a man for any cause of State can not be imprisoned but theay must shew ther reson. and therfor faulty in that and oute of the Statute of Magna Charta as in 33 Hen. 6 and confirmd so by all the judges. For L[ondon]s Corp[oratio]ns, lett them follow the Law and not committ upon by Lawes, for theay cannot doo that.

May 17, 1621.[54]

Ed.: In considering pending bills seeking monopolies and price fixing.

Sir Edward Coke. That there is 19 patents for monopolies, concealments, and penal laws, tearing the flowers from the Crown. In the 44 of Eliz., by

---

53. [*Ed.:* The notes by Sir Thomas Barringon of the House of Commans in 1621, May 5, 1621, in Notestein, Relf, and Simpson, *Commons Debates, 1621,* vol. 3, p. 172.

54. [*Ed.:* X Journal, May 17, 1621, f. 340.]

proclamation all of this nature was damned, and therefore I think it fit by petition to go to the King that all these may be damned.

June 2, 1621.[55]

> *Ed.:* In a debate concerning trade and customs.

Sir Edward Coke saith, that this motion of sir D. Digges is a worthy motion; for freedom of trade is the life of trade: that customers are called in latin *Publicani,* and every one knoweth, that Christ called publicans sinners; and we may justly match and call publicans customers, and customers sinners; for they cozen and deceive both the king and kingdom. He saith, he will never fear questioning for what he hath here said; for he hath here spoken old English, which is conscience. He knoweth he hath offended many, because it pleased this house to put him in the chair at the committee concerning monopolies; whereby he hath proceeded the more carefully. He would have those of the out ports, who shall desire to farm their customs, to offer good sureties: but, for the better furtherance of trade, he would have an order of declaration entered here, that none of those patents of monopolies, which have been here condemned, should be put in execution during this adjournment or cessation.

November 22, 1621.[56]

> *Ed.:* Here Coke prefaces the reports of three members of the Lords.

Sir Edward Coke. I am to make report of three speeches of three great lords. 1, The Lord Bishop of Lincoln, Lord Keeper of the Great Seal of England. 2, The Lord Digby. 3, The Lord Treasurer. But first I will begin with myself. I am in this case at a great disadvantage, for it appears their speeches were *premeditates meditationes*[57]; mine must needs be *properatus.*[58] They (no doubt) had conference one with another before, and *collatio peperit artes et perficit*

---

55. [*Ed.:* Cobbett, *Parl. Hist.,* I, 1291.]
56. [*Ed.:* X Journal, November 22, 1621, f. 404.]
57. [*Ed.:* considered thoughts.]
58. [*Ed.:* sudden.]

artes.[59] I marked how everyone of them spake in his own element, and that hath ever been the order in parliaments, but I am sure I am out of my element. The first of them was a divine and excellent orator for persuasion. The second was my Lord Digby who was ambassador, and he was set forth in the King's negotiation. The third was my Lord Treasurer who was to speak concerning the treasure of the kingdom. They are all in the vigor of their age. I am in declining. They have had it from the fountain, I from the streams. And thus much of myself. Now I come to their speeches.

December 3, 1621.[60]

> *Ed.:* In a debate on the foreign and domestic policy implications of an alliance by royal marriage with Spain.

Sir Edward Coke answereth something that hath not been answered. *Melius est recurrere quam male currere, satius est recurrere quam praecurrere.*[61] Hath not every man the marriage of his own child, yea, the king cannot dispose of the marriage of my son. If lands descend from another ancestor, the king cannot have the wardship and marriage, the father living. These are inseparable prerogatives of the Crown and king. Marriage and leagues, war and peace, they are *arcana imperii*[62] and not to be meddled with. If they were a petition of right that required an answer, I would never prefer it or give my consent to the preferring of it; but it's only a petition of grace. The Prince his marriage must move either directly or indirectly from the King. Now we have heard the Lords say that Janus his temple must be opened; the voice of Bellona must be heard and not of the turtle. Nay more we heard that his Majesty must either abandon his children or engage himself in war. The King of Spain maintains 6 armies, his forces have gotten the Palatinate, so then we must fight against the Spaniards. But we desire that we might fight against Spain. We say that the hope of the marriage with Spain is the cause of the insolency

59. [*Ed.:* conference begets and perfects professional skills.]

60. [*Ed.:* X Journal, December 3, 1621, ff. 467–68.]

61. [*Ed.:* It is better to run back than to run badly; it is more satisfactory to run back than to run precipitately forward.]

62. [*Ed.:* government secrets (the essentials of statecraft).]

of the papists. We advise nothing but what his Majesty liketh, for surely it
will avert the hearts of many that he should marry with any but a protestant.
For marriage with strange women the scripture saith *cauti sitis ne avertant
corda vestra et sequamini deos alienos.*[63] To do this by way of petition is good
and hath no hurt in it. If it please his Majesty he may take this petition for
a ground and lay it by or else make use of it when the match is next moved.
He may give it life if he please and quash it at his pleasure, for we draw not
a bill to bind but a petition, precedents whereof you may have divers. Edward
3 did confer with his Commons concerning his marriage. 42 Edw. 3. No. 7,
a foreign prince did abuse him and he being weary of arms was for a treaty,
and they dissuaded him from peace and persuade him to take his sword in
hand because a just war was better than a dishonorable peace. That the Commons may argue, debate and dispute of the estate of the kingdom which
concerns the good of it. 4 Hen. 5, a league was to be made between the King
of England and Sigismund, King of the Romans, by act of parliament and
there is an act for it. The writ is our guide. *Nil nisi prudentia aut ratione fecit
vetustas.*[64] The king calleth the parliament *pro magnis arduis et urgentibus ne-
gociis nos statum et defensionem regni nostri ac statum et defensionem ecclesiae
concernentibus etc.*[65] Now judge if ever cause were more urgent than this or
did concern the state, kingdom and commonwealth. *Ecclesiam Anglianam* are
the words of the writ and doth not this concern religion?

December 15, 1621.[66]

> *Ed.:* In a debate on the King's prerogative on the privileges and liberties
> of his subjects.

Sir Edward Coke. Silence would smite my conscience. *Cum aequali dubium,
cum principe stultum, cum puero poena[m], cum puella pudorem.*[67] One out of

---

63. [*Ed.:* You must be careful not to turn away your hearts and follow strange gods.]

64. [*Ed.:* Past ages made nothing without prudence or reason.]

65. [*Ed.:* for great, hard and urgent business concerning us, the estate and defence of our realm, and
the estate and defence of the Church, etc.]

66. [*Ed.:* X Journal, December 15, 1621, ff. 509–510.]

67. [*Ed.:* With an equal, doubt; with the prince, foolishness; with a boy, punishment; with a girl,
shame.]

Ireland would not dispute with the king. The king as the sun *in summo gradu*[68] hath his full light. In the 39 Edw. 4, the liberties of the court is the law of the court. 19 Hen. 6. When the law groweth dangerous, they may be freed by parliament. How can great men be punished, their burthen is pulled off. We must have another interpretation. He would have us have any other style as *nulli vendimus.*[69] The king will not sell justice. The law no custom but by custom, that is, particular laws. The King doth not mean to take our privileges away. But that a Committee of the whole House for we can have no proxies but we represent others. That a committee be appointed on Monday.

December 17, 1621.[70]

Sir Edward Coke saith, that we have now, by this last message, as he conceiveth, an allowance of our Privileges, which indeed are our's by law, by custom, by precedent, and by act of parl. That he thinketh, if we did set down our privileges and liberties, it would clear us of all those rubs. He wisheth, that himself were a sacrifice, so as there were a good and perfect correspondency and right understanding between the king and the house, as he hopeth there is: That one Walter Clerk, being a burgess for Chippenham, was fined for a riot in time of parl. at the king's suit; which encouraged also one Rob. Basset to sue the said Clerk, on an action of trespass; and also one John Payne sued the said Clerk to an outlawry, and laid him up in the Fleet: but hereupon this house of parl. would do nothing till they had their burgess again. Those of the king's side said then, that, for the king's suit, *Non omittas propter aliquam libertatem;*[71] and it was then also alledged, on the behalf of this house, that the king calleth the burgesses here for the service of the kingdom; and if one of them may be taken from us, all may like-wise by the same right.

. . .

Sir Edward Coke would have us make a Protestation for our Privileges: That he can tell us when both houses did sit in parl. together, both the lords and the commons: That the demand of the privileges of this house, by the Speaker

---

68. [*Ed.:* in the highest degree.]
69. [*Ed.:* to no one shall we sell.]
70. [*Ed.:* Cobbett, *Parl. Hist.,* I, pp. 1352, 1355.]
71. [*Ed.:* do not omit on account of any liberty.]

was after they began to be questioned: and, at first, when the demand of the privileges was made to the kings of this realm, it used to be done still at the first meeting of the parl.; and in this manner, that, if the house might not have their privileges and liberties, they would sit silent. He would have us make our protestation for our privileges, and then send the same to the king, that he may see it.

C. 1625
Subsidies

The parliament of 1625, the first of Charles I, was a much less controversial parliament than that of either 1621 or 1624, but it grew more heated as it progressed. Coke began the first parliament moderately, withholding his motion on the first day to appoint a committee of grievances. Coke, however, opposed both heavy taxes and the Duke of Buckingham's influence and policies.—*Ed.*

June 22, 1625.[1]

Ed.: Responding to a motion for a committee of grievances or for good harmony between the King and Parliament.

Sir Edward Coke gave 3 reasons against making committees for grievances and courts of justice: first, the danger of infection by drawing the meaner sort of people about us, which was the judicial reason of the adjourning of the term; 2, there have been no grievance[s] since the King came to the crown; 3, we have yet received no answer of our last grievances, therefore we are first to begin to petition his Majesty for that; and hereafter let us be careful to present our grievances in such time that we may have an answer before the breaking up of the parliament.

1. [*Ed.:* Bedford MS. 197, June 22, 1625, 5, *reprinted in* Janssen and Bidwell, *Proceedings in Parliament, 1625.*]

Speeches in Parliament 1625

June 23, 1625.[2]

Ed.: In a debate on the privileges of a member of Parliament taken into execution in an action for debt.

Sir Edward Coke. The liberty of parliament the heartstring of parliament. 2 questions: Whether Sir William Cope shall have his privilege for the last parliament or this.

14 Hen. 4, the knights could have no wages because the parliament dissolved and the King's death.

Privilege holds as well upon prorogation as adjournment. 31 Hen. 6, the parliament prorogued. The Duke of York, regent, sued the Speaker in the vacation and had a judgment. The Commons desired their Speaker.

Ed.: In a debate concerning the problems associated with the perceived increase in the numbers of priests and Jesuits.

Sir Edward Coke.[3] *Non intellecti nulla est curatio morbi.*[4] Diseases kill not men for the most part, but the neglect of cure in due time. So in the politic body, 4 causes of the swarming of these locusts: [1,] suffering of them in the land with impunity; 2, begging of recusants; 3, dependence upon landlords and great men. To appoint a committee to look over the former petitions and answers.

June 24, 1625.[5]

In the Committee of the Whole House

Ed.: Considering petitions concerning the exercise of religion.

Sir Edward Coke. We have not yet touched the center point of the decay of religion. Where prophecy ceases, the people perish. A great part of the realm

---

2. [*Ed.:* House of Commons, Draft Journal, MS. 3409, H.L.R.O., June 23, 1625, 133.]
3. [*Ed.:* Committee Book, MS. 3410, H.L.R.O., June 23, 1625, 157.]
4. [*Ed.:* There is no cure for a disease which is not understood.]
5. [*Ed.:* Committee Book, June 24, 1625, 158, reprinted in Janssen and Bidwell.]

without teaching. To petition the King to have this in some sort remedied. A precedent for this in the midnight of popery: *quinquagesimo*[6] of Edw.3, n. 96, the Commons complained of this to the King, this long before Luther. To desire the King that he would call his bishops to him and advise with them.

June 30, 1625.[7]

Ed.: In a debate on the assessment of subsidies.

Sir Edward Coke. Ordinary charges the King should bear alone; but *ubi commune periculum commune auxilium.*[8] In extraordinary he may require relief. 27 Edw. 3, the King told his subjects he demanded no aid because he had good officers. The King's revenue as it is, is able to supply his ordinary. Ancient parliaments did so limit their gifts, that they might meet again. Till 31 Eliz. never but one subsidy granted, and Sir Walter Mildmay, though he were a great officer, spoke against it then. But since that time there has been no such thing. 35to.3 subsidies, 6 15[s]; 39to, 3 subsidies, 6 15[s]; 43to, 4 subsidies, 8 15[s]; etc. And it is not to be forgotten that the tonnage and poundage which yields 160,000*l. per annum,* and the subsidies of the clergy 20.000*l. per annum,* are all by gifts of parliament. The time for these two subsidies he would have October and April.

August 2, 1625.[9]

Ed.: Considering the censure of Canon Richard Montague, for publishing books contrary to the current orthodoxy.

Sir Edward Coke (having spoken before, yet being permitted contrary to the orders of the House to speak again). That the privilege of the House of Commons was the heartstring of the commonwealth. We are the general inquisitors, but for the point of doctrine not to judge but to transfer: *pro de-*

---

6. [*Ed.:* in the fiftieth.]
7. [*Ed.:* Bedford MS, June 30, 1625, 18v.]
8. [*Ed.:* where there is mutual danger, mutual assistance.]
9. [*Ed.:* Bedford MS, August 2, 1625, 41v.]

fensione Ecclesiae,[10] given as one cause of calling parliaments in all the ancient writs; and when both Houses have done their duties it will come to the King at last. 18 Hen.3, the parliament beseech the King not to pardon those who were condemned in parliament. 15 Edw.3, John of Gaunt and the Lord Latimer were questioned for giving the King ill counsel. No man, not John of Gaunt himself, is to be excepted. Many men (and I myself) will speak in parliament that which they dare not speak otherwise.

August 5, 1625.[11]

Ed.: In debate concerning the use of treasury revenues for war.

Sir Edward Coke spoke. In King Edward the 3d's time, who was a valiant and a wise king, the clergy did petition the King for 3 things: for the maintenance and preservation of religion, for a peaceable government, and for the continuance and increase of love between the King and his subjects, was that petitioned then, and is it not needful now. He is afraid some ill star has ruled that has brought us hither. But the place where he is now, in the Divinity School, puts him in mind not to fear any evil but to put our trust in God. For surely we have a gracious and a religious King. And are there no more precedents to this purpose? Yes, in the time of that stout and valiant King Henry the Fourth you shall find that the Commons, perceiving things to go awry, did resort unto the King by petition who rectified the same. See the records of Hen.4.

Two things are urged against us very strongly to give, first our engagement, secondly, the King's necessity. For the first, our engagement by the House. It was not other but if that the King would turn his weapon against the right enemy, they would supply him in a parliamentary course.

And for the other argument of necessity, I find in Bracton, a father of our law, that there is a threefold necessity: *necessitas affectata, inevitabilis aut invincibilis, et improvida.*[12] That this is not *affectata* in his conscience he dares acquit the King. That it is *invincibilis,* or *inevitabilis,* he does not believe. God

---

10. [*Ed.:* for the defence of the Church.]
11. [*Ed.:* Petyt MS 538-8, August 5, 1625, 134v-9, reprinted in Janssen and Bidwell.]
12. [*Ed.:* Necessity may be [1] pretended, [2] inevitable or invincible, or [3] unexpected.]

forbid that his Majesty should be put to that pinch. We have no invasions, no eighty-eights. That it is *improvida* he does verily believe. And therefore he thinks that in respect that it has grown by improvidence and is not inevitable, not to be supplied by the House.

Cannot the King as well live off his revenue as his ancestors? King Edward the 3d maintained wars in France 14 years before he had supply. Offices ought to be held and used by men of experience and understanding, of good years, judgment, and discretion, to execute such offices. Or else they were void in law, and so be our [books and] law cases: 3° *Eliz.,* Dyer, Skrogges's case and many other books. And a kingdom can never be well governed where unskillful and unfitting men are placed in great offices and hold the great offices of the kingdom. For if they are inexperienced and unskillful themselves, they cannot execute them or make choice of fit men under them by reason of want of experience and judgment. Neither are young and unskillful persons to be trusted with such great offices. Besides multiplicity of offices to be held by one man is a great prejudice to the merit of honor and his Majesty's well-deserving subjects. And by this means that which was wont to be thought fit to advance divers as a reward of their good service or a token of his Majesty's favor and grace and bestowed only upon men of great desert both of king and kingdom, is now held and engrossed by one man only which is neither safe for his Majesty nor profitable unto the kingdom. And whereas the king[s] might and anciently have rewarded many by one of these great offices upon one of his servants whom he found to be most fit for it and another and by such means keep his revenue to himself, it is now come to pass that by engrossing of offices his Majesty's Exchequer stands charges with many pensions for the reward of service at least alleged. Nay, his ancient crown land granted away to gratify men in this kind.

The office of Admiral is the greatest office of trust about the King, for the benefit of the kingdom, it being an island consisting of trade, and therefore requires a man of great experience and judgment (which he cannot attain unto in a few years), and such a one as shall have spent his time in the understanding of it. And he says for his part were he to go to sea he had rather go with a man that had been once on the seas and able to guide and manage a ship or fleet than with him that had been 10 times at the haven.

The Master of the Ordnance was anciently a tradesman until 37 Hen. 8 and then it was conferred on a nobleman and ever since it has been in the nobility and was never well governed.

4° Ric.2 such granting of offices wrought a great disquiet in the state. 3 Hen. 7 oppression by subsidies made [a] rebellion. 14 Hen.8, when as great taxes were laid upon northernmen by the means of the Cardinal, the Earl of Northumberland being employed in the same the people slew him; the King he laid it upon his Council, his Council on the judges, and the judges on the Cardinal, and there it rested.

It has been told us that by the late King's neutrality the wars increased, *neutralitas nec amicos parit nec inimicos tollit*,[13] and as the case now stands it is a good project for the parliament and a worthy action to bring the King, that he may be able to subsist of his own estate which is now in a consumption. And the ship has a great leak which may be stopped yet, but if it be not stopped in time, it will all come to nought. And subsidies never given for the ordinary but for the extraordinary expenses of the King.

No state can subsist of himself in an honorable estate except it has 3 things.

First, free ability to support itself for his own necessaries and defense against any sudden invasion.

Secondly, that it must be able to aid his allies and foreign friends.

Thirdly, to reward his well-deserving servants. The ordinary to be discharged by the ordinary.

The causes of defect [are] not for want of income, but through the ill ordering of it, which grows either by wasting or surcharging it. And therefore the remedy must be accordingly There is *medicina removens* and *medicina renovans*.[14] He moves to have a committee to recollect the heads for memorials, which are great enemies to the revenue of the crown whereof fraud is one and instances what hurt it does in the customs. The officers bought their offices dear and they wink at the merchant. And then to make up all, there must be a medium and so the farmers grow rich. How is it else that he that was but a broken merchant lately, by farming the customs awhile, is now become worth 40 to 50,000 *l.*

Another is new-invented offices with large fees. 12 Edw.4, a complaint of the like nature for an office of Surveyor of the Brewer[s] with a large fee. And old offices with new fees [and new offices with new fees] to be repealed as by the law they may be with the love of the people and honor and profit of the

---

13. [*Ed.:* Neutrality does not win friends or remove enemies.]
14. [*Ed.:* medicine which removes [and] medicine which renews.]

King. President of York to cease, president of Wales to cease; they are both needless charges for the people who had rather to live under the government of the common laws. The western men had the same honor as may appear by the statute of 32 Hen.8, but they desired to be governed by the common laws and to shake off that honor. Another not to monopolize offices *singula officia singulis teneantur sicut judices,*[15] every officer to live off his office and not to beg other things.

If the old offices and old orders were kept there would be no need of new tables and therefore Sir Simon Harvey by his will should out of his offices. And voluntary annuities and pensions to be retrenched are not bought and sold, and a new market kept of them as now it is. And all unnecessary charges and portage money twelve *d.* of the pound taken away whereas they make great gain of it themselves.

And overmuch bounty is another thing that is to be restrained. For here is no friend to the King or state that seeks a fee farm or a new office. The statute of 4 Hen.4: no man ought to beg any thing of the crown till the King be out of debt. This statute is called Brangwyn, which is Welsh for a white crow. They are like a crow ever craving, and for their sins they are white. In the time of want and dearth, as now it is, costly apparel, diet, and Lady Vanity is to be abandoned.

And thus much for *medicina removens*. Now for *medicina renovans*. The King has 31 forests, and parks almost without number. Every one of them is a great charge to the crown. And therefore those to be peopled, and what greater honor can be to the King than by building of churches and increasing of his people without doing wrong to others to grow rich. Besides, Ireland, which is now a very plentiful and rich nation (pray God it be not monopolized), by Holinshed it appears that in King Edward the 3d's time yet it did yield clearly unto the crown 30,000 *l.* per annum and now is a great charge to the crown.

His project. There is no farmer that had any lease made unto him by King James but will give half a year's rent, with all his heart, to have the same confirmed by King Charles. And if the King will take these courses he did hope, as old as he was, to live to see King Charles to be styled Charles the Great.

15. [*Ed.:* Single offices should be held by single individuals, as in the case of judges.]

6 Edw. 3, *numero* 4°, a[nd] 5 Edw. 3, *numero* 5°. The Commons did petition the King to live off his own estate and there it is alleged that the ordinary revenue should maintain the ordinary charge. 27 Edw. 3, *numero* 9°, the King did not make a new charge to an old office.

6 Edw. 1 and 1 Hen. 5 upon an extraordinary aid and grievance the Commons show that the King ought to keep himself within his compass.

That shop boys be not taken from their shops and placed in the office of Green Cloth.

5 Hen. 4. 11 Hen. 6 *numero* 24 *et* 25, the Lord Cromwell being then Treasurer acquainted the Commons with the King's revenue and his goings out and prayed them that the[y] would take a course to keep the King within his revenue. And in 1° Hen. 7 and 11 Hen. 7 the Commons confined his Majesty to his revenue.

August 10, 1625.[16]

Ed.: In debate on the Supply.

Sir Edward Coke, who said, "That two leaks would drown any ship. That *solum & malum concilium*[17] was a bottomless sieve. An officer should not be, *cupidus alienae rei, parcus suae; avarus republicae; super omnia expertus. Misera servitus est, ubi lex incerta aut incognita.*[18] That in the 11th Hen. 3. Hubert de Burgh, chief justice, advised the king that Magna Charta was not to hold, because the king was under age when that act was made. He was created earl of Kent, but degraded for this some time after. In the 16th Hen. 3. Segrave, chief justice, was sentenced for giving sole counsel to the king against the common-wealth. That it was *malum consilium* to press more Subsidies when they had given two; and to bring them hither only for 40,000*l*. And, lastly, offered to give 1000*l*. out of his own estate, rather than grant any Subsidy now." The result of all which was, resolution was then agreed on, "That a committee of the whole house should be appointed at eight o'clock the next morning, to consider what return to make to his maj's message delivered this day."

---

16. [*Ed.:* Cobbett, *Parl. Hist.,* II, 35.]

17. [*Ed.:* the ill advice of one person.]

18. [*Ed.:* covetous of another's property, sparing with his own, greedy with the state, his finger in every pie. It is miserable slavery where the law is uncertain or unknown.]

D. 1628
Petition of Right

Parliament was focused at the outset on *The Five Knights' Case,* in which citizens were committed to prison not for crimes created by parliament or for avoiding a parliamentary tax but for not paying loans that were in theory voluntary but were in fact coerced by the King. Their writs of *habeas corpus* had been denied by the newly obedient King's Bench. Seventy-six men lingered in prison over the winter. Charles I's opening address, warning members not to meddle in his affairs, helped little. Coke, elected independently by two separate constituencies, but seated only for one, was by then at the extreme of his opposition to Charles, although his deep loyalty to the Crown was a continuing theme in his actions. Coke moved early for a committee of the whole to consider both grievances of Parliament and the King's supply, or tax support for military or other unusual expenses. Commons passed a remonstrance against Charles's unilateral raising of money from tonnage and poundage. Coke argued for the protection of *habeas corpus,* moving for a Petition of Right, which was drafted on his lines and voted up. There were numerous arguments over details, particularly over the King's use of martial law, which Coke opposed. The House of Lords introduced an amendment to save the "sovereign power of the Crown." Coke persuaded the Commons to defeat the amendment. The Lords, influenced largely by Coke, who represented Commons to them, agreed with the amendment's removal. The King, advised by Buckingham, initially gave an evasive answer that would not amount to acceptance of the Petition as law. Coke denounced Buckingham as the cause of the King's insult to parliament. The Lords and Commons made a new joint address to Charles I, asking him to assent. Charles I assented to the Petition of Right as a statute of the realm, and the Commons granted him his supply, having already passed five subsidies, or emergency grants and specialized taxes on goods.

During the ongoing debates on the Petition of Right, other debates on religious issues occupied considerable attention, and Parliament passed laws against religious error.—*Ed.*

March 20, 1628.[1]

Ed.: In debate on the elections of members and of certain government officials.

Sir Edward Coke. It behooves us with all endeavor to labor that the kingdom be kept in unity. The devil put in this. This is not to cut the member but to strike the root. They must have men of gravity. These men make a separation between king and people. I beseech God this Machiavellian trick be found out and punished.

. . .

Sir Edward Coke. We passed divers excellent laws last parliament. Let a note be made of them, and let them be delivered to the House upon Monday morning.

. . .

Sir Edward Coke.[2] I have spent my youth in Suffolk, my age in Buckinghamshire, and had a thought never more to have seen a parliament. I desire there may be no precipitation but that a few days may be allotted to consider. For questionable elections, I humbly move they may be examined in order as they come.

March 21, 1628.[3]

Ed.: Describing an unwritten, but proposed bill to bring in the names of recusants.

1. [*Ed.:* "Proceedings and Debates," f. 8v. In Johnson, Cole, Keeler, and Bidwell, *Common Debates 1628.* vol. II, p. 34. (hereinafter *CD, 1628.*)]

2. [*Ed.:* Stowe Ms. 366, March 20, 1628, 5.]

3. [*Ed.:* Harleian MS, March 21, 1628, f. 289v, in *CD, 1628,* II, 44.]

Sir Edward Coke[4] said that to draw a committee before we have a bill, and it be read, is not usual. Let it be first read, for we must have a subject, a foundation, and that is it we must work upon.

> *Ed.:* In debate on the limits of property forfeiture or loss of life before attainder or conviction.

Sir Edward Coke said, in 4to Hen. 6, the Chancellor of England did use to take a theme, and divide it, and speak of some subject therein. And that was, "While we have time let us do some good." So I, at this time, "Let us do something." Mr. Speaker, nothing is more precious to a man in this life than liberty. Imprisonment is a heavy punishment; and yet just in many cases. The law gives remedy if a horse or a sheep be taken. If a man be in prison, God forbid but the law should give remedy. It doth give remedy, you know right well. There is a *habeas corpus*[5] that the judges cannot deny. Nay, there is a writ called *de homine replegiando*,[6] grounded upon Magna Carta. If a man be unjustly committed, there is a writ, and secret of law in it. But many do think that this writ is gone. So saith Stanford; he gave his opinion of 28 Edw.3. but he comes with that of 42 Edw.3, a law made that all statutes made against Magna Carta should be void; but this writ is grounded upon that; then it stands. Thus the secret of law. If they repeal the act first, the law resolves we have laws made that men should not be long detained in prison. If the keeper of a jail keeps me in prison, and do not sue out a commission of free deliverance, he loses his prison. So that the prison is but a surety to bring a man forth, if he have no surety. But shall a man be in perpetual imprisonment? That is against the law of the land. For seeing a man hath surety for himself, God forbid the law should hold him in prison. The law is curious in this, touching the liberty or freedom of a subject. To give strength to the law, I have penned a bill. I do not doubt but this bill will have many oppugners. Therefore I keep my reasons till the time.

The bill read, entitled An act against long and unjust detainment of men in prison.

---

4. [*Ed.:* Harleian MS, March 21, 1628, 291v–92, in *CD, 1628*, II, 45.]

5. [*Ed.:* produce the body [a writ to review the legality of an incarceration.]]

6. [*Ed.:* For replevying a man; a writ of bail for one incarcerated neither for a crime nor by royal command.]

It recited that by the laws of the realm, no person in prison, or committed to prison, for any offense done, or supposed to be done, ought to be detained; but justice in convenient time is to be executed, that, if he be innocent, he may be acquitted and delivered. It is desired that no person now in prison, or restrained of liberty, or which shall be, by commandment or other warrant, for any contempt done or supposed to be done, shall, after the end of this session, be kept in prison. If he be not delivered within two months after the parliament, he shall within two months be set at liberty until an accusation be alleged. And for default of such discharge, the parties shall be freely discharged from all offenses committed by them within two months. And if any such person shall not be set at liberty, he shall be acquitted of all offenses whatsoever.

March 22, 1628.[7]

> *Ed.:* In a debate on the King's Request for supply, focusing on his abilities with regard to taxes and loans.

Sir Edward Coke. The way I shall take, I am absolutely to give supply to his Majesty, yet with some caution. To tell you of foreign dangers and inbred evils, I will not do it. The state is inclining to a consumption. It is curable. I fear not foreign enemies. God send us peace at home. For the disease I will propound remedies. I'll speak nothing out of my head, but from my heart and out of acts of parliament. I am not able to fly at all grievances, but only at loans. Let us not flatter ourselves, who will give subsidies if the King may impose what he will, and if after a parliament the King may enhance what he pleaseth. I know the King will not do it. I know he is a religious king free from personal vices, but he deals with other men's hands and sees with other men's eyes. Will any give any subsidy that he may be taxed after parliament what they please? The King cannot tax any by way of loan. I differ from them that would have it go by way of grievance, but I would have it go alone.

I'll begin with a notable record, it cheers me to think of it: 25 Edw.3, *num.* 16. It is worthy to be writ in letters of gold. Loans against the will of the subject

---

7. [*Ed.:* Proceedings and Debates, ff. 14–14v, in *CD, 1628,* II, 64–65.]

are against reason and the franchises of the land, and they desire restitution. What a word is that "franchise." Villeins *in nativo habendo*,[8] their lord may tax them high or low, but this is against the franchise of the land for freemen. "Franchise" is a French word, and in Latin it is liberty. In Magna Carta, *nullus imprisonetur*[9] nor put out of his liberty or franchise. 9 Hen.3, *cap.* 29 have been confirmed by good kings 33 times. 12 Hen.3, *sententias lata super cartas*.[10] The Magna Carta is called *carta libertates et franchisae*.[11] *Rot. pat.*, 21 Hen.3, *mem. 4, Carta libertatis quia liberos facit*,[12] and to overthrow it makes slaves.

42 Edw.3, they make a law that all laws against Magna Carta are void. Edw.1, statute *de confirmatione cartarum*,[13] no benevolence nor aid shall be but by assent of the realm; 25 Edw.1, which expounds Magna Carta. 34 Edw.1, *nullum tallagium seu auxilium per nos ponetur sine voluntate baronum, etc.*[14] They were wise, they unfolded much in few words. *Tallagium* comes *a talliare*,[15] from cutting. You shall not cut a part of my substance without my will, and that is tailoring excises of bread and wine. It is cutting if you cut any part of the subject. No tallage shall be done; the word *tallagium* was in the Conqueror's time. W. Conqueror, *volumus ut omnes liberi homines habeant terras suas in pace sine omni tallagio, ita quod nihil exigatur nisi per communem concessum*,[16] as appears by Mr. Lambarde's ancient laws, etc.

Objection: 34 Edw.1. is no act of parliament.

Answer: 'Tis true it is in the form of a charter, but yet an act of parliament. 9 Ric.2, *rot.* 10, the King cannot raise supply but by assent of parliament. 5 Ric.2, many undone by loans.

Objection: May not enemies come in, and in such a time of necessity may not loans be?

Answer: 13 Hen.4, *rot. parl.*, 10 *et* 18, no tallage or subsidy for defense of

8. [*Ed.*: For having a villein; a writ to apprehend a villein who had run from the lord's state.]

9. [*Ed.*: no one shall be imprisoned.]

10. [*Ed.*: the sentences [decisions] made upon the charters, a statute passed in 1228 codifying some rulings made on the basis of the charters.]

11. [*Ed.*: the charter of freedom and franchise.]

12. [*Ed.*: the charter of liberty, because it makes men free,]

13. [*Ed.*: for confirmation of the charters,]

14. [*Ed.*: no tallage or aid shall be imposed by us without the consent of the barons.]

15. [*Ed.*: *Tallagium* [tallage, or tax] comes from *talliare* [to cut.]

16. [*Ed.*: We will that all free men shall have their lands in peace without any tallage, so that nothing will be exacted except by reason of a common concession,]

the realm or sea shall be without act of parliament, for parliaments ought to be every year.

Fortescue, *cap.* 34 *et* 35, shows how in other countries they set impositions at will, but the king of England *per se aut ministros tallagium aut subsidium non potest imponere sine assensu totius regni.*[17] Escuage, you know, may be uncertain, and though it be done in respect of tenure, yet being uncertain it cannot be without act of parliament.

Hen.7 got a benevolence of his people and he made a promise in parliament not to do the like again, 11 Hen.7, *cap.* 10, *rot.* 16 Henry 8, the great cardinal made a commission to take the sixth part of all plate. When they came into Norfolk and Suffolk they rose and would not pay it. The King laid it on the Council and said "I never consented to this commission." 34 Hen.8, "*Quinzime,*" *br.*9, no tallage can be without act of parliament. I do but gild gold to constrain a man to lend. None can be sure of his own.

Question: What will you do?

Answer: I would have this loan an act of parliament, and as a preface to an act of subsidies, and woven into it, and let the other grievances be in all humility tendered to his Majesty. And I do not despair. His Majesty is most free of all his predecessors.

March 24, 1628.[18]

Ed.: In a debate over a bill for conscripting soldiers, considering the role of Deputy Lords Lieutenant.

Sir Edward Coke. When they shall come to it the deputy lieutenants have a greater excuse than everyone knows of. I'll tell them how the law stands at this day. When I was a student I could not understand two statutes that concern this point: 5 Hen.2, *cap.* 10, 18 Hen.6, *cap.* 19. I was in a wood; never any book case explained them, and those statutes say that if any soldier be returned by indenture, and returned by record, for the terms to serve their master, etc.,

17. [*Ed.:* A tallage or subsidy cannot be imposed by him or his ministers without the assent of the whole kingdom.]

18. [*Ed.:* Proceedings and Debates, f. 16, in *CD, 1628,* II, 79–80.]

I found a precedent of an indenture of a soldier of Erpingham. *In republica sunt servanda jura belli.*[19] Sir John Erpingham was sent for to the King and treated with him for the soldiers, and came down into the country and got his tenants and others that went with him. See for this 48 Edw.3; 9 Edw.4, 16; 21 Edw.4, 75. It was an excellent law, that the poor man went with his lord and master, but for an Englishman to go with a stranger, what misery is it? They must not be *sine fide et sine sede*[20] that are captains. It must be with one that he may live with when he returns. In Edw.3 times there came a new course, men were pressed. I had rather live under a sharp law than under no law, *et nihil novum sub sole,*[21] the same course was then as is now. Then they pressed men, and 25 Edw.3, *cap.* 8, it was enacted that no man shall find arms and munition but by his tenure. There's a negative law; 4 *et* 5 *Phil. et Mar., cap.* 2 was but for a time. Now they have new courses and new discipline. But now we are without law. I hold the deputy lieutenants lie under the stroke of the law for what they do. Let there be a committee of soldiers and others of my profession to pen a law for them. For the love of God and safety of the realm, let it not be said that there wants laws that touch government, that we may live under a law and not other men's discretions.

    . . .

Ed.: In a debate on supply.

Sir Edward Coke.[22] I am heartily glad that I find a concurrence in matter and judgment. It concerns us in point of honor. It is a tender point to a king. I would not have so great a price set on it as honor. The King hath precedency. We will consider of supply and grievances too. Both were propounded. The order gives the supply the precedency. We cannot give the King honor; he hath all honor. It was the purpose of the House to look into grievances. If loans be not taken away from us, we cannot do what we desire.

    . . .

19. [*Ed.:* The laws of war are to be preserved in the commonwealth.]
20. [*Ed.:* without faith and without a fixed abode.]
21. [*Ed.:* and there is nothing new under the sun,]
22. [*Ed.:* Proceedings and Debates, f. 18, in *CD, 1628,* II, 84.]

In the Committee for Religion

Ed.: In debate concerning lease laws relating to recusants.

Sir Edward Coke.[23] The proclamation touching recusants and the commission for composition, to speak freely, is a toleration. When I was Attorney, when a lease was made of recusants' lands, there was a special covenant that they should not come into a recusant's hand, as now it doth. What doth it differ from a toleration? If there be such a commission, 'tis against the law. This man that hath it is to be brought here, and to be examined how many recusants he hath compounded with, and to bring all the commissions in.

March 25, 1628.[24]

Committee of the Whole House

Ed.: In a debate concerning a subject's liberties in his person and in his property, the Parliamentary response to *The Five Knights' Case.*

Sir Edward Coke. I like the motion well to have time given. The matter is very weighty, and of very great consequence. *In medio tutissimus ibis.*[25] I shall ever be as ready to maintain the King's prerogative as any man. I have been twice sworn to it, and it was resolved 3 *Jac.* at the parliament that the King's prerogative is the supreme part of the laws of the realm. No other state is like this.

Divisos ab orbe Britannos.[26] We have a national law appropriate to this kingdom. If you tell me of other laws, you are gone. I will only speak of the laws of England. This question is a question of law. That Mr. Attorney may have something to answer, I will say somewhat, and I shall speak with reverence; and I would not speak were it not that my gracious King I hope shall hear it. It is not I, Edward Coke, that speaketh it. I shall say nothing, but the

---

23. [*Ed.:* Proceedings and Debates, f. 18v, in *CD, 1628*, II, 85.]
24. [*Ed.:* Proceedings and Debates, ff. 21–21v, in *CD, 1628*, II, 100–101.]
25. [*Ed.:* You shall go most safely in the middle, or moderate way.]
26. [*Ed.:* The British are separated from the rest of the world.]

records shall speak. I shall be ready to convert myself on better reason. *Errores ad sua principia referre est refellere.*[27] This opinion grows out of Westminster I and Mr. Stanford, that these men shall not be bailed: those that are in for murder or by command of the King or of his justices or of the forest, Stanford accordingly. In every text mark the context. The command of the King is in the King's Bench, which is there *coram rege,* and *per preceptum regis,*[28] is the command of the judges of the King's Bench, and the other justices of the Common Pleas.

And in the same time I will show you that the command of the King is meant by the judges. Westminster 1, *cap.* 9, if men follow not with hue and cry they shall be amerced by the by King. 2 Ric.3, 11, *non in camera regis sed in curia regis,*[29] and it shall be by the justices. Westminster 1, *cap.* 20, *de malefactoribus in parcis,*[30] 'tis a grievous law. He shall be fined at the King's will, that is at the will of the judges. The King distributes his power by the judges. Westminster 1, *cap.* 26 and 29, it is given to the King, it is meant the judges. The same men that made that law made that question, and by the King is meant the King's justices. 1 Ric.2, *cap.* 12, mentions the warden of the Fleet, etc., if not by the King's [writ] or by the commandment of the King. H.4. took it literally; one was in execution in the Fleet, the King sent him for a soldier, but that ought to be by a command from some court. 5 *Mariae* 162; 13 *Eliz.* 297, Westminster 1 say, none shall be bailable by the command of the King; it must be taken by some courts of justice. For the reasons of the judgment I heard them not nor understand them. I will speak *in rem* and not *in personam.*[31] *Pasch.,* 18 Edw.3, *rot.* 33, *coram rege,*[32] Bildeston's case. Edw.3 first made a warrant showing no cause to apprehend a man, and had a writ under the great seal to deliver this man to the Tower till further order should be taken by the King. This command came not verbally or by any signification, but by writ, and he lay two years in the Tower, and there the King commanded that he should be brought into the King's Bench, which was by *habeas corpus,* and there before Scott, the Chief Justice, they asked whether there were any

27. [*Ed.:* To trace errors to their beginning is to bring them to an end.]
28. [*Ed.:* before the king [and] by the king's command,]
29. [*Ed.:* not in the king's chamber but in the king's court,]
30. [*Ed.:* concerning wrongdoers in parks,]
31. [*Ed.:* to the matter and not the person.]
32. [*Ed.:* before the king [i.e. in the King's Bench],]

other cause of his commitment and the lieutenant said aright *nihil nisi breve praedictum*,[33] and they said that it is not cause sufficient, and so he was delivered. There was the King's writ and yet without cause. Then came another writ to show that they should have information that he coined the King's coin, and proclamation was made, and a short day given. This was not sufficient cause.

16 Hen.6, "*Monstrans de faits*"[34] 182, the King cannot command any to be imprisoned. 1 Hen.7. 4b, the King cannot arrest any man. Fortescue, *cap.* 8. concurs with the former. I never read one opinion against it. No free man ought to be committed but the cause must be showed in particular. If it be for treason or murder the particular must not be showed, but the general must. If he escape and break prison, if there be a particular cause, he shall suffer as if he were condemned for the fact. Commit him generally; if the jailer and he join together, it is fineable only. 1 Ric.2. *de Frangentibus Prisonam*,[35] the cause for which he is taken, etc. If the cause be not set down he may escape. I will conclude with the chiefest authority, the Acts of the Apostles, 25 *cap.* verse the last: It is against reason to send a man to prison and not to show the cause. What I speak it is that my Sovereign be truly informed of the laws, which I dare say he will defend with his sword, as well as his predecessors. I have now given a preparative to Mr. Attorney, according to the old course of physic, which is before you purge a man to give him a preparative. I have much more in store.

. . .

Sir Edward Coke. No restraint ever so little, but it is an imprisonment.

. . .

Sir Edward Coke. For us to touch anything that the King's prerogative can reach unto, it is dangerous. For employment in the King's service, shall we not leave that to the King and trust him therewith? 18 E.2, Beaumont was of the Great Council, and of the Privy Council. The King desired his counsel, to employ him abroad. He refused and was fined and imprisoned for it. I was employed to go to Ireland. I was willing to go and I hoped (if I had gone) to have found some Mompesson there. I would have gone, else I should have been fined and imprisoned.

33. [*Ed.:* nothing except the aforesaid writ,]
34. [*Ed.:* showing the record, demonstrating the legal basis for a claim or judgement.]
35. [*Ed.:* Concerning those that break prison,]

. . .

Sir Edward Coke. Qui bene distinguunt, bene docent.[36] I put my case of a great lord to give his counsel and to be an ambassador. The King cannot press soldiers to go beyond the seas. 1 Edw.3. is for soldiers but not for others things.

March 26, 1628.[37]

In the Committee of the Whole House

> *Ed.:* In a debate over supply, especially concerning appropriations and impressment and confinement of men for naval vessels.

Sir Edward Coke. These are matters of great weight. The course of this House is to deliberate well before we order. Let every man have a copy and keep it secret. Some things are general. If they were in particular we might give a better answer. It is desired to pay some arrears. We must know what they are, and we must consider the ability of the country to pay these, for we are to serve the country. What these arrearages are, none know.

. . .

Sir Edward Coke. Confinements in a foreign country or in a man's house is all one. This is a new-growing evil. *Venienti occurrite morbo.*[38] It is against Magna Carta. *Liber homo non imprisonetur.*[39] In Queen Elizabeth's time it was resolved no free man should be confined to any place whatsoever. Did that blessed Queen confine recusants till a law was made? And shall men that are no delinquents be confined?

It is much against the liberty of the subject that a Norfolk man should be confined to Cumberland. Let it be ordered that it is the ancient and undoubted right of the subjects of England not to be confined to a particular place but by act of parliament.

> *Ed.:* Concerning an oath administered by the commissioner of a loan.

---

36. [*Ed.:* He who makes good distinctions teaches well.]
37. [*Ed.:* Proceedings and Debates, f. 24v, in *CD, 1628,* II, 122–25.]
38. [*Ed.:* Remedy the growing disease.]
39. [*Ed.:* A free man is not to be imprisoned.]

Sir Edward Coke. One thing hath been moved. These loans were done by commission. No commission can be granted but it must be warranted by law, as a writ, a commission of jail delivery of *nisi prius,* etc., in all these it is *factum secundum legem Angliae.*[40] All commissions must not be new, but such as are in the register or in the Chancery. 18 Edw.3, all novel inquires and these adulterate commissions were damned by parliament. 9 Hen.4, *num.* 36, the King would regulate mariners by a commission, and it would not be, for that there was no such form. 1 *Eliz.,* a commission was granted to the Earl of Bedford to determine the right of an office in the Common Pleas, and they committed the poor man, who was delivered by a *habeas corpus.*

Ed.: Concerning the progress of debate, at the end of the morning session, addressing Edward Littleton, the speaker.

Sir Edward Coke. I never saw that moderation in any parliament as is used in this. Men ought to speak pertinently. When you hear a man not speak to the question, you in the chair are to stand up and take him off.

March 27, 1628.[41]

Ed.: This follows the reading of a petition from a conference with the Lords.

Sir Edward Coke. It joys my soul to see this care for the honor of God and His worship. One thing would be added. The Jesuits do now live in our realm. If we do nothing against them, I pray God they do nothing against us.

March 29, 1628.[42]

In the Committee of the Whole House

Ed.: Concerning the King's inability to imprison a freeman without cause.

---

40. [*Ed.:* done according to the law of England.]
41. [*Ed.:* Proceedings and Debates, f. 27v, in *CD, 1628,* II, 145.]
42. [*Ed.:* Proceedings and Debates, ff. 35–36, in *CD, 1628,* II, 190–193.]

Sir Edward Coke. This is *questio juris.*[43] They that have spoken pithily and learnedly, and that with all reverence to his Majesty and the Council. I said before I gave them a preparative that removed the humors, *humores moti* and not *remoti corpus destruunt.*[44] They that argued for the King would not answer what was said. They slighted it as nothing to the purpose. There is a figure called   *simulatio*[45] that (God forgive me) I used when I was in their places, that that we cannot answer we scorn and slight. I will leave this question as naked as Aesop's crow.

Duo sunt instrumenta ad omnes res confirmandas et confutandas: ratio et auc-toritas.[46] They that speak here must beat upon reason.

1. I shall produce therefore some reasons, first from the universality of the persons whom this concerns. *Commentaries, 236,* it is maxim that the common law hath so admeasured the King's prerogative that in no cause it can prejudice the inheritance of the subject, and how doth this absolute authority that is pretended concern not only the commonalty but the lords and all spiritual persons and all officers? For if he be committed and be called on for his office, his office is forfeited. It concerns all men and women, and therefore it deserves to be spoken of in parliament. This may dissolve this House, for we may be all thus committed.

31 Hen.6. *rot. 27, rot. parl.,* no member of the parliament can be arrested but for felony, treason, or the peace, and all here may be committed, and then where is the parliament? Sure the Lords will be glad of this; it concerns them as well as us.

2. The second reason is from the indefiniteness of the time, *non definitur in lege.*[47] Had the law given this prerogative it would have set some time to it, else mark what would follow. I shall have an estate of inheritance for life or for years in land or property in my goods, and I shall be a tenant at will for my liberty, and I shall have property in a goose and not liberty in my person. *Perspicua vera non sunt probanda.*[48]

Objection: When you were Chief Justice you did otherwise than now you

---

43. [*Ed.:* a question of law.]
44. [*Ed.:* Humours destroy the body when disturbed, not when they are removed.]
45. [*Ed.:* pretence.]
46. [*Ed.:* There are two instruments for confirming and refuting all things: reason and authority.]
47. [*Ed.:* it is not defined in law.]
48. [*Ed.:* Obvious truths do not need to be proved.]

speak. I would have another speak truth: Wray was wont to say letters of great men were letters of justice. When I was a student I wondered what he meant. His meaning was that letters in that kind do let justice, or further it. Nothing fell out in my place of justice, but I kept a note of it. Beckwith was committed and no cause showed. We meant to bail him, and then came the lords' letter that we should bail him (God be thanked for it) and the letter was kept and my note saith so. Sir John Broket was committed and no cause showed, and perhaps the judges would have delivered him, and then came a letter from the lords (God be thanked). The Council Table must be maintained, or the commonwealth will perish.

Objection: There was a *mandatum regis*[49] and the party was remanded. I deny that I ever was at any disputation in my place of any judgment that was given. I confess freely when I read Stanford only, perhaps I was of his opinion; but when I saw such a company of authorities against it, God forbid that I should follow my guide when my guide goes wrong. 12 Hen.7. Yew's case, he was committed *tam pro felonia quam per mandatum domini regis:*[50] the attorney, seeing the court would deliver him, *retraxit mandatum suum.*[51]

If the King had such as prerogative for which there was only an opinion of one judge in Queen Mary's time, shall that weigh down so many acts of parliament and precedents as are on our sides?

The *remittitur quousque,*[52] what means the *quousque?*[53] That is *quousque secundum legem terrae deliberatur*[54] but it is not *quousque curia advisari vult.*[55] In Hen.6. Markham was then a lawyer, and Edward the fourth asked him if the King might arrest one. The laws to the King are *quoad directionem* and not *quoad correctionem.*[56]

Fortescue, *cap. 8, nullus rex Angliae proprio ore*[57] can commit any; it is too

49. [*Ed.:* command of the king.]
50. [*Ed.:* both for a felony and by command of the lord King:]
51. [*Ed.:* withdrew his mandate.]
52. [*Ed.:* let him be sent back until [etc.].]
53. [*Ed.:* until.]
54. [*Ed.:* until he shall be delivered according to the law of the land.]
55. [*Ed.:* until the court will be advised.]
56. [*Ed.:* for direction and not for correction.]
57. [*Ed.:* no king of England by his own mouth.]

low a thing for him. 8 Hen.4, the King has distributed his judicial power to the courts of justice and ministers of justice, and it is too low for so great a monarch as the King is to commit men to prison. 18 Edw.3, *rot.* 33, Bildeston's case. *Sed quaesitum est del lieutenant si alia esset causa. Qui respondit non habuit nisi breve praedictum. Sed quia videtur curie breve non esse sufficient[em] ideo deliberatur.*[58] Here's a court that cannot be daunted with any fear. Now to your balance that is in your hands that sits in the chair. Put in Stanford and 21 Edw.1 (though it was nothing) into one balance, and into the other put 7 acts of parliament, 3 book cases, and the precedents; sure *haec via non ducit in urbem.*[59] For my reading, I never read any opinion or record against it.

There must be added that if any be committed for a just cause he ought not to be detained long in prison. By the Statute of Gloucester, if a man be imprisoned he shall remain there till the next coming of the justices, but there must be a time. Westminster 2, *cap.* 29, *rex concedit*[60] that none shall be long in prison, *ne diu detineantur in prisona.*[61] 8 Hen.4, if one have a jail and sue not a commission of jail delivery it is a forfeiture.

Ed.: Criticizing the precedential merit of an opinion in which Coke had allowed the Privy Council to commit a prisoner without bail.

Sir Edward Coke. This report moves me not. That report is not yet 21 years old, but under age, being 13 *Jac.* In truth when I read Stanford I was of his opinion, but after looking into those records before mentioned I was of another mind. He brings an ill time of 13 *Jac.;* there were many of the traitors of the powder treason then committed *per mandatum concilii.*[62] For the report, those apocrypha reports, there's no credit to be given to them. It was done by some young student that did mistake. It was no judgment of the court, but the student's own making.

---

58. [*Ed.:* But the lieutenant was asked whether there was any other cause; and he answered that he had none except the aforesaid writ; but because it appeared to the court that the writ was insufficient, he was therefore delivered.]

59. [*Ed.:* this road does not lead to the city.]

60. [*Ed.:* the King grants . . .]

61. [*Ed.:* . . . that they shall not be long detained in prison.]

62. [*Ed.:* by command of the council.]

March 31, 1628.[63]

In the Committee of the Whole House

> *Ed.:* In debate about a petition of both Houses concerning recusants, considering the effect of the precedent of 13 Jac.

Sir Edward Coke. The glass of time runs out, and some things cast amongst us have retarded us. When I spake against the loans and this matter I expected blows, and somewhat was spoken, though not to the matter. Concerning that which I did when I was a judge, I will say somewhat. Indeed a motion was made, but no argument or debate or resolution upon advice. I will never palliate with this House. There is no judge that hath an upright heart to God and a clear heart to the world but he hath some warrant for everything he doth. I confess when I read Stanford and had it in my hands I was of that opinion at the Council Table. But when I perceived some members of this House were taken in the face of this House and sent to prison, and when I was not far from that place myself, I went to my book, and would not be quiet till I had satisfied myself. Stanford was my guide and my guide deceived me; therefore I swerved from it. I have now better guides. Acts of parliament, and of other precedents, these are now my guides. I desire to be freed from the imputation laid upon me.

As for the intended judgment, I fear (were it not for this parliament) it had been entered. A parliament brings judges and all other men into good order. If a clerk had drawn this he would have done it by a precedent, and no precedent warrants it, and therefore some other did it.

This draft of the judgment will sting us, *quia nulla causa fuit ostenta, ideo ne fuit bayleable,*[64] and so it appears by the records. I persuade myself Mr. Attorney drew it. I had a copy of my Lord Anderson's report of 34 *Eliz.* long ago. I durst not vouch it as it was in that copy, for it was apocrypha, and did not answer his gravity that made it, and yet it was cited in the King's Bench that all the judges of England ruled it.

---

63. [*Ed.:* Proceedings and Debates, ff. 36v–37, in *CD, 1628,* II, 213.]
64. [*Ed.:* because no cause was shown, therefore he was not bailable.]

April 1, 1628.[65]

In the Committee of the Whole House

Ed.: This is a discussion of a book of writs compiled by Lord Anderson.

Sir Edward Coke. Of mine own knowledge this book was all writ with my Lord Anderson's own hand, and I had a copy of it in Queen Elizabeth's time. It is no flying report of a young student. I was Solicitor then, and Treasurer Burghley was as much against commitment as any of this kingdom; it was the white staves that made the stir. I know who it was that offended; it was not done by all. It was one that laid men in corners and dark places. Let us now go to the question.

. . .

Ed.: In a discussion about the inability to hold a suspect without cause.

Sir Edward Coke. When one is in one prison and brought thence into the King's Bench by *habeas corpus,* he cannot be bailed, if he be not in *Maresc.,* and if he be not bailed he is remanded to the prison from whence he came.

April 2, 1628.[66].

In the Committee of the Whole House

Ed.: This is a debate about the grant of supply for war.

Sir Edward Coke. When I considered from whence those articles came, and with what consideration they were molded, I doubted whether I should speak or not, but finding a way to speak out of a record, I will tell you my opinion. When poor England stood alone, and had not the access of another kingdom, and yet had more and as potent enemies as now it hath, and yet the King of England prevailed.

---

65. [*Ed.:* Proceedings and Debates, ff. 40–40v, in *CD, 1628,* II, 229–31.]
66. [*Ed.:* Proceedings and Debates, ff. 42v–43, in *CD, 1628,* II, 248–50.]

42 Edw.3, *num.* 2, in the parliament roll, the King and the parliament gave God thanks for his victory against the kings of Scotland and of France. He had them both in Windsor Castle as prisoners. What was the reason of those conquests? Four reasons were given: 1, the King was assisted by good counsel; 2, there were valiant men; 3, they were timely supplied; 4, good employment.

8 Ric.2, *num.* 3, the King was environed with the Flemings, Scots, and French, and the King of England prevailed.

17 Ric.2, *num.* 1, wars were in Ireland and Scotland. The King of England prevailed, and thanks were given to God here, and I hope we shall live to give God thanks for our King's victories.

13 Ric.2, *num.* 1, the King was environed with Spaniards, Scots, and French, and yet the King of England prevailed. I am now in no fear of Scotland.

Henry the fourth was a great warrior. The Bretons were a trouble to him. Calais assaulted, Ireland besieged, other troubles, but the King of England prevailed.

7 Hen.4, one or two great men about him so mewed him up that he took no other advice but from them. The Chancellor took this theme or text in his speech at the parliament, *Multorum consilia requiruntur in magnis. In bello qui maxime timent sunt in maximis periculis.*[67] Let us give and not be afraid of our enemies; let us supply bountifully, cheerfully, and speedily, but enter not into particulars. King Solomon's rule is *qui repetit separat,* nay *separat foederatos.*[68] We are united in duty, etc., to the King. The arrearages will of necessity separate us; *quae causa,*[69] it is a wonderful thing. This will turn us out into other discourses. Follow Solomon's rule, *qui repetit separat.*[70] The King hath 80 score thousand pound a year for the Navy, and to scour the Narrow Seas. It hath been taken, and we are now to give it, and shall we now give more to guard the seas besides, when that it is taken without our gift, and diverted another way? For the 1,000 horse and 10,000 foot, a pure defensive war is a vast thing, yet in an island defensive war is the safest. It is a great thing to have such an army. I will not speak against it, but in general I would give the King a bountiful supply. It shall never be said we deny the

67. [*Ed.:* The advice of many people is required in great things. Those who are most afraid in war are in the greatest danger.]

68. [*Ed.:* he who strikes again divides, nay divides the allied forces.]

69. [Ed for what reason,]

70. [*Ed.:* he who strikes again divides.]

King all supply. I think myself bound; where there is *commune periculum*[71] there must be *commune auxilium.*[72] The King, in King James his father's time, was an excellent means to procure all these excellent laws we then had, whereby is prevented all these worms, these locusts, the caterpillar, the informer, monopolizer, and concealer. We are in hand to have a fast. It shall be expedient that we pray that the King have good counsel and valiant men, and what we give be well employed.

April 3, 1628.[73]

In Conference with the Lords

Ed.: A Report to the House of Lords concerning Acts of the House of Commons dealing with the liberties of subjects.

Sir Edward Coke. "Your lordships have heard 7 acts of parliament in point, and 31 precedents summarily collected, and with great understanding delivered; which I have perused, and understand them all thoroughly: 12 of the precedents are *in terminis terminantibus,*[74] a whole jury of precedents, and all in the point. I am transported with joy, because of the hope of good success in this weighty business, your lordships being so full of justice, and the very theme and subject both promise success; which was *corpus cum causa,* the freedom of an Englishman, not to be imprisoned without cause shewn; which is my part to shew, and the reason and the cause why it should be so; wherein I will not be prolix; for to gild gold were idle and superfluous."—After that he had cleared some doubts made of the Statute of Westminster, which saith, 'That the sheriff, and others, in some cases, may not replevin men in prison,' he proceeded further and said, "That all those arguments offered unto you in this last conference, are of a double nature. 1. Acts of parliament. 2. Judicial precedents. For the first I hold it a proper argument for your lordships; because you, my lords temporal, and you, my lords spiritual, gave your assent unto

---

71. [*Ed.:* mutual danger.]

72. [*Ed.:* mutual assistance.]

73. [*Ed.:* Cobbett, *Parl. Hist.,* II, 266–71.]

74. [*Ed.:* in exact or determinative boundaries (directly on point).]

those acts of parl.; and therefore, if these cannot persuade you, nothing can. For the 2nd, which are judicial precedents, it is *Argumentum ab authoritate*,[75] and *Argumentum ab authoritate, valet affirmative;*[76] that is, I conceive (through it be no good argument to say negatively) the present judges gave no opinion in this point. 3. It is good law, which I fortify with a strong axiom. *Neminem oportet sapientiorem esse legibus.*[77] Now these two arguments being so well pressed to your lordships by my colleagues, I think you may wonder what my part may be: it is short but sweet; it is the Reason of all those Laws and Precedents; and reason must needs be welcome to all men: for all men are not capable of understanding the law, but every man is capable of reason. And these reasons I offer to your lordships, in affirmance of the antient laws and precedents made for the Liberty of the Subject, against Imprisonment, without cause expressed. 1. *A re ipsa.* 2. *A minori ad majus.*[78] 3. From the remedies provided. 4. From the extent and universality of the same. 5. From the in-definiteness of the time. 6. A fine.—The first general reason is, *A re ipsa,* even from the nature of imprisonment, *ex visceribus causae;*[79] for I will speak nothing but ad idem, be it close or other imprisonment; and this argument is threefold; because an imprisoned man upon will and pleasure, is 1. A bond-man. 2. Worse than bond-man. 3. Not so much as a man; for *mortuus homo non est homo;*[80] a prisoner is a dead man. 1. No man can be imprisoned upon the will and pleasure of any, but he that is a bond-man and villain; for that imprisonment and bondage are *propria quarto modo*[81] to villains: now *propria quarto modo,* and the Species, are convertible; whosoever is a bond man may be imprisoned, upon will and pleasure; and whosoever may be imprisoned, upon will and pleasure, is a bond-man. 2. If Freemen of England might be imprisoned at the will and pleasure of the king, or his commandment, then were they in worse case than bond-men or villains; for the lord of a villain cannot command another to imprison his villain without cause, as of disobedience, or refusing, to serve, as it is agreed in the Year-Books.'—And here he said, 'That no man

---

75. [*Ed.:* an argument from authority,]
76. [*Ed.:* An argument from authority has affirmative value;]
77. [*Ed.:* No one ought to be wiser than the laws.]
78. [*Ed.:* 1. From the thing itself. 2. From lesser to greater.]
79. [*Ed.:* the heart of the case;]
80. [*Ed.:* A dead man is no man.]
81. [*Ed.:* appropriate in the fourth way (according to the universality of the same).]

should reprehend any thing he said out of the books or records. He said, he would prove a freeman, imprisonable upon command or pleasure without cause expressed, to be absolutely in a worse case than a villain; and if he did not make this plain, he desired their lordships not to believe him in any thing else; and then produced two Book-Cases, 7 Edw. 3.; A prior had commanded one to imprison his villain; the judges were ready to bail him, till the prior gave his reason, that he refused to be bailiff of his manor, and that satisfied the judges. Second Case, 33 Edw. 3. Title Trespass 253. in Faux Imprisonment: it was of an abbot, 'who commanded one to take and detain his villain; but the cause being demanded, he gives it, because he refused, 'being thereunto required to drive his cattle. Ergo, Freemen imprisoned, without cause shewn are in worse case than villains, that must have a cause shewn them why they are imprisoned. 3. A Freeman imprisoned, without cause, is so far from being a bond-man, that he is not so much as a man; but is indeed a dead man, and so no man. Imprisonment is in law a civil death; *perdit domum, familiam, vicinos, patriam,*[82] and is to live amongst wretched and wicked men, male-factors, and the like. And that death and imprisonment was the same, he proved by an argument *ab effectis,*[83] because, they both produce the like im-mediate effects: he quoted a book for this; 'If a man be threatened to be killed, he may avoid feofment of lands, gifts of goods, &c. So it is if he be threatened to be imprisoned: the one is an actual, the other is a civil death. And this is the first general argument, drawn *a re ipsa,* from the nature of imprisonment, to which *res ipsa consilium dedit.*[84]—The second general Reason he took from his books; 'For, he said, he had no law, but what, by great pains and industry, he learned at his book; for, at ten years of age, he had no more law than other men of like age. And this second reason is, *à minori ad majus:*[85] he takes it from Bracton, '*Minima poena corporalis est major qualibet pecuniaria.*'[86] But the king himself cannot impose a fine upon any man, but it must be done judicially by his judges, *per justitiarios in curia, non per regem in camera;*[87] and so it hath been resolved by all the judges of England. He quoted 3 Rd.

82. [*Ed.:* He loses his home, his family, his neighbours, his country,]
83. [*Ed.:* from this effect.]
84. [*Ed.:* the thing itself gives counsel.]
85. [*Ed.:* from the minor to the major:]
86. [*Ed.:* The least corporal punishment is greater than a pecuniary penalty.]
87. [*Ed.:* by justices in court, not by the king in his chamber;]

2. The third general Reason is taken from the number and diversity of remedies, which the laws give against imprisonment, *viz. Breve de Homine replegiando; de Odio & Atia; de Habeas Corpus;* an appeal of imprisonment. *Breve de Manucaptione.* The two latter of these are antiquated; but the writ *de odio & atia*[88] is revived, for that was given by the statute of Magna Charta, cap. 29. and by statute of 42 Edw. 3. it is declared, That all statutes made against Magna Charta, are void. Now the law would never have given so many remedies, if the freemen of England might have been imprisoned at will and pleasure.—The fourth general Reason is from the extent and universality of the pretended power to imprison; for it would extend not only to the commons of this realm, and their posterities: but to the nobles of the land, and their progenies: to the bishops and clergy of the realm, and their successors. And he gave a cause why the commons came to their lordships, '*Commune periculum commune requirit auxilium.*'[89] Nay, it reached to all persons, of what condition or sex, or age, soever; to all judges and officers, whose attendance is necessary, &c. without exception; and therefore an imprisonment of the such extent, without reason, is against reason.—The 5th general Reason is drawn from the indefiniteness of the time, the pretended power being limited to no time, it may be perpetual during life and this is very hard. To cast a man into prison, nay, to close prison, and no time allotted for his coming forth, is a hard case, as any man would think that had been so used. And here he held it an unreasonable thing, that a man had a remedy for his horse or cattle, if detained, and none for his body thus indefinitely imprisoned; for a prison, without a prefixed time, is a kind of hell.—The 6th and last argument is, 'A Fine;' and *sapiens incipit à fine;*[90] and he wished he had begun there also. This argument he made threefold. *Ab honesto.*[91] This being less honourable. *Ab utili.*[92] This being less profitable. *A tuto.*[93] This imprisonment, by will and pleasure, being very dangerous for the king and kingdom.' 1. *Ab honesto.* It would be no honour to a king or kingdom, to be a king of bondmen

---

88. [*Ed.:* Writ requiring the sheriff to determine whether the charge is based only on hatred and ill will, in which case bail should be granted.]

89. [*Ed.:* A common danger requires common assistance.]

90. [*Ed.:* The wise man begins from the end;]

91. [*Ed.:* From what is honourable.]

92. [*Ed.:* From what is useful.]

93. [*Ed.:* From what is safe.]

or slaves; the end of this would be both *dedecus & damnum,* both to king and kingdom, that in former times hath been so renowned. 2. *Ab utili.* It would be against the profit of the king and kingdom, for the execution of those laws before remembered, Magna Charta. 5 Edw. 3. 28 Edw. 3. 42 Edw. 3. whereby the king was inhibited to imprison upon pleasure. You see, quoth he, that this was *vetus querela,*[94] an old question; and now brought in again, after seven acts of parliament: I say, the execution of all these laws are adjudged in parliament to be for the common profit of the king and people; and he quoted the Roll, 'This pretended power being against the profit of the king, can be no part of his prerogative."—He was pleased to call this a binding reason, and to say, 'That the wit of man could not answer it; that great men kept this Roll from being' printed, but that it was equivalent in force to the printed Rolls. 3. *A tuto.* It is extremely dangerous to the king for two respects; 11, of loss; 2, of destroying the endeavours of men. First, if he be committed without an expression of the cause, though he escape, albeit in truth it were for treason or felony, yet this escape is neither felony nor treason; but if the cause be expressed for suspicion of treason or felony, then the escape, though it be innocent, is treason or felony. He quoted a case in print like a reason of the law, not like a remittitur at the rising of the court, for the prisoner *traditur in ballium, quod breve regis non fuit sufficiens causa;*[95] i.e. the king's command. He quoted another famous case. The commons in parliament, incensed against the duke of Suffolk; desire he should be committed: the lords and all the judges, whereof those great worthies, Prescot and Fortescue, were two, delivered a flat opinion, That he ought not to be committed without an especial cause. He questioned also the name and etymology of the writ in question, *corpus cum causa; ergo,*[96] The cause must be brought before the judge, else how can he take notice thereof? Lastly, he pressed a place in the gospel, Acts 25, last verse, where Festus conceives it an absurd and unreasonable thing, to send a prisoner to a Roman emperor, and not to write along with him the cause alledged against him; send therefore no man a prisoner, without his causes along with him, *hoc fac & vives.*[97] And that was the first reason, *à tuto,*[98]

---

94. [*Ed.:* an old dispute.]
95. [*Ed.:* is delivered on bail, that the king's writ was not a sufficient cause;]
96. [*Ed.:* body with cause (an alternate form of *habeas corpus*).]
97. [*Ed.:* do this and you will live.]
98. [*Ed.:* that of avoiding risk,]

that it was not safe for the king, in regard of loss, to commit men without a cause.—The 2nd reason is, That such commitments will destroy the endeavours of all men. Who will endeavour to employ himself in any profession, either of war, merchandise, or of any liberal knowledge, if he be but tenant at will of his liberty? for no tenant at will will support or improve any thing, because he hath no certain estate; ergo, to make men tenants at will of their liberties, destroys all industry, and endeavours whatsoever. And so much for these six principal Reasons,

Taken
- A re ipsa.
- A minori ad majus.
- A remediis.
- From the Extent and Universality.
- From the Indefiniteness of the Time.
- A fine.

Loss of
- Honour.
- Profit.
- Security.
- Industry.

These were his reasons.—Here he made another protestation, "That if remedy had been given in this case, they would not have meddled therewith by no means; but now that remedy being not obtained in the king's bench, without looking back upon any thing that hath been done or omitted, they desire some provision for the future only. And here he took occasion to add 4 Book-Cases and authorities, all in the point, saying, That if the learned counsel on the other side, could produce but one against the liberties, so pat and pertinent, Oh! how they would hug and cull it. 16 Hen.6. Tit. Monstrance de Fait, 182. by the whole court, the king in his presence cannot command a man to be arrested, but an action of false imprisonment lieth against him that arresteth: if not the king in his royal presence, then none others can do it: *Non sic itur ad astra.*[99] 20 Hen. 6. 4. Hussey reports the opinion of Markham, chief-justice to Edward the Fourth that he could not imprison by word of mouth; and the reason, because the party hath no remedy; for the law leaves every man a remedy of causeless imprisonment: he added, that Markham was a worthy judge, though he fell into adversities at last by the lord Rivers's means, Fortescue, chap. 18. *Proprio ore nullus regum usus est*[100] to imprison any man, &c. 4. Eliz. a blessed queen, renowned for justice and religion. Pl. 235. The com-

99. [*Ed.:* He does not in this way achieve immortality (lit. is [not thus] gone to the stars).]
100. [*Ed.:* It is not proper that any rule be used.]

mon law hath so admeasured the king's prerogative, as he cannot prejudice any man in his inheritance; and the greatest inheritance; and the greatest inheritance a man hath, is the Liberty of his Person, for all others are accessary to it; for this he quoteth the Orator, *Major Haereditas, venit unicuique nostrum, a jure & legibus quam a parentibus.*[101] And these are the 4 authorities he cited in this point; now he propounded and answered two objections; 1st in point of state; 2ndly in the course held by the commons. 1. *Obj.* 'May not the privy-council commit, without cause shewed in a matter of state where secrecy is required? would not this be an hindrance to his maj.'s service? *Answ.* 'It can be no prejudice to the king as to matter of state, for the cause must be of higher or lower nature. If it be for suspicion of treason, misprision of treason, or felony, it may be by general words couched; if it be for any other thing of smaller nature, as contempt, and the like, the particular cause must be shewed; and no *individuum vagum,*[102] or uncertain cause to be admitted. 2. *Obj.* 'If the law be so clear as you make it, why needs this declaration and remonstrance in parliament? *Answ.* The subject hath in this case sued for remedy in the king's bench, by *Habeas Corpus,* and found none; therefore it is necessary to be cleared in parliament."—Here sir Edward Coke ended his discourse: and then he made a Recapitulation of all that had been offered unto their lordships, That generally their lordships had been advised by the most faithful counsellors that can be, *viz.* dead men; these can't be daunted by fear nor muzzled by affection, reward, or hope, of preferment; and therefore your lordships might safely believe them; particularly, their lordships had 3 several kinds of proofs. 1. Acts of Parliaments, judicial precedents, good reasons. 1. You have had many antient acts of parliament in the point, besides Magna Charta; that is, 7 acts of parl. which indeed are 37, Magna Charta being confirmed 30 times; for so often have the kings of England given their royal assents thereunto. 2. Judicial precedents of grave and reverend judges, *in terminis terminantibus,* that long since departed the world, and they were many in number. Precedents being 12, and the judges 4 of a bench, made 4 times 12 and that is 48 judges. 3. You have, as he termed them, *vividas rationes,*[103] manifest and apparent reasons.

---

101. [*Ed.:* A greater inheritance comes to every one of us from the law and the statutes than from our parents.]

102. [*Ed.:* vague particulars,]

103. [*Ed.:* manifest reasons,]

Towards the conclusion, he declared, That they of the commons have, upon great study and serious consideration, made a great manifestation unanimously, *nullo contradicente*,[104] concerning this great Liberty of the Subject; and have vindicated and recovered the body of this fundamental liberty, both of their lordships and themselves, from shadows; which some times of the day, are long, sometimes short, and sometimes long again; and therefore we must not be guided by shadows; and they have transmitted to their lordships not *capita rerum*,[105] heads or briefs; for these *compendia* are *dispendia*;[106] but the Records at large, *in terminis terminantibus.*' And so he concluded "That their lordships are involved in the same danger, and therefore, *ex congruo & condigno*,[107] they desired a conference; to the end their lordships might make the like Declaration as they had done, '*commune periculum commune requirit auxilium*;'[108] and thereupon take such further course, as may secure their lordships and them, and all their posterity, in enjoying of their antient, andoubted, and fundamental liberties."

April 4, 1628.[109]

In the Committee of the Whole House

Ed.: In a debate concerning subsidies and taxes.

Sir Edward Coke. This House was never yet divided. I came hither this day to give subsidies, and the King hath furthered me. If we should go away without giving, what rumors would there be, and what distractions in the town! Some have moved for poll money. I would have no new thing. I would have no constraint in wardships and subsidies. Let a man have a good pennyworth in his own land. Let it go by assessment. For poll money, there are divers precedents, but all with ill success. 4 Ric.2, *num.* 15, he demanded money by the

---

104. [*Ed.:* with no one speaking against.]
105. [*Ed.:* heads of things.]
106. [*Ed.:* Collections . . . waste.]
107. [*Ed.:* for the sake of congruence and equal dignity.]
108. [*Ed.:* mutual danger requires mutual assistance.]
109. [*Ed.:* Stowe MS, 366. April 4, 1628, 48v–49, in *CD, 1628*, II, 308.]

poll. It caused a rebellion where the rude multitude chopped off many a good man's head. 4 Hen.7, there was a new device to raise money, but the gentlemen of Yorkshire would not pay to that rate, whereupon the Duke of North-um-berland being sent amongst them, they chopped off his head also. In the country (for which I serve) the gentlemen are not much aforehand, and the poor are very poor. I agree with him that rung at the fore-bell, 5 subsidies to be paid between this and Christmas.

April 8, 1628.[110]

In the Committee of the Whole House

> *Ed.:* In a debate on a grievance from the regulation and quartering of soldiers.

Sir Edward Coke. There is a secret of law what may a lieutenant do by law. Before 27 *Eliz.* there were no continued lieutenants but upon certain occasions, as occasion did serve, like the High Commission Court, which was never but upon some occasions, for it is very dangerous to have it standing; no appeal can be from it. In time of peace a lieutenant can do nothing but according to law. Pasch., 39 Edw.3 *rot.* 92, *coram rege.* Thomas Lancaster in Edw.2 made an insurrection and was taken *flagrante crimine,*[111] and they gave judgment without indictment, and he was beheaded. *Sed pro eo quod non fuit arrainatus sed secundum leges, etc., et cur res fuit aperta; ideo fuit reversum,* that is, *tempus pacis.*[112] If the courts of justice be open, none ought to be executed. Nothing must be done but according to law, and it is adjudged that he was unlawfully put to death. If there be an uproar, if the King's courts be open you can do no martial law. 1 *Edw.3, pars prima,* Roger de Mortimer was executed by martial law when the King's court was open, and his heir had an assize and reversed it. Two laws will never stand in England: if the courts be open, no martial law. 14 Edw.3, 122, the   is more plain. Pasch., 28 Edw.3, rot. 33,

---

110. [*Ed.:* Proceedings and Debates, ff. 54v–55, in *CD, 1628,* II, 362–63.]

111. [*Ed.:* While the crime was flagrant, or during the crime.]

112. [*Ed.:* But because he was not arraigned according to the laws, etc., and [the king's court] was open, therefore it was reversed [that is,] time of peace.]

Worcester *coram rege,* Mortimer, Earl of March, was none of the best men, but you must punish him by law, else you make him innocent. He was taken and without judgment had his head chopped off, and his heir came and re-covered all.

This billeting of soldiers in my house is dangerous. *Domus est tutissimum refugium.*[113] One says, keep soldiers from idleness, or else *nihil cogitat nisi de ventre et venere.*[114] You hear how fruitful they are. There are 4,000 men now billeted. No doubt but upon an humble petition his Majesty, hearing of it, will take a course with them. The King of Denmark wants men; send them thither. Let a subcommittee draw a petition. If this vermin be in the country, it will disable and dishearten the country. No doubt his Majesty will meet us half way.

April 9, 1628.[115]

> *Ed.:* Considering a disputed election result for Coventry, in which two sheriffs returned results.

Sir Edward Coke. The words of the statute are, citizens free and residents be chosen, and no other. The judgement of the election is the right of them that sit here, and not the return of the sheriff. When I was Speaker this question was then, and it was answered the election is free and they may choose a stranger, and that law was made for the benefit of the citizen, and *quilibet potest renunciare juri pro se ipso.*[116] They may disclaim their own liberty, and give away their own liberties, and when they choose them by way of impli-cation this makes them freemen: and I was chosen in Cornwall, where I was never free nor resident, and I was then Speaker. The sheriff is not judge. He is to return according to the major number, and this House is to judge of it. In Buckinghamshire the county did elect one, and the sheriff would not return him because he was outlawed, and 1 *Jac.* he was here and punished.

This sheriff was called in and brought to the bar, and kneeled, and there confessed his fault that he did it out of ignorance, and confessed that Mr.

---

113. [*Ed.:* A house is the safest refuge.]
114. [*Ed.:* [They] think of nothing but filling their belly and sating their lust.]
115. [*Ed.:* Proceedings and Debates, ff. 56–57, in *CD, 1628,* II, 376–79.]
116. [*Ed.:* anyone is able to renounce a law made for his benefit.]

Greene and Mr. Purefoy had the plurality of voices, but because they were not residents he did not return them.

...

Ed.: Considering a warrant to dispatch troops, by a lawyer who was not a lieutenant empowered to dispatch them.

Sir Edward Coke. This gentlemen made a warrant for fear. *Habemus reum confitentem,*[117] he himself confesseth it. We have rules and they guide us. *Melius est omnia mala pati quam malo consentire.*[118] It is writ in every honest man's heart not to consent to ill. This man made a warrant when no warrant was made to him. 11 Ric.2, the judges, amongst whom was Bealknap, gave this opinion against his conscience and said it was out of fear; but at home he could not sleep but, said he, "I deserve 3 H's: a hurdle, a halter, and a hangman." After 1 Hen. 4, in the parliament roll, it is said that no man hereafter shall excuse himself by fear. I say cowards fear; *Vir sapiens est robustus.*[119] He will never shrink for fear. *Nihil est timor sed perditio.*[120] It betrays succors. It is no answer to say he hath given his judgment from fear. I mislike a man that differs from me in fear. This man is not *laicus* but *doctus.*[121] His credit is his life. Let our censure be *ad correctionem,* not *ad destructionem.*[122] His offense is great; this almanac must serve for the meridian of England. This example will prove more and try more than twenty points of doctrine, and it will strike far. *Solus Deus errare non potest.*[123]

April 10, 1628.[124]

Ed.: Debating the King's or the house's authority to adjourn or recess by prorogue.

---

117. [*Ed.:* We have a defendant who confesses,]
118. [*Ed.:* It is better to suffer every wrong than to consent to evil.]
119. [*Ed.:* The wise man is robust.]
120. [*Ed.:* Fear is nothing but desperation.]
121. [*Ed.:* not a layman but learned.]
122. [*Ed.:* for correction, not destruction.]
123. [*Ed.:* Only God is incapable of error.]
124. [*Ed.:* Proceedings and Debates, f. 60v, in *CD, 1628,* II, 400.]

Sir Edward Coke. I am as tender of the privileges of this House as of my life, and they are the heart-strings of the commonwealth. The King makes a prorogation, but this House adjourns itself. The commission of adjournment we never read, but say, "This House adjourns itself." If the King write to an abbot for a corody for a varlet, if it be *ex rogatu,*[125] though the abbot yields to it, it binds not. Therefore I desire that it may be entered that this is done *ex rogatu regis.*[126]

April 12, 1628.[127]

Ed.: Responding to a message from the King, which attempted to pressure the house to grant the supply quickly and to ignore their grievances.

Sir Edward Coke. Crede mihi, bene qui latuit, bene vixit.[128] I may say, *bene dixit qui bene tacuit.*[129] This message may prove gracious. It stands on 5 parts. First, his Majesty tells us he hath given us timely notice of his supply and of his expectation. Secondly, that he finds a stop. This we must clear or refer it to a committee, that we chalk out our proceedings, and if we can, let us open our stop, and show that we so proceeded as never subjects did. Thirdly, that he expects that we apply ourselves to his Majesty's affairs. My soul and all this House (for we have all one soul and one judgment and affection to the King) agree to that. Fourthly, that his Majesty's affairs (his affairs are the affairs of the kingdom) and ours proceed together, and not one to interrupt the other. Let us speak it with all reverence, we were the unworthiest men that ever lived or took any English air if we give not supply to the King, and to make provision for our liberties. If we be not interrupted with grievances, we shall end all, if his Majesty will give us a gracious answer, and to expedite them will expedite us. As for the conclusion, that shall never fall out, God forbid. Let us with all speed address ourselves to show there is no stop on our side, and prepare our grievances.

---

125. [*Ed.:* by desire,]
126. [*Ed.:* by the king's desire.]
127. [*Ed.:* Proceedings and Debates, f. 64v, in *CD, 1628,* II, 431–32.]
128. [*Ed.:* Believe me, he who has kept himself well hidden has lived well.]
129. [*Ed.:* He has spoken well who has kept silent.]

April 14, 1628.[130]

> *Ed.:* On Lord Suffolk's allegation that John Selden had destroyed records and had uttered sedition.

Sir Edward Coke. I persuade myself that that great Lord spake not of himself. Razing records is felony, and sure that noble Lord was informed that a record was razed, and that was felony. I expect that that worthy gentleman shall be an ornament to the law. But this toucheth not him but this House. The charge is heavy for razing records reported by a great Lord of noble blood. We are bound to stand by him and acquit him. Let us find out the author. If this be not righted, never employ any more. I will not speak of the Bishop of Durham, that lately presumed to offend in this kind. 21 *Hen.* 8, when the statute of nonresidence came in and bribes of the clergy suppressed, Bishop Fisher said it was want of faith; down goes the church, look to Bohemia. The House would not sit, but the Bishop made a friar's distinction and said he meant not the House of Commons, but Bohemia, and this was then accepted of. I hope this will not hinder the business. Set down the words *in verbis conceptis*[131] and desire justice of the Lords.

April 15, 1628.[132]

In the Committee of the Whole House

> *Ed.:* In debate on the regulation and quartering of soldiers, and the grievance for it, against an argument for the King's power, based on Coke's report of Lord Sanchar's case, 9 Reports 117.

Sir Edward Coke. I am glad there is no other authority than is cited. We touch not the King's power. The King hath power to grant commissions of oyer and terminer, but the manner now is only the question. The King may pardon felonies, no man disputes it; but if a pardon be good in a particular

---

130. [*Ed.:* Proceedings and Debates, ff. 66v–67, in *CD, 1628,* II, 448.]
131. [*Ed.:* in the words as solemnly uttered.]
132. [*Ed.:* Proceedings and Debates, ff. 73v–74, in *CD, 1628,* II, 466.]

cause, we do dispute every day. We do not innovate but what was done in the best kings' times. The martial law belongs to the Constable and Marshal. We set down in what times the martial law is to be executed. Those commissions now granted are not in the old form. Admit the King hath a power, that power may be regulated by act of parliament. 13 Ric.2, *cap.* 2, the King, willing to ordain remedy, hath declared the power of the Constable and Marshal: that the Constable is to have cognizance touching deeds of arms and war out of the sea, and also war within the sea that cannot be determined by the common law. The military men may find fault with the gentlemen of the long robes that dispute this power. I honor that profession. We will teach them how to use martial law.

April 17, 1628.[133]

In Conference with the Lords

Ed.: This is the second conference on the Liberty of the Subject.

Sir Edward Coke began thus:—'Your lordships have well perceived how fairly, and with what respect, we have dealt with you, and ever shall. We brought up unto you what we had resolved on; and not only that, but the cause and grounds of our resolutions, and all our records; the like whereof was never done in parliament and we are to maintain what we did. The natural and the politic body have a great resemblance and proportion: and as the natural body hath symptoms of good or evil health, so we hold it a good symptom for us, that Mr. Attorney was so long and so loth to come to it. My lords, we will break order rather than defer the business. This conference is between the two houses. Mr. Attorney is no member of your house: he attends you; but his voice is with us: yet we are so willing to proceed, that we will take no hold of threads: let him say what he can, we will allow him a voice here, where he ought not to speak. We have *delegatam potestatem, tantum permissam, quantum commissam;*[134] and therefore, for all new matter of this conference, we come with ears, not with tongues. For the resolutions of the

---

133. [*Ed.:* Cobbett, *Parl. Hist.,* II, 294.]

134. [*Ed.:* a delegated power, only permitted insofar as it has been committed;]

judges, we are glad of them; and we are confident never a judge in England will be against what we have resolved. We can say nothing to it; it is new matter; but we will report it faithfully to our house.

. . .

Sir Edward Coke[135] spake next. 'As,' said he, 'the centre of the greatest circle is but a little prick, so the matter ever lies in a little room; but weighty businesses are spun out to a high length. This he said, was more weighty than difficult: his part was little; he would run over Mr. Attorney's Reasons briefly; and, said he, '*summa sequar vestigia rerum.*[136] This tenet of theirs was expressed shortly and significantly: it was a wonder for him to hear the Liberty of the Subject should be thought incompatible with the regality of the king; for *nihil tam proprium est imperii, quam legibus vivere,*[137] saith Bracton. Nay further, *Attribuit rex legi quod lex ei; dominium enim & imperium exercere, sine lege, non potest.*[138]—First he, said, Mr. Attorney seemed to intimate, that, in this *speciale mandatum*[139] a cause should be conceived to blind the judges, when other matter was intended. He had heard indeed of that sentence, *Qui nescit dissimulare, nescit regnare;*[140] but he held it no good divinity; for David, in the 119th Psalm, desires 'a sound heart;' that is, a heart without dissimulation: ergo no king should cover to dissemble in his mandates. Then for that case of rebellion, in Ireland, he said, it was *bona terra, mala gens.*[141] But, he said, O'Donnel's children lost nothing by the bargain; *periissent nisi periisset:*[142] for they were better brought up here in the true religion, instead of popery. Besides, they have lost nothing, for their blood was tainted. It was charity to keep them. A strange proviso, that a thing happening once in 100 years should overthrow and marr so many statutes in continual use, against the old rule, '*Ad ea quae frequentius accidunt, jura adaptantur!*'[143] And he never heard of such an objection.—In the next Reason, he said, Mr. Attorney came close to

135. [*Ed.*: Cobbett, *Parl. Hist.*, II, 323–28.]
136. [*Ed.*: I will trace only the high points.]
137. [*Ed.*: nothing is so appropriate to supreme power as to live by the laws,]
138. [*Ed.*: The king bestows on the law what the law bestows on him; for he cannot exercise dominion and supreme power without law.]
139. [*Ed.*: a special mandate [scope of office].]
140. [*Ed.*: He who does not know how to dissemble does not know how to govern;]
141. [*Ed.*: a good land, but a bad people.]
142. [*Ed.*: they would have perished if he had not perished:]
143. [*Ed.*: The laws are adapted to those things which occur frequently.]

him, and said he was glad he had awaked him. That a king is trusted in greater things, as war, money, pardons, denisons; *ergo, &c. Negatur,* said he, for the liberty of the person is more than all these; it is *maximum omnium humanorum bonorum,*[144] the very sovereign of all human blessings: yea, but the king may make money of brass, (saith *Dionysius Halicarnasseus*) or other base metal, as he heard queen Elizabeth say, that her father, king Henry the eighth. did hope to live so long, till he saw his face in brass; i.e. in brass money. He said this was a main point: and that whatever the king's power was by the common law, yet was it qualified by acts of parl. And no man will deny but the king may limit himself by acts of parl.—He cited 9 Ed. 3. c. 4. 3 Hen. 5. c. 1. that the money must be of weight sterling; ergo, it must now be of the lay and fineness of sterling. In another statute, 'de dimissione denariorum,' it is required the coin should be *de legali metallo; ergo, not illegitimate.*[145] Why must the king have the mines of gold in my land, but for the use of his mint and coining? He cited also a law of King Edgar, C. 8. and of Canutus, C. 8. that no money should be current but of gold and silver. And for Pardons; they are also limited, in wilful murder; as he proved out of the 4 and 25 Edw. 8. And this he said by the way. Now his part was short; he had before expressed what books and warrants they had for their tenet. If he be a little more earnest than seems fitting, he craves your lordships pardon; it concerns him near. He takes occasion here to say (under reformation) his reasons were not answered, or not fully. He touched upon his former reason from imprisonment; that it is a badge of a villain to be imprisoned without cause; that this and *saller luy haut & bas sont propria quarto modo* to villains;[146] this he presents with all reverence; for we, said he, speak for the future times only: our king is good, and the council most gracious; but *non nobis nati sumus;*[147] it is for our posterity that we desire to provide, rather than for ourselves, that they be not in worse case than villains; for to be imprisoned without cause shewn, is to be imprisoned without cause at all. *De non apparentibus & non existentibus, eadem est ratio.*[148]—He agreed with Mr. Attorney in the enumeration of all the kinds of Habeas Corpus; and if they two were alone, he did not doubt but they

144. [*Ed.:* the greatest of all human goods,]
145. [*Ed.:* of lawful metal: therefore, not unlawful.]
146. [*Ed.:* Tallaging high and low are the proper signs, in the fourth manner.]
147. [*Ed.:* It was not for us that we were born;]
148. [*Ed.:* Things not appearing come under the same reasoning as things non-existent.]

should agree in all things. Only, he said, that for a freeman to be tenant at will for his liberty, he could never agree to it; it was a tenure that could not be found in all Littleton.—Then he also touched his former argument from universality; that the lords, the bishops, and all are jumbled and involved in this universality. Law doth privilege noblemen from arrests: this new doctrine, like the little god Terminus, yields to none. Nay, the judges themselves, when they should sit on the Bench, must be walking towards the Tower. Then he fell to a protestation, that he intended no prejudice at all to the king for matters of state; for the honourable must be maintained in honour, or this common-wealth could not subsist; but the question was, Whether they ought not to express the cause? He repeated again Plowden, 4 Eliz. pl. 236. The common law hath so admeasured the king's prerogative, as he cannot prejudice any man in his inheritance. He cited also 42 Edw. 3. c. 1. to prove that all judgments given against Magna Charta are void.—Next he was pleased to say, He was not so well dealt with in one particular as he expected: For a student's report should not have been cited against him. He desired Mr. Attorney to remember, he had not *veritatem ex cathedra;*[149] or infallibility of spirit; that was for the Pope. He said, he misgrounded his opinion upon 33 Hen. 6. which being nothing to the purpose, he is now assured his opinion is as little to the purpose.—Here he took notice of an objection, What, can you arrest none without a process or original writ? Why, the suspected fellow will run away? To which he answered, that process signifies the whole proceeding: and cited a rule in law, *Quando lex aliquod concedit, concedere videtur id, sine quo res ipsa esse non potest.*[150] The law gives process and indictment; *ergo,* gives all means conducing to the indictment. And this answers all Mr. Attorney's cases of watchmen and constables."

. . .

—"*Sir Ed. Coke* put your lordships in mind, that you had the greatest cause in hand, that ever came into the Hall of Westminster, or, indeed, into any parliament. My lords, said he, your noble ancestors, whose places you hold, were parties to Magna Charta; so called for weight and substance, for, oth-erwise, many other statutes are greater in bulk; as Alexander, a little man,

---

149. [*Ed.:* truth by reason of [the papal] chair;]

150. [*Ed.:* When the law grants something, it is deemed to grant everything without which the thing itself cannot be.]

called *magnus*[151] for his courage. And you, my lords, the bishops, said he, are commanded *fulminare*,[152] to thunder out your anathemas against all infringers of Magna Charta. (*Sententia lata super Chartas*).[153] And all the worthy judges that deserved their places, have ever had Magna Charta in great estimation. Now, as Justice hath a sword, so it hath a balance, *Ponderat haec causas, percutit ille reos.*[154] Put together, my noble lords, in one balance 7 acts of parliament, records, precedents, reasons, all that we have spoken, and that of 18 Edw. 3. whereto I found no answer; and, in God's name, put into the other balance what, Mr. Attorney hath said, his wit, learning, and great endowments of nature; and, if he be weightier, let him have it; if not, then conclude with us. You are involved in the same danger with us; and therefore we desire you, in the name of the commons of England, represented in us, that we might have cause to give God and the king thanks for your justice, in complying with us."—And here rested Sir E. Coke.

Ed.: In response to a call from the Lords for a further conference on the Liberties of the Subject, and a journal from the Commons of 1621, recording Coke's views then of Magna Carta.

Sir Edward Coke.[155] We speak our consciences as it is for the present. We sometimes change our opinions upon better reason. Also it is dangerous for us to allow this, for the Clerk with his pen may mistake in setting down words. Perhaps he mistook. Shall this conclude us? The Clerk may leave out somewhat, and say then some opinion were so. That shall not bind us. Let us answer that we will think of it, and give what answer shall be fit for us to give. It is not fit the book be any evidence against us. The Clerk's office is not to take our sayings, but to take the orders of the House only.

151. [*Ed.:* the great.]
152. [*Ed.:* to cast lightning bolts,]
153. [*Ed.:* opinion on the Charters [a statute].]
154. [*Ed.:* The case weighted in the one, the guilty punished by the other.]
155. [*Ed.:* Stowe MS 366, f. 77, in *CD, 1628,* II, 512.]

April 18, 1628.[156]

> *Ed.:* Debating the Liberty of the Subject, Coke draws an analogy between the rights of the subject to refuse an office and Richard de Pembridge's refusal of the Lieutenancy of Ireland.

Sir Edward Coke. For foreign employments there is a difference when the party is the King's servant and when not. 46 *Edw.* 3, *rot.* 33 *in dorso;* this was the time when the law was in its height. Sir Richard Pembridge was a baron and the King's servant and Warden of the Cinque Ports. He was commanded to go into Ireland and to serve as deputy there, *penitus recusavit, propter quod idem rex reducens in memoriam incensa beneficia ei impensa et propter inobedientiam suam et ingratitudinem, etc.*[157] Note that Ireland is part of the kingdom of England. What punishment had he? He was not committed, yet the King was highly offended because he had offices and fees and lands *pro servitio suo impenso.*[158] The King seized his lands and offices *et conservationem Quinque Portuum et Castrum Pembroke et custodiam forestae, etc., et custodiam haeredis J.S. durante minoritate commissam sibi per regem, volens quod praedictus non intromitteret et dat officia, etc.*[159] I went to the parliament roll, and in 47 *Edw.*3 there was another precedent for foreign employment. They that have offices and lands *pro concilio aut servitio impenso,*[160] if they refuse, those lands and offices so given were seized, but no committment.

---

156. [*Ed.:* Proceedings and Debates, ff. 78–78v, in *CD, 1628,* II, 540–541.]

157. [*Ed.:* he utterly refused on account of which the king called to mind the innumerable benefits bestowed on him, and, because of his disobedience and ingratitude, etc.]

158. [*Ed.:* for his service given.]

159. [*Ed.:* and the keeping of the Cinque Ports and Pembroke Castle, and the keeping of the forest, etc., and the wardship of the heir of J. S. committed to him by the king during the minority, willing that the aforesaid [Richard] should not intermeddle, and gave the offices, etc.]

160. [*Ed.:* for advice or service given,]

April 18, 1628[161]

In the Committee of the Whole House

> *Ed.:* In a debate on the jurisdiction of martial law over conscripts, Coke responds to an argument by Sir Henry Martens, that martial law displaces common law.

Sir Edward Coke. I shall maintain *jus belli. Maxime conservanda sunt belli jura.*[162] The civilian that expounded 13 *Ric.*2, his exposition corrupts the text. God send me never to live under the law of conveniency or discretion. He saith also both laws stand together cumulative. Bring it to a court of justice. Shall the soldier and justice sit on one bench? The trumpet will not let the crier speak, *non bene convenient.*[163] He vouched 4 *et* 5 *Phil. et Mar.* and the proviso there. That is one of the causes the statute was repealed. This is to go out of the text. The question must be determined by the law of England, and the martial law is bounded by it. If you bring me other laws it is not to the purpose. The common law is the great and principal law. Take a case mixed with the civil law, the common law carries it, 22 *Hen.*4. The civilians enjoy their lands by the common law, and not by the civil law. *Quod intempestivum injucundum.*[164] I will first show what is the time of peace, which is when the courts of Westminster are open, for when they are open then you may have a commission of oyer and terminer; and where the common law can determine a thing, the material law cannot. Pasch. 14 *Edw.*3, in the Exchequer, in the Earl of Kent's case. Hen.2 grants a fair to St. Ives rendering 50 *li.* per annum, and after, by another charter, he granted that if the profits of the fair be interrupted by reason of war, he should not pay the rent after the King grants the rent to the Earl of Kent. In a *scire facias* the abbot pleads that it was *tempus belli,*[165] and thereupon issue was joined. 18 *Edw.*2, "*Quare*

---

161. [*Ed.:* Proceedings and Debates, ff. 81–81v, in *CD, 1628,* II, 545–46.]
162. [*Ed.:* the law of war. The laws of war are important to be preserved.]
163. [*Ed.:* They do not well go together.]
164. [*Ed.:* What is inappropriate is unpleasant.]
165. [*Ed.:* time of war.]

Impedit," 175, the issue was passed if it were a time of war or of peace, and nothing is there ajdudged; but in 14 *Edw*.3 the record saith that the said issue ought to be judged by *recorda regis,* it shall not be tried by a jury but by the records. Whether martial law may be in time of peace, 21 *Edw*.4, 10, *de termino Trinitatis nihil, quia tempus duelli et non tenuit.*[166] 1 *Hen*.4, all the appeals of things done within the realm shall be tried by the good law, so called *in opposito* in the cruel war. If two men go into a foreign nation and there fight and one is killed, the martial law tries it by way of appeal according to the civil law. 13 *Hen*.4, fol. 5, *accordant.* Drake slew Doughty beyond sea. Doughty's brother desired an appeal in the Constable and Marshal's court, and Wray and the other judges resolved that he might there sue. We make no law, we must not mediate *ubi lex non distinguit.*[167] To hang a man *tempore pacis*[168] is dangerous. I speak not of prosecution against a rebel. He may be slain in the rebellion, but after he is taken he cannot be put to death by the martial law. Pasch., 39 *Edw*.3, *rot.* 49; 28 *Edw*.2, *num.* 13, when the courts are open martial law cannot be executed. 5 *Hen*.4, *num.* 39, Wilman's case, the Constable and Marshal desired an addition to their commission, and they proceeded against some according to that power; but because it was not according to their ancient power it was void, for they cannot do anything according to that additional power, and there was a prohibition to stay their proceedings by virtue of that additional power. 6 *Hen*.7, 4, 5, the King granted a leet and that there should be cognizance of rape, and the grant was void. So, if the King grant to the justices of the Common Pleas to hear felonies. The civilian provided for himself, and said the commission is only for actual soldiers, but the commission goes to all soldiers, and all that shall join with them. And who shall judge of this, who are soldiers and who they are that join with them? There are now 60 articles to which that commission hath reference; 40 of them are written in blood. How shall the soldier know how to obey them? They are not under the Great Seal. The Council of York had a commission with reference to instructions. When I was judge in the Common Pleas, we granted prohibitions, and after, King James caused them to be added to the commission itself.

166. [*Ed.:* for Trinity term, nothing, because it was the time of battle and it was not held.]
167. [*Ed.:* where the law makes no distinction.]
168. [*Ed.:* in time of peace.]

April 21, 1628.[169]

Ed.: Reporting on the conference with Lords, held on April 17.

Sir Edward Coke. I will tell you how I began. The Lords and we stayed an hour for Mr. Attorney before he came. When he came I made a protestation, and I observed it was a good symptom, he was so loath to come to it. I said he was by order of parliament not to speak. If he had any voice at all, his voice was here with us; but the case was such that to expedite it we would break any order. My part fell into reason. He said there was an incompatibility between a monarchy and our resolution. But I said *nihil est tam proprium monarchiae quam leges et sine legibus non potest esse imperium.*[170] He said that sometimes the true cause must be concealed and hid. But I said that holds not in law; *qui nescit dissimulare nescit vivere.*[171] He put a case of Irish rebels that were put in the Tower. I answered it was charity to keep them. And Sir Dudley Digges answered they are to lie there till they find good sureties for their good behavior, which they are not able to do, and also *ad ea quae frequentius accidunt jura adaptantur,*[172] and that case has not fallen out but seldom. He leaped over seven statutes by the art of simulation, and four cases he put by way of simile, as money, the King may make it of what metal he please, etc., and therefore he may imprison. It is a plain *non sequitur.* But I answered this case of coining by the statute of 25 *Edw.* 3 and 9 *Hen.* 5, all money must be of the lay of sterling. I told him what I heard Queen Elizabeth say of her father's nativity that was cast, and that he should live till he saw his face brass, and so he did. Copper payment is no payment. But it was further answered, admit the King abase his money, he himself suffers more than the subject. So if he make war (which was another of the Attorney's similes) he and the subject are both involved there. To pardon a malefactor, or to make a denizen (which were his other cases), the King may lose by it. Therefore may he imprison? A strange argument, a simile. He said the judges

---

169. [*Ed.:* Proceedings and Debates, ff. 83–83v, in *CD, 1628,* III, 5–6.]

170. [*Ed.:* Nothing is so appropriate to monarchy as laws, and supreme power cannot exist without laws.]

171. [*Ed.:* He who knows not how to dissemble knows not how to live.]

172. [*Ed.:* The laws are adapted to things which occur frequently,]

knew wherefore Monson was committed, so I said the judges know wherefore the gentlemen were committed.

Then came a serjeant at law. He had 5 damnable and desperate reasons.

1. That our conclusion tended to an anarchy and not to a monarchy.

2. If this be yielded to, it is to put the sword into the King's hand with one hand, and to pull it out with another.

3. You must allow the King to govern by the law of state or else there is no power there.

4. This question is too high a question to be determined where the persons are to receive irreparable loss.

5. This raised up dust in all our faces. If the King demanded money by way of loan and the party refuse and be committed, will you have the cause brought up in a *habeas corpus?*

So he dealt most unjustly and rashly, and I move that we may have a conference with the Lords about him. As for the resolution of the judges, they say they neither determined one nor other, and it is no judgement. They comply with us.

April 22, 1628. [173]

Ed.: Prior to his speech, committing a bill, the speeches were these:

Mr. Jordan. An act for the further punishing of adultery and fornication.

Mr. Jordan. I did always look that this bill should find many opposers but, Mr. Speaker, this is no laughing matter. I humbly move according to the motion of a lawyer in the last parliament that those that find themselves guilty of this vice would speak against the commitment of this bill, but those that are against it would speak for it.

They cry, "Commit it! Commit it!"

Sir Edward Coke. I see you all cry, "Commit it! Commit it!" and you laugh at it as you say so but, good Mr. Speaker, it is the bill, not the sin, which we would have committed.

173. [*Ed.:* Stowe, April 22, 1628, 97–97v, in *CD, 1628,* III, 26.]

April 25, 1628.[174]

In the Committee of Grievances

> *Ed.:* In debating the effect of a Common Council which was an act by the City of London, to imprison a man for non-payment of forced loans assigned to the City, a portion of which he was involuntarily assigned.

Sir Edward Coke. This is of more weight than difficulty. A Common Council may take place in four cases: 1, for the government of the City according to the laws of the realm. 2, for the common profit, as for mending ways, etc., so as it exceed not law and reason. 3, to regulate trades and to prevent fraud, as a halfpenny for a cloth that is measured and searched, etc. 4, an ornament to the City upon a victory. But to compel a man to lend money to purchase land, etc., it is altogether unlawful. The King dealt only with the Mayor and Court of Aldermen, and not with this party.

April 26, 1628.[175]

In the Committee of the Whole House

> *Ed.:* Debating proposals from the Lords sent to commons as a counter-offer to their proposals on the Liberty of the Subject. The three propositions were to declare Magna Carta and six later statutes to be still in force, that according to Magna Carta, the subjects have a fundamental propriety in their goods and liberty in their person, that he confirms these as in ancient times, that he will act according to common law, and that he would not extend his prerogative to diminish the propriety in goods or liberty of their persons.

Sir Edward Coke. This is case of great consequence, and we are to deal tenderly. This is the wheel that turns that great business of the House. That

---

174. [*Ed.:* Proceedings and Debates, f. 91v, in *CD, 1628*, III, 77–78.]
175. [*Ed.:* Proceedings and Debates, f. 99, in *CD, 1628*, III, 94–96.]

that I speak is for future times. We see what an advantage they have that are learned in the law in penning articles, above them that are not, how wise soever. Our resolutions are plain and open and clear. What theirs are we are to dispute. We have resolved *nemine contradicente*,[176] "that no free man," etc. This is according to my conscience and knowledge. The first proposition for Magna Carta and the six other statues, the words are good, but they conclude nothing in what cases they are in force. Is it if any be imprisoned without cause? And there's not a word of that. Also they conceive these statutes are explanatory, and they mention not 36 *Edw.* 3. I delight in the King's grace, but will you have Magna Carta as a grace? Our petition is a petition of right, and the King is to do it in right.

For the second proposition, that "according to Magna Carta" we have "propriety," etc., that determines nothing. The question is what is *lex terrae*?[177] Therein some differ. If I have any law, *lex terrae* is the common law.

For the third, we shall out of grace enjoy our ancient fundamental liberties. Is it not right? I know not what "fundamental" is. It is Holborn Latin.[178] I understand not fundamental liberty or propriety. We gain nothing by all those. He will "graciously" confirm all our "just liberties." We are in a round. The King's Council say they may commit us without cause shown, and all is out of grace, and as our ancestors did under the King's "best progenitors." Who are his best progenitors, they that had best possessions, or best virtues? I never read who was the best king. Also there wants the word "predecessors." The bishops therefore are gone.

The fourth has more danger in it than is meant, that within "all cases" within "the common law," etc. That concerns the liberty of the subject. His Majesty would "proceed," etc. Shall we seclude all the statutes and customs, and he not proceed according to the common law? And yet the common law must now yield to the law martial. I am sure the martial law is here meant. The common law must yield to it.

For the fifth, I will point at it. I understand not much in it. His Majesty's prerogative "intrinsical." It is a word we find not much in the law. It is meant that intrinsical prerogative is not bounded by any law, or by any law qualified.

176. [*Ed.:* with no one speaking against,]
177. [*Ed.:* the law of the land.]
178. [*Ed.:* The Latin learned by lawyers.]

We must admit this intrinsical prerogative an exempt prerogative, and so all
our laws are out. And this intrinsical prerogative is entrusted him by God and
then it is due *jure divino*,[179] and then no law can take it away. Then it follows
that for defense, etc., if his Majesty "shall find" cause to commit, he may. We
are but where we were. We cannot yield to this, that he should have power
to commit any, and within "convenient time" he shall declare the cause; and
this is that we all strive for, and the kings contended for it before Magna Carta,
and could never prevail; and the confirmation is in general to be shown, if it
be *per mandatum domini regis*,[180] or "for matter of state"; and then we are
gone, and we are in a worse case than ever. If we agree to this imprisonment
"for matters of state" and "a convenient time," we shall leave Magna Carta
and the other statutes and make them fruitless, and do what our ancestors
would never do. We shall say "for matter of state" and "a convenient time"
a man maybe committed without cause. 20 *Hen.* 3, there was a little point in
law to be changed for *antenati* before marriage. *Sed responderunt omnes comites
et barones* (there was no duke nor marquess then), "*Nolumus leges Angliae
mutare.*"[181] I would never yield to alter Magna Carta. We are now about to
declare and we shall now introduce and make a new law, and no king in
Christendom claims that law, and it binds the subject where he was never
bound. Never yet was any fundamental law shaken but infinite trouble ensued.
The statute of *non clameum:*[182] the common law was that you were to make
claim in one year: that was taken away, and then came such troubles as they
were never quiet till 4 *Hen.* 7. So the law was that no man should will his
lands by testament: now we have that law altered, and now five parts of the
suits in Westminster Hall are upon that point. It is true *rerum progressus os-
tendunt multa quae [in] initio praecaveri non possunt.*[183] Shake Magna Carta,
and we know what will come of it. You have a rule in building, *lapis male
positus non est removendus.*[184] Have we come up thither, and declared what
the law is, and shall we go back and consent of these commitments? Consider
the trust we reposed in the Lords. We showed them our evidence. We desire

179. [*Ed.:* by divine law,]
180. [*Ed.:* by command of the lord king,]
181. [*Ed.:* But all the earls and barons answered: "We will not change the laws of England."]
182. [*Ed.:* [statute of] non-claim:]
183. [*Ed.:* The progress of events reveals many things which cannot be foreseen at the outset.]
184. [*Ed.:* A misplaced stone is not to be removed.]

them to declare the like, but to be against us we begged it not. If the Lords will not comply with us, but make any hesitation, I doubt not our gracious Sovereign will comply with us.

April 28, 1628.[185]

> *Ed.:* Discussing a subpoena of member Sir Simeon Steward, who was bound by a recognizance not to assert his privileges as a member of the house.

Sir Edward Coke. There was a fault on all sides. The recognizance is upon record. He is now bound not to make any use of his privilege. A man elected cannot refuse; he must serve his trust. He can make no proxy; he sits for many a thousand. It was ill done to do this. Let us send for the recognizance.

. . .

In the Committee of Lawyers

> *Ed.:* Later that afternoon, the subcommittee of lawyers met to discuss a bill more fully protecting the Liberty of the Subject under Magna Carta. Selden spoke first of the need to set down Magna Carta in the form of 13 Hen. 4.

Sir Edward Coke.[186] 1 *Hen.* 8, it was in the parliament roll that no loan or privy seal shall be without parliament. When I was Attorney I saw it, but now it is lost. 5 *Ric.* 2, *num.* 11, divers merchants are undone by loans. 9 *Ric.* 2, *rot.* 60, to the same purpose. 13 *Hen.* 4, *num.* 10 *et* 18, no loan or aid for guarding of the realm. Westminster 1, *cap.* 1, none shall come to eat in the house of any prelate or any other. Let us recite all these laws in the bill.

---

185. [*Ed.:* Proceedings and Debates, f. 95v, in *CD, 1628,* III, 124.]
186. [*Ed.:* Proceedings and Debates, f. 99, in *CD, 1628,* III, 130–31.]

April 29, 1628.[187]

In the Committee of the Whole House

> *Ed.:* Here, Coke reports the framing of the Petition of Right to the Committee of the Whole House.

At a committee for the whole House concerning the framing of a bill for the liberties, Sir Edward Coke reports from the committee.

Sir Edward Coke. First, they agreed to set down 3 capita: 1, propriety of goods; 2, liberty of person; 3 and lastly, billeting of soldiers; and also the particular statutes that are in force: Magna Carta, *cap.* 29; 25 *Edw.* 1, the first part of it. 34 *Edw.* 1, *De Tallagio Concedendo;* 5 *Edw.* 3; *cap.* 1; 25 *Edw.* 1, *num.* 16; et 25 *Edw.* 3, *cap. 4;* 28 *Edw.* 3; 36 *Edw.* 3, *num.* 9, 20 *et* 24; 37 *Edw.* 3; 42 *Edw.* 3, *num.* 12; 1 *Ric.* 3, *cap.* 2. In this law we looked not back, for *qui repetit separat;*[188] and we have made no preamble other than the laws before mentioned, and we desired our pen might be in oil and not in vinegar.

The bill was exhibited and read.

An act for the better securing of every free man touching the propriety of his goods and liberty of his person:

Whereas it is declared and enacted by Magna Carta that no free man is to be convicted, destroyed, etc.: and whereas by a statute made in Edw. 1, called *De Tallagio non Concedendo,* and whereas by the parliament 5 *Edw.* 3 and 4 *Edw.* 3 and 29 *Edw.* 3, etc.; and whereas the said Great Charter was confirmed and that the other laws, etc., be it enacted that Magna Carta and these said acts of explanation and other the acts be put in due execution, and that all judgments, awards, and rules given or to be given to the contrary shall be void; and whereas by the common law and statutes it appears that no free man ought to be committed by command of the King, etc., and if any free man be so committed, and the same returned upon a *habeas corpus,* he ought to be delivered or bailed.

Be it enacted now that no free man shall be committed by the King or

---

187. [*Ed.:* Proceedings and Debates, ff. 100–100v, in *CD, 1628,* III, 149–51.]

188. [*Ed.:* who repeatedly (criticizes) divides (others) (an allusion to Ecclesiasticus.)]

Privy Council, and the cause ought to be expressed; the same and no other being returned upon a *habeas corpus* shall be delivered or bailed.

And whereas by the common law and statutes every free man has a propriety in his goods and estate, as no tax, tallage, etc., nor any soldier can be billeted in his house, etc.; be it enacted that no tax, tallage, loan shall be levied, etc., by the King or any minister without act of parliament, and that none be compelled to receive any soldier in his house against his will.

. . .

Sir Edward Coke. If the King should have this prerogative, he should lose most by it, and if the naked truth could appear to his Majesty he should see that no flowers of his crown should be violated, and the subject made worse than a villein. But for that that no cause should be shown upon the commitment, the honest man and the honest judge shall be most miserable, he that has an upright heart to God. I was committed to the Tower and all my books and study searched, and 37 manuscripts were taken away, and 34 were restored, and I would give 300 *l.* for the other 3. I was inquired after what I had done all my life before. So then there may be cause found out after the commitment, and the commitment is fearful. All men's mouths are open against the party, and our friends afraid as well to come to us. I think the acts of parliament include these questions in substance, but it is only implied. It is not now without occasions that we insist upon this. Were there ever such violations offered? Were there ever such commissions and oaths?

Objection [by Sir Dudley Digges]: Shall we do that to the King now that never was done before?

Answer: Why, was there ever such violations? And is not the King named in Magna Carta, at least by way of implicity? And 36 *Edw.* 3 and 25 *Edw.* 3 names the King and his Council.

May 1, 1628.[189]

In the Committee of the Whole House

Ed.: Discussing a message from the King to the House asking whether the

---

189. [*Ed.:* Proceedings and Debates, f. 105, in *CD, 1628,* III, 189.]

House would not accept his promise to abide by his word to abide by the law.

Sir Edward Coke. We receive comfort from his Majesty's gracious care over us. We dispute here of our liberties, but his Majesty's care watches over us. Now is the axe laid to the root of the tree. That that proceeded from his Majesty is great. His Majesty desires us to let him know whether we will rely upon his gracious promise or no. Let us consider of it against tomorrow.

May 2, 1628.[190]

In the Committee of the Whole House

Ed.: Debating whether to accept the King's word or to press for the Petition of Right.

Sir Edw. Coke. That Royal Word had reference to some message formerly sent: his majesty's word was, That they may secure themselves any way, by bill, or otherwise, and he promised to give way to it: and to the end that this might not touch his majesty's honour it was proposed, that the bill come not from this house, but from the king: 'We will and grant, for us and our successors, that we and our successors will do thus and thus.' And it is to the king's honor that he cannot speak but by record.

Others desired the house to consider, when and where the late promise was made: was it not in the face of both houses? Cruel kings have been careful to perform their promises; yea, though they have been unlawful, as Herod: therefore, if we rest upon his majesty's promise, we may assure ourselves of the performance of it. Besides, we bind his maj. by relying on his word. We have laws enough; it is the execution of them that is our life, and it is the king that gives life and execution.

190. [*Ed.:* Cobbett, *Parl. Hist.,* II, 344.]

May 3, 1628.[191]

In the Committee of the Whole House

> *Ed.:* On the same matter of relying on the King's word or insisting on the Petition of Right.

Sir Edward Coke. Misconceiving is the mother of misdoing. Sure I am misreports bring forth delays. We will not Strain or enlarge anything. We agree upon the substance.

. . .

Sir Edward Coke. I find we err much in sending messages. 2 *Hen.* 4, *num.* 10, the King ought not to take any information what is done here till it be resolved here.

. . .

> *Ed.:* On the same matter.

Sir Edward Coke. Futura sunt contingentia.[192] Let us absolutely confess we do not encroach on his prerogative.

May 6, 1628.[193]

In the Committee of the Whole House

> *Ed.:* On the same matter.

Sir Edward Coke. Let us go in a parliamentary way. For any not to rely on the King it is not fit trust. In him is all the confidence we have under God. He is God's lieutenant. Trust him we must. Was it ever known that general words were a sufficient satisfaction to particular grievances? Was ever a verbal

---

191. [*Ed.:* Proceedings and Debates, ff. 108–108v, in *CD, 1628,* III, 234–236.]

192. [*Ed.:* Future things are contingent.]

193. [*Ed.:* Proceedings and Debates, f. 113, in *CD, 1628,* III, 271–72.]

declaration of the King *verbum regium?*[194] When grievances be, the parliament is to redress grievances and mischiefs that happen. Imprisonments are our grievances, billeting of soldiers, unnecessary loans, etc. Did ever parliament rely on messages? They ever put up petitions of their grievances, and the King ever answered them. The King's answer is very gracious, but what is the law of the realm? That is the question. I put no diffidence in his Majesty. The King must speak by a record, and in particulars, and not in general. Let us have a conference with the Lords, and join in a petition of right to the King for our particular grievances. Did you ever know the King's messages come into a bill of subsidies? All succeeding kings will say, "You must trust me as well as did your predecessors, and trust my messages." But messages alone never came into a parliament. Let us put up our petitions; not that I distrust the King, but because we cannot take his trust but in a parliamentary way.

May 7, 1628.[195]

In the Committee of the Whole House

> *Ed.:* Discussing the Commissions of the King's Lieutenants and the Instructions for Martial Law.

Sir Edward Coke. It is agreed that the articles are not now for this climate. They are not under the Great Seal, and so no man can have warrant from them, and so not according to law. For the commission itself—the learned man himself disliked these words, that it go to any but to soldiers—then this commission must be against law. 41 *Edw.* 3 an annuity granted for counsel; the counsel is to be given in that profession the grantee is of. *Secundum discrecionem vestram*—it is *per leges* to discern *quid sit justum*,[196] but it is a great difference that is between jurisdiction and execution. Execution is in *debellando et in bello* when it is *flagrante crimine*,[197] but may they now in time of peace execute this martial law? Without all question they cannot. I observe

---

194. [*Ed.:* the royal word.]
195. [*Ed.:* Proceedings and Debates, f. 115v, in *CD, 1628,* III, 307.]
196. [*Ed.:* "According to your discretion" (means to discern) by the laws what is just,]
197. [*Ed.:* in combat and in war, (when it is for) a flagrant crime,]

in all the commissions, if it be for a thing done within the realm there the commissions go only *per incarceracionem corporis, etc., judicandum legibus.*[198] Show me an act of parliament against 5 *Hen.* 4, no. 24, 25.

May 9, 1628.[199]

In Conference with the Lords on May 8, 1628.

> *Ed.:* Presenting the Commons' view to promote the Petition of Right.

I pray your Lordships to excuse us, for we have been this day till one of the clock about the great business, and (blessed be God) we have dispatched it in some measure; and before this time we were not able to attend your Lordships, but I hope that this meeting will prove to be a great blessing to us. My Lords, I am commanded from the House of Commons to express the singular care and affection they have of concurrence with your Lordships in these urgent affairs and proceedings in this parliament, both for the good of the commonwealth and principally for his Majesty. And this I must say in this particular: if we had hundreds of tongues we were not able to express that desire which we have of that concurrence with your Lordships; but I will leave that without any further expression.

My Lords, it is evident what necessity there is, both in respect of ourselves and our posterities, to have good success of this business. We have acquainted your Lordships with the reasons and the grounds, and after we had some conference we received from your Lordships five propositions, and it behooves me to give your Lordships some reasons why you have not heard from us before now. For in the meantime, as we were consulting of this weighty business, we have received divers messages from our great sovereign the King, and they consisted of five parts:

First, that his Majesty would maintain all his subjects in the just freedom both of their persons and estates.

Secondly, that he will govern us according to the laws and statutes.

---

198. [*Ed.:* by imprisonment of the body, etc.; one should judge according to the laws.]
199. [*Ed.:* Proceedings and Debates, ff. 116v–118v, in *CD, 1628,* III, 338–41.]

Thirdly, that we shall find much confidence in his royal word, (I pray observe it).

Fourthly, that we shall enjoy all our rights and liberties with as much freedom as ever any subjects have done in former times.

Fifthly, that whether we shall think it fit, either by way of bill or otherwise, to go on in this great business, his Majesty would be pleased to give way to it.

These gracious messages did so work upon our affections that we have taken them into deep consideration. My Lords, when we had those messages (I deal plainly, for so I am commanded by the House of Commons), we did consider in what way we might go for our most secure way (nay, yours). We did think it the safest way to go in a parliamentary course, for we have a maxim in our House of Commons, and written on the walls of our House, that old ways are the safest and surest ways.

And at last we fell upon that which we did think (if that your Lordships did consent with us) is the most ancient way of all, and this is, my Lords, *via fausta*,[200] both to his Majesty, to your Lordships, and to ourselves; for, my Lords, this is the greatest bond that any subject can have in any parliament: *verbum regis*.[201] This is an high point of honor, but this shall be done by the Lords and Commons assented unto by the King in parliament. This is the greatest obligation of all, and this is for the King's honor and our safety.

Therefore (my Lords), we have drawn a form of a petition, desiring your Lordships to concur with us therein. For we do come with an unanimous consent of all this House of Commons, for there is great reason your Lordships should do so, for your Lordships be involved in the same. *Commune periculum* requires *commune auxilium*.[202] And so I have done with the first part. And now I shall be bold to read that which we have so agreed on. I shall desire your Lordships that I may read it, which he did, and is as follows.

Ed.: Coke's language following is the Petition of Right, as considered by the Lords and as adopted, modified only by two lines added at the Lords' behest on May 11 and 20. The final petition was adopted on June 2.

---

200. [*Ed.:* through love,]
201. [*Ed.:* word of the King.]
202. [*Ed.:* Mutual danger (requires) mutual assistance.]

To the King's most excellent Majesty:

Humbly show unto our Sovereign Lord the King, the Lords spiritual and temporal, and Commons in this present parliament assembled, that whereas it is declared and enacted by a statute made in the time of the reign of King Edward the first, commonly called *Statutum de Tallagio Non Concedendo,* that no tallage or aid should be laid or levied by the King or his heirs in this realm without the good will and assent of the archbishops, bishops, earls, barons, knights, burgesses, and other the free men of the commonalty of this realm, and by an authority of parliament held in the XXVth year of the reign of King Edward the Third, it is declared and enacted that from thenceforth no person should be compelled to make any loans to the King against his will, because such loans were against reason and the franchises of the land. And by other laws of this realm it is provided that none shall be charged by any charge or imposition called a benevolence, or by such like charge; by which the statutes beforementioned, and other the good laws and statutes of this realm, your subjects have inherited this freedom, and they should not be compelled to contribute any tax, tallage, or aid, or other like charge not set by common consent in parliament. Yet, nevertheless, of late divers commissions directed to several commissioners in several counties, with instructions, have issued; by pretext whereof your people have been in divers places assembled and required to lend certain sums of money to your Majesty. And many of them, upon their refusal so to do, have had an unlawful oath administered unto them, and have been constrained to become bound to make appearance and to give attendance before your Privy Council, and in other places, and others of them have been therefore imprisoned, confined, and sundry other ways molested and disquieted; and divers other charges have been laid and levied upon your people in several counties by lord lieutenants, deputy lieutenants, commissioners for musters, justices of peace, and others by command and direction from your Majesty, or your Privy Council, against the laws and free customs of the realm.

And where also by the statute called the Great Charter of the Liberties of England, it is declared and enacted that no free man may be taken or imprisoned, or be disseized of his freehold or liberties, or his free customs, or be outlawed or exiled, or in any manner destroyed, but by the lawful judgment of his peers, or by the law of the land; and in the 28th year of the reign of King Edward the Third it was declared and enacted by authority of parliament that no man, of what state or condition that he be, shall be put out of his lands or tenements, nor taken, nor imprisoned, nor disinherited, nor put to death without being brought to answer by due process of law.

Nevertheless, against the tenor of the said statutes, and other the good laws and statutes of the realm to that end provided, divers of your subjects have been of late imprisoned without any cause shown, and when for their deliverance they were brought before your justices by your Majesty's writs of *habeas corpus,* there to undergo and receive as the court should order, and their keepers commanded to certify the causes of their detainer, no cause was certified, but that they were detained by your Majesty's special command, signified by the lords of your Privy Council, and yet were returned back to several prisons without being charged with anything to which they might make answer according to the law.

And whereas of late great companies of soldiers and mariners have been dispersed into divers counties of the realm, and the inhabitants against their wills have been compelled to receive them into their houses, and there to suffer them to sojourn against the laws and customs of this realm, and to the great grievance and vexation of the people; and whereas also by authority of parliament, in the 25th year of the reign of King Edward the Third, it is declared and enacted that no man shall be forejudged of life or limb against the form of the Great Charter and the law of the land; and by the said Great Charter and other the laws and statutes of this your realm, no man ought to be adjudged to death but by the laws established in this your realm, either by the customs of the said realm, or by acts of parliament; and whereas no offender of what kind soever is exempted from the proceedings to be used, and punishments to be inflicted by the laws and statutes of this your realm; nevertheless, of late time divers commissions under your Majesty's Great Seal have issued forth by which certain persons have been assigned and appointed commissioners with power and authority to proceed within the land, according to the justice of martial law, against such soldiers or mariners or other dissolute persons joining with them as should commit any murder, robbery, felony, mutiny, or other outrage or misdemeanor whatsoever, and by such summary course and order as is agreeable to martial law and as is used in armies in time of war, to proceed to the trial and condemnation of such offenders, and them to cause to be executed and put to death according to the law martial. By pretext whereof some of your Majesty's subjects have been by some of the said commissioners put to death, when and where, if by the laws and statutes of the land they had deserved death, by the same laws and statutes also they might, and by no other ought to, have been judged and executed.

And also sundry grievous offenders, by color thereof claiming an exemption, have escaped the punishments due to them by the laws and statutes of this your realm by reason that divers of your officers and ministers of justice have unjustly refused or forborne to proceed against such offenders according to the said laws and statutes upon pretense that the said offenders were punishable only by martial law, and by authority of such commissions as aforesaid; which commissions, and all other of like nature, are wholly and directly contrary to the said laws and statutes of this your realm.

They do therefore most humbly pray your most excellent Majesty that none hereafter be compelled to make or yield any gift, loan, benevolence, tax, or such like charge, without common consent by act of parliament. And that none be called to make answer, or to take such oath, or to give attendance, or to be confined, or otherwise molested or disquieted concerning the same, or for refusal thereof. And that no free man, in any such manner as is before mentioned, be imprisoned or detained. And that your Majesty would be pleased to remove the said soldiers and mariners, and that your people may not be so burdened in time to come. And that the aforesaid commissions for proceeding by martial law may be revoked and annulled. And that hereafter no commissions of like nature may issue forth to any person or persons what-soever to be executed, as aforesaid, lest by color of them any of your Majesty's subjects be destroyed or put to death contrary to the laws and franchises of the land.

All which they most humbly pray of your most excellent Majesty as their rights and liberties according to the laws and statutes of this realm. And that your Majesty would also vouchsafe to declare that the awards, doings, and proceedings to the prejudice of your people in any of the premises shall not be drawn hereafter in consequence or example. And that your Majesty will be also graciously pleased, for the further comfort and safety of your people, to declare your royal will and pleasure, that in the things aforesaid all your officers and ministers shall serve you according to the laws and statutes of this realm, as they tender the honor of your Majesty and the prosperity of this kingdom.

May 12, 1628.[203]

> *Ed.:* Discussing a hearing on procedural failings in the election in Cornwall, the deputy lieutenants of Cornwall were summoned to appear before the house. On the question, which they raised by letter, of whether they may be represented by counsel.

Sir Edward Coke. To say a man shall have counsel in every cause—if in the Star Chamber they confess it, they are to be *ore tenus*[204] and to have no counsel; and if in any action a man confess the fact, he is to have no counsel for so much as he has confessed.

May 13, 1628.[205]

> *Ed.:* The deputy lieutenants of Cornwall refused to appear before the house, claiming their service to the King required they stay in Cornwall, for which they were condemned to the Tower, after which Coke observes . . .

Sir Edward Coke. I had rather give account to God for mercy than for justice. The end of all punishment is *poena ad paucos, metus ad omnes.*[206] These gentlemen have ill fortune that have light[ed] on gentlemen of this House of great worth and service. That that moves me is that they have entered into the King's breast as to say: His Majesty will be justly provoked, and suppose that we countenanced you against him. Thus they climb up to the King's heart. The acknowledgment below draws no blood. Let them do it.

May 17, 1628.[207]

> *Ed.:* On a petition by Turkish merchants, imprisoned for nonpayment of an import on currants.

---

203. [*Ed.:* Proceedings and Debates, f. 121, in *CD, 1628,* III, 370.]
204. [*Ed.:* by word of mouth.]
205. [*Ed.:* Proceedings and Debates, f. 123v, in *CD, 1628,* III, 388–89.]
206. [*Ed.:* a penalty imposed on the few may be a terror to all.]
207. [*Ed.:* Proceedings and Debates, f. 129, in *CD, 1628,* III, 450.]

Sir Edward Coke. This petition brings in question the right of impositions which is clear cannot be imposed, and so this House did resolve. If impositions be set they will be multiplied, and when trade is overburdened merchandise will cease. For the imposition upon currants, I know Fleming was then Chief Baron, and they conferred with other judges who differed from them in their opinion. This 2s. is now super-added. We know the King's wants to be great, and so never questioned this revenue. Shall this moderation of ours bring in these new impositions? Why is this seizure? The goods ought not to be seized for nonpayment of the new imposition. Let the parties have a replevin.

. . .

> *Ed.:* Reporting on a Conference with Lords held mid-day on the pending Petition of Right.

Sir Edward Coke[208] reports from the conference that the Lord Keeper spoke to this purpose.

First he mentioned the great care and correspondency of the Houses, then the happy hopes of a good issue for, at the last conference, he said, the study was to sweeten all things for the King, and since that the debate of the Upper House had been wholly spent in the argument of imprisonment. The Lords, he said, had resolved nothing conclusively, but by way of addition, to make the petition easy and passable with his Majesty, presented some few words to be added at the end. The Lord Keeper read those words for, he said, he would not alter the narrative nor the prayer of the petition. Lastly he desired all convenient expedition, and left it to the House to consider whether they would sit this afternoon or no; if they would, the Lords would do so also. The words of addition were these:

> We humbly present to your Majesty this petition not only with a care of preserving our own liberties, but with due regard to leave entire your sovereign power wherewith your Majesty is trusted for the protection, safety, and happiness of your people.

208. [*Ed.:* Stowe MS 366, May 17, 1628, 174–74v, in *CD, 1628,* III, 454.]

May 19, 1628.[209]

> *Ed.:* Debating a bill to remove the four counties nearest to Wales from the jurisdiction of the Marches of Wales.

Sir Edward Coke. We are about the King's revenue, let us withdraw unnecessary expenses. This question grows upon 23 Hen. 8, that there shall be a President and Council of Wales and the Marches. I know these counties have ever sued to be discharged, but these four counties were never part of the Marches of Wales *18 Edw. 2, Ass, 82. ass. direct al vic de Shropshire; vic returne, que le lieu ou fuit in le Marches de Wales ubi breve domini regis non currit. 1. E. 3. dower direct al vic de Shropshire, et fuit dit que it gist en lieu ou de Marches de Wales ubi breve domini regis non currit, 7 Edw. 3, 9, acc. 3 Ric. 2. num. 29 et 30,* parliament roll, *les counties complain que ils fuer counties et nul parte del Wales, et ils prie aide par les inroades, etc. 6 Hen. 4, 9, scire facias, vic de Salop returne que il fuit in Marches de Wales et breve domini regis non currit la. 23 Hen. 6., cap. 5; 32 Hen. 6, cap. 4, Marches est ubi limits, etc.*[210] as Northumberland is part of the Marches of Scotland. There was an Earl of the Marches but he was never Earl of Shropshire. There is a council in York. 32 Hen. 8., in the general pardon, the King was at a great charge to found a council in Cornwall, etc. Then the Cornish men petitioned the King they might live under the law, and not under a president.

> *Ed.:* Reporting on the conference with the Lords, held earlier that day, on the Petition of Right and the Lords' proposed amendment.

---

209. [*Ed.:* Proceedings and Debates, f. 130v–131, in *CD, 1628,* III, 466–68.]

210. [*Ed.:* 18 Edw. II in [Fitzherbert's Abridgement, title] *Assise,* 82, an assize directed to the sheriff of Shropshire; the sheriff returns that the place where [etc.] was in the marches of Wales where the lord king's writ runs not. 1 Edw. III, dower directed to the sheriff of Shropshire, and it was said that it lies in the marches of Wales where the lord king's writ runs not. 7 Edw. III, 9, agrees. 3 Ric. II, nos. 29 and 30 in the parliament roll, the counties complain that they were [*blank*] counties and no part of Wales, and they pray aid by the inroads, etc. 6 Hen. IV, 9, in *scire facias,* the sheriff of Shropshire returns that it was in the marches of Wales and the lord king's writ does not run there. 23 Hen. VI, chapter 5. 32 Hen. VI, chapter 4, marches is where limits, etc.]

Sir Edward Coke reports from the conference. We began and showed the reasons and grounds we had to refuse their propounded alterations. We began with the word "pretext" but that must be construed according to the precedent matter. But for that word we were content to yield to it.

Secondly, for that the loan was "upon urgent occasions," etc., to that we said [first,] all loans were against law. Secondly, it might imply some loans upon pressing occasions were lawful. Thirdly, it was not agreeable to our conclusion for our prayer was, "that no loan," etc. Fourthly, if we allege urgent reasons, reasons of state, we must look into what is passed that may hinder us in our ends. The Bishop of Lincoln said that this was but to make the matter more sweet and passable, and that the King was jealous of his honor and desirous to render himself fair to posterity. But the good Bishop said it was no weighty matter but, he argued, if the King cannot take loans, no not even when urgent and pressing occasions were, [then] much less when there were none. I replied that *optandum in legibus ut judici quam paucissima relinquuntur,*[211] and let us leave nothing to posterity, and it is not a fit shaft for our quiver for us, the House of Commons, to say lands were "upon urgent affairs," etc.

Thirdly, "unlawful oath," we think it is unlawful, and I said there was never a Lord there but thought so. The Lord Keeper said this oath was not in the commission but in the instructions. Also, the Lord President said that oath was but to discover a practice in some that dissuaded, and not for them that refused. The Lord Saye replied that it was his own collection, and that he had no warrant from the House so to say. Also they say that the Lords, most of them, were employed in the loan. I replied, under terms of sweetness we must not go from our ends; and though the words were not in the commission, yet they were in the instructions that were printed, and if the party refused, every such party was examined, nay witnesses were examined. These were *primae impressiones,* and let us *principiis obstare.*[212] As for the Lords, I would not meddle with them. But for the gentlemen that were used therein, I said I hoped well of this parliament, and that a general pardon will amend all; but in itself the Great Seal is to protect men from wrong. This seal was used to oppress men.

211. [*Ed.:* It is desirable in laws that as little as possible be left to the judge,]
212. [*Ed.:* (These were) cases of a new kind, (and let us) oppose them from the very beginning.]

Fourthly, for the words "Privy Council" they would have it "at London."
I said the truth of the cause was not at London, but before the Council. Also,
we hope this will be a law for hereafter.

Fifthly, for the words "superior power." I said that was to leave a word for
the King and his council, but I think this and the former was yielded unto
by the Lords.

Sixthly, as for martial law. I said it is difficult to say when the King's army
is on foot, and how many men make an army, and if they be on foot. If they
be not in war they can hang none. The Lord Keeper replied if a rebellion be
in the farthest parts, if you stay for an attainder, all is lost. I answered, there
is a difference. If they resist the King's power you may slay them in the field,
but for jurisdicton afterwards they must be tried by law. Also, we complain
of what is done in time of peace. The noble Duke said, I would fain know,
if a general lead an army and there are those that are disobedient, that will
obey nothing so that the expedition does nothing but bring home *damnum
et dedecus,*[213] shall we come to the common law? I asked if this case were within
the land or without. He said he meant without. Then, said I, the Marshal
and Constable may try it. The Lords said they came with an intent to bring
all to a happy end, and that they would acquaint their House with what was
done. The Duke said that he would do his best service to make a good end
of this parliament, and to do the best service he could for King and people.

As for the word "pretext," it is ordered that it be yielded unto.

May 20, 1628.[214]

In the Committee of the Whole House

Ed.: Reporting on that day's conference with Lords.

Sir Edward Coke reports from the conference with the Lords. Lord Keeper
1, delivered their desire of correspondence with this House; 2, that the Lords
agreed to all parts of our petition and waived all their alterations, except the

---

213. [*Ed.:* damage and disgrace,]
214. [*Ed.:* Journal of the House of Commons, Tuesday, May 20, 1628, p. 116, in *CD, 1628,* III, 491.]

word "pretext" and the word "unlawful." 3 reasons to alter that last word: 1, it was too high and too rigid; "unlawful" may be against the law of God, nature, and reason; 2ly, it may be understood against the law divine and moral; [3ly] that they will instead of "new and unlawful" change it to an oath "not warranted or warrantable by the laws or statutes of this realm." Desired expedition; if we would sit this afternoon they would. Desired to know our mind in that.

. . .

In the Committee of the Whole House

Ed.: Debating the House's response to the Lords' response, and arguing against their broad amendment by adding a new final paragraph.

Sir Edward Coke.[215] This is *magnum in parvo.*[216] This is propounded to be a conclusion of our Petition. It is a matter of great weight; and, to speak plainly, it will overthrow all our Petition; it trenches to all parts of it; it flies at Loans, at the Oath, at Imprisonment, and at Billetting of Soldiers: this turns all about again. Look into all the petitions of former times; they never petitioned wherein there was a saving of the king's sovereignty. I know that prerogative is part of the law, but "Sovereign Power" is no parliamentary word. In my opinion it weakens Magna Charta, and all the statutes; for they are absolute, without any saving of "Sovereign Power"; and should we now add it, we shall weaken the foundation of law, and then the building must needs fall. Take we heed what we yield unto: Magna Charta is such a fellow, that he will have no "Sovereign." I wonder this "Sovereign" was not in Magna Charta, or in the confirmations of it. If we grant this, by implication we give a "Sovereign Power" above all laws. Power in law, is taken for a power with force: the sheriff shall take the power of the county; what it means here, God only knows. It is repugnant to our Petition: that is, a Petition or Right, grounded on acts of parliament. Our predecessors could never endure a *salvo jure suo,*[217] no more than the kings of old could endure for the church, *Salvo honore Dei & ec-*

---

215. [*Ed.:* Cobbett, *Parl. Hist.,* II, 357. (May 17, 1628).]
216. [*Ed.:* a great thing in a small package.]
217. [*Ed.:* saving his right.]

clesiae.[218] We must not admit of it, and to qualify it is impossible. Let us hold our privileges according to the law: that power that is above this, is not fit for the king and people to have it disputed further. I had rather, for my part, have the prerogative acted, and I myself to lye under it, than to have it disputed.

May 24, 1628.[219]

Ed.: Debating a request from the Lords for a conference with the House, seeking a large committee from both sides to consider the Petition or other approaches to the same business.

Sir Edward Coke. I like not that we should say that this is not a parliamentary way. A negative is dangerous, and when wise men differ in opinion—*quod dubitas, ne feceris.*[220] This addition came not out of our quire but from the Lords, and we have conferred with them and better we had never meddled with this than to add this that is in fair terms. And at first I was taken with it, and it seemed glorious, but now I see it was as dangerous a thing as ever came in parliament. Now shall we decline all, and come to new propositions, and declarations, and what? To accommodate? Let us know if the Lords be satisfied or not. If they be not, then it must sleep. If I have any understanding this addition wounds the fundamental laws. Let us go to the Lords and say, if you be not satisfied give us your reasons.

May 26, 1628.[221]

Ed.: Reporting on a conference with the Lords that day, in which they agreed to drop the remaining requests for amendments to the Petition.

Sir Edward Coke reports to the House from the Lords, thus. I am almost dead for joy. *A Domino factum est istud, et est mirabile in oculis nostris,*[222] etc.

---

218. [*Ed.:* saving honour to God and the Church.]

219. [*Ed.:* Proceedings and Debates, ff. 151–151v, in *CD, 1628,* III, 598.]

220. [*Ed.:* do not do anything about which you are doubtful.]

221. [*Ed.:* Stowe MS 366, May 26, 1628, 192v, in *CD, 1628,* III, 614.]

222. [*Ed.:* This has been done by the Lord, and it is marvellous in our eyes. (A quote from the Vulgate, Psalm 117:23).]

My Lord Keeper said he had many times delivered from the Lords words of friendship and good correspondency to the House of Commons, but now their Lordships were resolved not to show words but deeds for a good issue towards the happiness of King and kingdom. Concerning the petition of right, he said in a matter of such weight their Lordships have proceeded with long and serious debate since the last conference. But now they were, *in omnibus,*[223] agreed with us, and stood upon no alterations but those which were already granted: the word "means" for "pretext" and "not warrantable by the laws and statutes of this kingdom" instead of the word "unlawful." The petition, he said, remains with you; and as the Lords have already voted it in the Upper House, so they expect we should do here; and having so done, they said they would move the King for a speedy hearing. There remains yet one excellent circumstance. The Lords do desire that, as we do touch upon military matters in our petition, so we would take into consideration the right regulating of them; and by way of bill to settle the charge and the office of deputy lieutenants; and thus I hope you shall see a blessed end of this parliament.

May 27, 1628.[224]

> *Ed.:* Presenting the final Petition of Right from the Commons to the Lords.

May 27. The commons sent a message to the lords, by sir Edw. Coke, and others, "To render them their most hearty thanks, for their noble and happy concurrence with them all this parliament: and they acknowledged that their lordships had not only dealt nobly with them in words, but also in deeds. That this Petition, which they were now to deliver, contained the true liberties of the subjects of England, and a true exposition of the Great Charter, not great for the words thereof, but in respect of the weight of the matter contained therein, the Liberties of the People: that their lordships concurring with the commons, had crowned the work; and therefore they doubted not, but as the first parliament of king James was called *felix parliamentum,*[225] so this might be justly stiled *parliamentum benedictum.*[226] Sir Edward concluded with the

---

223. [*Ed.:* in all respects.]
224. [*Ed.:* Cobbett, *Parl. Hist.,* II, 372–73.]
225. [*Ed.:* happy parliament.]
226. [*Ed.:* blessed parliament.]

humble desire of the commons, that the lords would join with them to beseech his maj. for the more strength of this Petition, and the comfort of his loving subjects to give a gracious answer to the same in full parliament." This said, he delivered the Petition of Right, fairly engrossed; and then they withdrew into the Painted Chamber.

June 2, 1628.[227]

PETITION OF RIGHT.

The PETITION exhibited to his MAJESTY by the Lords Spiritual and Temporal, and commons in this present Parliament assembled, concerning divers RIGHTS and LIBERTIES of the SUBJECT, with the King's ROYAL ANSWER thereunto in full Parliament.

"To the King's most excellent maj.: humbly shew unto our sovereign lord the king, the lords spiritual and temporal, and commons, in parliament assembled, that whereas it is declared and enacted, by a statute made in the reign of king Edw. 1 commonly called, '*Statutum de Tallagio non concedendo,*' that no tallage or aid shall be laid or levied, by the king or his heirs, in this realm, without the good-will and assent of the archbishops, bishops, earls, barons, knights, burgesses, and other the freemen of the commonalty of this realm: and by authority of parliament, holden in the 25th year of king Edw. 3, it is declared and enacted that from thenceforth no person shall be compelled to make any loans to the king against his will, because such loans were against reason and the franchises of the land. And, by other laws of this realm, it is provided, that none should be charged by any charge or the position called a Benevolence, nor by such like charge; by which the statutes before mentioned, and the other the good laws and statutes of this realm, your subjects have inherited this freedom, that they should not be compelled to contribute to any tax, tallage, aid, or other like charge, not set by common consent in parliament: yet nevertheless, of late, divers commissions, directed to sundry commissioners in several counties, with instructions, have issued, by pretext whereof, your people have been in divers places assembled, and required to lend certain sums of money unto your maj. and many of them, upon their

227. [*Ed.:* Cobbett, *Parl. Hist.,* II, 374–77.]

refusal so to do, have had an unlawful oath administered unto them, not warrantable by the laws and statutes of this realm, and have been constrained to become bound to make appearance, and give attendance before your privy council, and in other places; and others of them have therefore been imprisoned, confined, and sundry other ways molested and disquieted: and divers other charges have been laid and levied upon your people, in several counties, by lords lieutenants, deputy lieutenants, commissioners for musters, justices of peace, and others, by command or direction from your maj. or your privy council, against the laws and free customs of this realm.—And whereas also, by the statute called, 'The Great Charter of the Liberties of England,' it is declared and enacted, that no freeman may be taken or imprisoned, or be disseized of his freeholds or liberties, or his free customs, or be outlawed or exiled, or in any manner destroyed, but by the lawful judgment of his peers, or by the law of the land. And in the 28th year of the reign of king Edw. 3. it was declared and enacted by authority of parliament, that no man, of what estate or condition that he be, should be put out of his lands or tenements, nor taken, nor imprisoned, nor disherited, nor put to death, without being brought to answer by due process of law: Nevertheless, against the tenor of the said statutes, and other the good laws and statutes of your realm, to that end provided, divers of your subjects have of late been imprisoned, without any cause shewed; and when, for their deliverance, they were brought before your justices, by your maj.'s writs of *Habeas Corpus,* there to undergo and receive as the court should order, and their keepers commanded to certify the causes of their detainer, no cause was certified, but that they were detained by your maj.'s special command, signified by the lords of your privy council; and yet were returned back to several prisons, without being charged with any thing, to which they might make answer by due process of law.—And whereas of late, great companies of soldiers and mariners have been dispersed into divers counties of the realm, and the inhabitants, against their wills, have been compelled to receive them into their houses, and there to suffer them to sojourn, against the laws and customs of this realm, and to the great grievance and vexation of the people:—And whereas, also, by authority of parliament, in the 25th year of the reign of king Edw. 3. it is declared and enacted, that no man shall be fore-judged of life or limb against the form of the Great Charter, and other the laws and statutes of this realm; and by the said Great Charter, and other the laws and statutes of this your realm, no man ought to be adjudged to death, but by the laws established in this your realm, either by the customs of the same realm, or by acts of parliament: and, whereas, no offender of what kind soever is exempted from the proceedings to be used, and punishments to be inflicted by the laws and statutes of this your realm: nevertheless, of late, divers commissions, under your Majesty's great seal, have issued forth, by which, certain persons have been assigned and appointed commissioners with power and authority to proceed, within the land, according to the justice of martial law against such soldiers and mariners, or other dissolute persons joining with them, as should commit any murder, robbery, felony, mutiny, or other outrage or misdemeanor whatsoever; and by such summary course and order, as is agreeable to martial law, and is used in armies in time of war, to proceed to the trial and condemnation of such offenders, and them to cause to be executed and put to death, according to the martial law: by pretext whereof, some of your majesty's subjects have been, by some of the said commissioners, put to death; when and where, if by the laws and statutes of the land they had deserved death, by the same laws and statutes also they might, and by no other ought to have been adjudged and executed: and, also, sundry grievous offenders by colour thereof, claiming an exemption, have escaped the punishment due to them by the laws and statutes of this your realm, by reason that divers of your officers and ministers of justice have unjustly refused, or forborn to proceed against such offenders, according to the same laws and statutes, upon pretence that the said offenders were punishable only by martial law, and by authority of such commissions as aforesaid; which commissions, and all others of like nature, are wholly and directly contrary to the said laws and statutes of this your realm:—They do therefore, humbly, pray your most excellent maj. That no man hereafter be compelled to make or yield, any gift, loan, benevolence, tax or such like charge, without common consent by act of parliament; and that none be called to make answer, or take such oath, or to give attendance, or be confined, or otherwise molested or disquieted concerning the same or for refusal thereof: and that no freeman, in any such manner as is before-mentioned, be so imprisoned or detained: and that your maj. will be pleased to remove the said soldiers and mariners; and that your people may not be so burdened in time to come: and that the aforesaid commissions for proceeding by martial law, may be revoked and annulled; and that hereafter no commissions of like nature may issue forth to any person or persons whatsoever, to be executed as aforesaid, lest, by colour of them, any of your majesty's subjects be destroyed or put to death, contrary to the laws and franchise of the land.—All which they most humbly pray of your most excellent maj. as their Rights and Liberties, according to the laws and statutes of this realm: and that your maj. would also vouchsafe to declare, That the awards, doings and proceedings, to the prejudice of your people, in any of the premisses, shall not be drawn hereafter into consequence or example: and that your maj. would be also graciously pleased for the further comfort and safety of your people, to declare your royal will and pleasure, that, in the things aforesaid, all your officers and ministers shall serve you, according to the laws and statutes of this realm, as they tender the honour of your maj. and the prosperity of this kingdom."

THE KING'S ANSWER.

"The king willeth, that Right be done according to the laws and customs of the realm; and that the statutes be put in due execution, that his subjects may have no cause to complain of any wrongs or oppressions, contrary to their just Rights and Liberties, to the preservation whereof, he holds himself, in conscience, as well obliged, as of his own prerogative."

June 3, 1628.[228]

> *Ed.:* Debating Sir John Elliot's proposition that the House must address continuing dangers to the Kingdom from religious controversy, foreign policy, military regulation, and taxes for the supply, suggesting a remonstrance.

Sir Edward Coke. I have had no conference with any, yet we may do it, *collatio peperit artem et confirmat artem.*[229] If I did think in my conscience that the King was truly informed of our dishonors and disasters, I would leave them to his wisdom. Let us join in an humble remonstrance, leaving all to his wisdom. Let us fly to him as our refuge; we are now in a miserable condition. Another thing is to be considered of: no king but must be able to live on himself, and to supply his allies. Who will aid him if he be not able to aid them? The King, I hope, shall never want that that is necessary; but it is our

---

228. [*Ed.:* Proceedings and Debates, f. 166, in *CD, 1628,* IV, 67.]
229. [*Ed.:* conference begets and strengthens professional skills.]

duty to look that his ordinary revenues may defray his ordinary charges that he may live on his own else he must live on us. I will not say how much his ordinary expenses are more than the ordinary revenue. But if things were restored as they were, all the hang-bys and encroachments, all must away. Let there be a restitution of his wardrobe and tables. If he would feed no more than he ought, he might yet subsist. And I think this would give wings to the parliament, and I hope we shall have a better answer than yet we have. I well like of this motion so as it be with all duty and humility, without restriction.

June 5, 1628.[230]

In the Committee of the Whole House

> *Ed.:* Considering a message from the King, warning the House he would not extend the parliament, and, in effect ordering them to consider no new business, especially nothing that would criticize him or his ministers. Coke's words here do not convey the shock and grief apparent in him and noted in various records, nor the acclaim with which other members greeted his attack on Buckingham.

Sir Edward Coke. We have dealt with that duty and moderation that never was the like, *rebus sic stantibus,*[231] after such a violation of the liberties of the subject. *Quicunque ausus est violare leges, non aliquos laedit cives, sed totam rem publicam evertere conatus est.*[232] Let us take this to heart. In 50 Edw. 3 they were then in doubt in parliament to name men that misled the King. They accused John of Gaunt, the King's son, and Lord Latimer, and Lord Neville for misadvising the King, and they went to the Tower for it. Now, when there is such a downfall of the state, shall we hold our tongues? How shall we answer our duties to God and man? 7 Hen. 4, parliament roll, *num.* 31 *et* 32; 11 Hen. 4, *num.* 13: there the Council are complained of, and were removed from the King. They mewed up the King and dissuaded him from the common good.

---

230. [*Ed.:* Proceedings and Debates, f. 196v, in *CD, 1628,* IV, 115.]

231. [*Ed.:* matters standing thus.]

232. [*Ed.:* He who dares to break the laws does not only hurt other citizens but attempts to overthrow the entire common weal.]

And why are we now required from that way we were in? Why may we not now name those that are the cause of all our evils? In 4 Edw. 3, and 27 Edw. 3, and 13 R. 2, the parliament moderated the King's prerogative. Nothing grows to abuse but this House has power to treat of it. What shall we now do? Let us palliate no longer; if we do, God will not prosper us. I think the Duke of Buckingham is the cause of all our miseries, and till the King be informed thereof we shall never go out with honor, nor sit with honor here. That man is the grievance of grievances. Let us set down the cause of all our disasters, and all will reflect upon him. As for going to the Lords, that is not *regia via*.[233] Our liberties are now impeached, we are required. It is not *vox regis*.[234] The Lords are not participant with our liberties.

June 6, 1628.[235]

In the Committee of the Whole House

> *Ed.:* Following a conciliatory note from the King, in considering the causes for the remonstrance begun on June 3.

Sir Edward Coke. We shall never know the commonwealth flourish but when the church flourishes. They live and die together. 1 Hen. 5, men were bold to speak in good and true causes, and they put up a petition and prayed execution of laws and prayed performance of promises. It is not credible to tell you of the increase of papists. If you have laws and they be not executed, it will patronize wicked doers. When Queen Elizabeth, in '88, had repelled the Spaniards, there was a conspiracy to poison our Queen, and no three years but some attempt was threatened. In the end of her time, one Wright went into Spain, and the King said the Catholics of England were as dear to him as his Castilians. And they promise him aid if he come hither, and they never left working till the powder treason. Popham told me of one Winchley, a papist, that was taken and carried into Spain and there was a counsel to invade England by reason of the papists. And one said that cannot be, papists are

233. [*Ed.:* the royal [high]way.]
234. [*Ed.:* the king's voice.]
235. [*Ed.:* Proceedings and Debates, ff. 173v–174, in *CD, 1628,* IV, 143–44.]

laid in jails. If there be so many recusants now we are not safe. They intend to make Spain a monarchy. If we proceed against these weapons, I fear no invasions. Let the laws be executed against papists. I saw a commission for a toleration. I dare say Queen Elizabeth would never have consented to the like.

June 7, 1628.[236]

In the Committee of the Whole House

> *Ed.:* Considering a commission of excises, directing all the Lords of the Council to levy money, but not enrolled as required.

Sir Edward Coke. This is a cause of great consequence. I commend them that revealed more *per lachrimas quam per risum.*[237] See now how these excises are disguised; nothing is unjust but is ashamed of light. All monopolies have fair pretenses but they are like apothecaries' boxes, *plus in titulo quam in* .[238] These excises are under the name of impositions, and sure to come to this commission. Usually the signature and the Great Seal go together. This came by immediate warrant from the King. Where is the warrant?

The Clerk of the Crown was called in again, and he said that Mr. Attorney's hand was to it and he drew it.

. . .

> *Ed.:* A further petition, accepting the King's answer to the Petition of Right, after which he granted his assent to the Petition as a statute.

The King came to the Lords House, and the House of Commons were sent for thither to the King, and then the Lord Keeper presented the humble petition of both Houses and said:

May it please your most excellent Majesty, the Lords spiritual and temporal

---

236. [*Ed.:* Proceedings and Debates, ff. 177–177v, in *CD, 1628,* IV, 181–82.]

237. [*Ed.:* by tears than by smiles.]

238. [*Ed.:* more on the label than in [the results].]

and Commons in parliament assembled, taking into their considerations that the good intelligence between your Majesty and your people does much depend upon your Majesty's answer unto their petition of right, formerly presented with an unanimous consent unto your Majesty, do now become most humble suitors unto your Majesty that you will be pleased to give a clear and satisfactory answer thereunto in full parliament.

The King's speech: The answer I have already given you was made with so good deliberation, and approved by the judgment of so many wise men, that I could not have imagined but it should have given you full satisfaction. But to avoid all ambiguous interpretations, and to show you there is no doubleness in my meaning, I am willing to pleasure you in words as well as in substance. Read your petition and you shall have an answer that I am sure will please you.

The petition was read and this answer: *Soit droit fait comme il est desire par le petition. C. R.*[239]

The King's speech: This I am sure is full, yet no more than I granted you in my first answer, for the meaning of that was to confirm all your liberties, knowing (according to your own protestations) that you neither mean nor can hurt my prerogative. And I assure you my maxim is that the people's liberties strengthen the King's prerogative, and the King's prerogative is to defend the people's liberties.

You see now how ready I have showed myself to satisfy your demands, so that I have done my part. Wherefore, if this parliament have not a happy conclusion, the sin is yours, I am free from it.

. . .

Ed.: Upon returning to the House, considering the King's answer.

Sir Edward Coke. Let us consider what is done. We have made a petition of right that is divided into many branches, and I am persuaded his Majesty's meaning was at first to give us as absolute and real an answer as now, and now it is: *Soit droit fait comme il desire.*[240] If this had been a private bill it is: *Soit fait comme il desire;* if a public: *Le Roy veult.*[241] But the King now says:

---

239. [*Ed.:* Let right be done as is desired by the petition. Charles, King.]
240. [*Ed.:* Let right be done as he desires.]
241. [*Ed.:* The king approves (lit., wills) it.]

Soit droit fait comme ils desire[nt]. We could never have had a better answer. If we have desired good things, it is granted. Let us so proceed as we may express our thankfulness, and let us all say amen, and communicate this joy to others.

June 11, 1628.[242]

In the Committee of the Whole House

> *Ed.:* Still considering the content of the remonstrance, whether concern over the forced loans should be in it.

Sir Edward Coke. This head is the fear of alteration of government. Now what greater fear can there be than when a general law is made for Lent and this is altered by proclamations? Proclamations come too high. For the loans, I have little reason to speak of them. I lent none, but it was said in my hearing that I had lent as much as any, and his Majesty was informed I did it with great alacrity. I was pressed to lend privately, but I denied. It was said that as wise and as learned as I had lent.

> *Ed.:* Considering whether to name Buckingham in the remonstrance, Coke is here responding to an argument by Sir Henry Marten, arguing from an idiosyncratic view of motion, divided between natural and violent, in which violent motion speeds up. Coke's response is nearer to Aristotle's view.

Sir Edward Coke.[243] I differ in the ground of him that spoke last. Natural motions go swiftest in the end. For the application, I say let us now be quicker in the end. I owe no duty to fear any but God and the King. I speak not out of malice, but out of duty. I will never palliate. I free my gracious Sovereign; he sees with other men's eyes and proceeds with other men's hands. This great Duke has monopolized many great offices. We free our Sovereign and lay all on his ministers, and the way to free him is to lay it where it is. If the judges

---

242. [*Ed.:* Proceedings and Debates, f. 184, in *CD, 1628,* IV, 243.]
243. [*Ed.:* Proceedings and Debates, f. 186, in *CD, 1628,* IV, 248.]

do not their duty it is their fault. We now go with a lamentable complaint as never was the like. Do not we know that Spain looks for a monarchy *in temporalibus?*[244] I see the weakness that is in the kingdom. Whose fault is it? They that misguide him. So we must name the Duke lest the aspersion lie on his Majesty.

June 13, 1628.[245]

> *Ed.:* Reporting on delivering, enrolling, and printing the Petition of Right.

Sir Edward Coke reports that he delivered the message yesterday to the Lords. And it was answered that the King's message shall be entered on record, and that the petition be in the parliament roll, and that it be sent to the courts and printed, and so they all agreed to what he desired. The question is how this shall be done. The petition ought of right to be entered. As for the entering of it, the King must send a writ, and recite the petition, and so send it to the courts, for so it was done in former times.

20. Edw. 3, *lunae post festum Epiphaniae magnum placitum inter Bohun, et le Count de Gloucester,*[246] when judgment was given there between them, both were fined, and by the King's writ this judgment was sent to the King's court to be enrolled.

28. Edw. 1, *rot. clauso membran.* 2, there is a writ to enroll Magna Carta and to see it observed, and so it has been used in all times.

This petition is a branch of Magna Carta. Let a committee consider on a writ to be drawn for the making of the writ.

My other message was about Maynwaring, his venemous book, and them that gave a warrant for that book, and to demand justice against him. To this was answered that their Lordships would take it into due consideration.

. . .

244. [*Ed.:* in temporal things.]

245. [*Ed.:* Proceedings and Debates, ff. 188–189, in *CD, 1628,* IV, 293.]

246. [*Ed.:* 20 Edw. III, on the Monday after the feast of the Epiphany, a great plea between Bohun and the earl of Gloucester.]

Ed.: Considering the commission for impositions and excises.

Sir Edward Coke. I observe some circumstances in this commission. It was the summons to the parliament. Sure some thought the parliament would not be. Let us go up to the Lords, they cannot but comply with us. I would be glad to hear of the projector, else we would never be quiet. There is a *pudor*[247] about it. Some great Lord[s] never knew it. The end of it was excises, for they are impositions, and to be sure he would have the word otherwise. Let us go up to the Lords and desire a conference, and let us complain of this commission and desire it may be cancelled, and if there be any enrollment of it, cancel it also. And that the projector may be punished and found out, let us vote it and pass our judgment.

. . .

Ed.: After adopting Coke's proposal to punish the author of the commission on excise, the house considered what topics, or heads, to include in the customary royal pardon for parliamentarians' actions.

Sir Edward Coke.[248] It is true if the King will grant a pardon, who can question what can be left out? But if he will have our consent to have it enacted the heads must be brought to us. When I was Attorney myself it was then questioned. I denied to send it, but I did after yield.[39] I would never refuse a pardon from God and the King, but let us require the heads of the Attorney.

. . .

Sir Edward Coke. 40 Edw. 3, the Commons did then send up a form of a pardon and desired it might be granted. And *21ᵐᵒ Jac.* the heads were produced.

[Ordered that Mr. Solicitor acquaint Mr. Attorney with the pleasure of the House that the heads be brought in.]

In Conference with the Lords

Ed.: Concerning the commission on excises.

---

247. [*Ed.:* shame.]
248. [*Ed.:* Proceedings and Debates, ff. 189v–190, in *CD, 1628,* IV, 295–96.]

Sir Edward Coke at the conference with the Lords about the commission for excises:

The concurrence between your Lordships and us in the urgent affairs of the commonwealth have invited us often to your Lordships, and conferences have produced trust, and trust, confidence. Though counsels be not to be judged by events, yet (blessed be God) our counsels and conferences have brought forth good effects. But, my Lords, I must contract myself. The subject of this conference is a commission; therefore we shall desire your Lordships to hear it read.

Which was done accordingly.

That that I shall say is of two parts. First, the observations out of the patent: 1, the persons to whom it was directed; 2, the authority that is committed; 3, the great penalty laid on them if they do it not; 4, the time.

First, the persons to whom it is directed are 33 Lords and others of his Majesty's honourable Privy Councils. 2dly, the authority committed to them is to consider how money may be levied by impositions or otherwise. It is true it is but a power to levy money by imposition. We do not find any thing raised (that is left to your Lordships); but to have a commission to levy money by imposition or otherwise, give us leave to fear that excises and whatever is comprehended in it was intended. Sure I am it is against the law. It is a very high breach of your Lordships' and our, the poor Commons', liberties. And yet this being ill in itself may produce a happy effect. The King and both Houses have given a judgment (the greatest that ever was) against this in the petition of right. And when this judgment is given, see how God's goodness has brought it to pass that this patent should be part of the execution of that judgment to damn it.

For the punishment, I do utterly dislike that clause "as you tender the King's honor" that that must come to a thing of this nature; and it is strange to me—I cannot dive into it—I leave it to your Lordships. For the time, it came out 27 days after the summons of parliament. All knew the parliament would descry this, but I hope it will now turn to good. I will not say it was kept secret.

That which I am to demand of your Lordships: first is that we have considered of the commission. We find it *ex diametro*[249] against the late judgment

---

249. [*Ed.:* in an exact line.]

in the petition of right; now, as we have condemned it, so your Lordships would concur with us as hitherto you have done.

Secondly, that this commission, as a thing directly against law, may be canceled: that if it be enrolled, a *vacat*[250] may be made of it, and if not, that order may be taken that it be not enrolled. 4thly, that the warrant may be damned and destroyed. 5thly, that it would please your Lordships in your wisdoms to take into consideration who is the projector of this device. And, if he could be found out, that some exemplary punishment may be according to justice inflicted upon him.

June 16, 1628.[251]

Ed.: Preparing to present the remonstrance to the King, in response to Sir John Elliot that the King first be told the parliament had voted him his subsidy.

Sir Edward Coke. Let there be no other introduction but to say the business is of that weight that it will admit no introduction.

June 18, 1628.[252]

Ed.: Concerning a petition from the executor of William Bowdler, who had died intestate leaving a sizable estate, but the Crown alleged Bowdler was a bastard, so his estate would be seized by the King rather than administered by the church; the petition, by Bowdler's son-in-law, was to determine whether the estate of bastards intestate was forfeit.

Sir Edward Coke. When I was sworn Attorney to Queen Elizabeth she said: Do not inform against any *pro domina regina sed pro domina veritate*,[253] I charge you do not oppress my subjects. And this then was a project in her time: an old man dying, a projector would pretend he was a bastard and so entitle the

250. [*Ed.:* a judgment vacating any order of record.]
251. [*Ed.:* Proceedings and Debates, f. 205v, in *CD, 1628,* IV, 334.]
252. [*Ed.:* Proceedings and Debates, f. 207v, in *CD, 1628,* IV, 362–63.]
253. [*Ed.:* on behalf of our lady the queen, but on behalf of our lady the truth.]

Queen; but when I was Attorney I ever did disclaim it. When he dies, the property without question is in the ordinary to dispose of, but the crown cannot claim it; and though the bastard have no kindred, yet he has friends that are *de carne*[254] who are to have it.

. . .

Sir Edward Coke had leave to speak again, who said: shall the King have title as supreme ordinary, shall the King be *quasi* an ordinary, as owner? He cannot, it is clear. When a bishop dies, his goods are called *multura episcopi*.[255] The King shall have his best horse and cup and his best cloak, *et mutam canum*,[256] that is his kennel of hounds; for they get their goods by the church and should leave them to the church. Now to have license to make their wills, the King had this. I know it cannot be put out of any book or record that the King should have this prerogative.

June 21, 1628.[257]

> *Ed.:* Debating a motion to ask the King for an adjournment.

Sir Edward Coke. Let us not send to the King to know how long we shall sit. Let us show the causes and the reasons why we desire to know the time. The bill of subsidy is very difficult, unless you will double it and make 1s., 2s., *non sic itur ad astra*.[258] No King is safe that is not able to defend himself, and to aid his allies, and to reward his well-deserving servants. Our great King cannot be able to subsist as things now stand if his ordinary revenue do not discharge his ordinary expenses. His house, as now it is, is *igni se dare*.[259] The King has want of money, what need superfluous expenses? Why should the Duchy of Lancaster continue? There is a Council of York. When Scotland was severed from us, it was then of some use, but now men's inheritances are carried by discretion. So for Wales (it is a marvelous thing) the subject's right

---

254. [*Ed.:* of the body.]
255. [*Ed.:* the bishop's mounter.]
256. [*Ed.:* and a pack of hounds.]
257. [*Ed.:* Proceedings and Debates, f. 211v, in *CD, 1628*, IV, 405.]
258. [*Ed.:* he does not in this way achieve immortality (lit. is gone to the stars).]
259. [*Ed.:* gives itself to the fire.]

is tried by *aliud examen*[260]—by witnesses, and not by juries. As for the house-hold, you will say: will you talk of that without the King's leave? But thus the parliament did in old time. 6 Edw. 3, *num. 4;* 50 Edw. 3, *num.* 5 and 160 especially in 7 Edw. 4 the subject took into consideration the revenue of the King, and how to regulate it. I will abate never a dish. Some have negative wits, I like them not.

For the forests, I hope to see men live where wild beasts do. Queen Eliz-abeth's pensions were all due, she had but 1,700 *l.* in voluntary pensions. I will not say what is now. I would take away all your new fees and new offices. I spoke of this at Oxford, I spoke of [*medicina*] *removens;* I will spare that now. I do not like we should go to the King in a heat.

. . .

In the Committee of the Whole House

> *Ed.:* Considering the impeachment and censure of a member for conspiring to alter the book of rates, in other words to raise the fees royal tenants paid.

Sir Edward Coke.[261] Here is sufficient to convict Sir Edmund Sawyer. Before, he said he never meddled with the book of rates and wished that he were hanged if he did, but now he confesses it. I love not that men should lay wagers that cannot be taken. Part of the words he confesses, the rest he does not remember. This is a great offense. This poisons the fountain. It is true we examine not upon oath, but usually in their discretion they that come here speak the truth, or else we can punish them. We will teach men to equivocate here. He is a member of this House, and therefore greater is the wrong to this House. I will parallel it with Longe's case in 8 Eliz. 4 *l.* was given to the mayor to be a burgess, and he was turned out of the House. Let Sir Edmund Sawyer be turned out of the House and go to the Tower.

260. [*Ed.:* a different jurisdiction.]
261. [*Ed.:* Proceedings and Debates, f. 213v, in *CD, 1628,* IV, 409.]

June 24, 1628.[262]

In the Committee of the Whole House

Ed.: Debating a bill against royal imposts.

Sir Edward Coke. The King has no manner of custom but by act of parliament. The ancient custom is upon wools and leather, but this came by parliament. And the subsidy on cloth, these impositions came by a pretended power in the King to impose in a time of necessity: *rot. finium, 3 Edw.* I, there is the demi-mark granted by the commonalty to the King; *rot. pat., 3 Edw.* I, *memb.* I, this custom was granted by the Lords and Commons. In 26 *Edw.* I, *returnum brevium, salvis nobis custumam lanae per communitatem concessam.*[263] 25 *Edw.* I there is a saving of the customs granted to the King by the commonalty.

The bill of tonnage and poundage excepts cloth but it was pretended that wool was pretermitted.

13 *Hen.* 4, *num.* 18, there can be no imposition, without an act of parliament, for the defense of the realm.

Also, every king has accepted poundage by act of parliament and, therefore, could not do it without a parliament. If the King now, in the face of the parliament, will take it without our grant, I fear to see it. We cannot now in this short time make a book of rates. We can do nothing; let us give him thanks for his answer to our petition, and let us humbly desire that no more be taken by him till it be granted by parliament.

. . .

Sir Edward Coke. Before 3 *Hen.* 5 it was never granted for life but then, he being a victorious prince, his Commons gave it to him; and he said that it should never be drawn into example, for it was thought that never king should have the like occasion as he then had. In Hen. 6 his time it went but for years, H. 7 got it for life. It is a good warning for us to look what we do. Without a book of rates we cannot grant it, and never had king impositions granted him.

---

262. [*Ed.:* Proceedings and Debates, ff. 216v–217v, in *CD, 1628,* IV, 447–49.]

263. [*Ed.:* the return of writs, saving to us the custom of wool granted by the commonalty.]

VI

Appendix I:
Official Acts Related to
Sir Edward Coke's
Career

A. The High Commission
(Coke refuses to appear), 1611

Ed.: Coke, the great critic of the High Commission, was ordered to sit as its member, with this result. Coke's notes of this conference were first printed in volume 12 of the *Reports,* at 88.

High Commission.
(1611) Michaelmas Term, 9 James I.

Memorandum, that upon Thursday, in this term, a High Commission in Causes Ecclesiasticall was published in the Great Chamber of the Arch-bishop at Lambeth, in which I, with the chief Justice, chief Baron, Justice Williams, Justice Crook, Baron Altham, and Baron Bromley, were named Commissioners, amongst all the Lords of the Councill, divers Bishops, Attorney and Solicitor, and divers Deans and Doctors of the Cannon and Civil Lawes; and I was commanded to sit by force of the said Commission, which I refused for these causes:

1. For this, that I, nor any of my Brethren of the Common Pleas, were acquainted with the Commission, but the Judges of the Kings Bench were.

2. That I did not know what was contained in the new Commission, and no Judge can execute any Commission with a good conscience without knowledge; and that alwaies the gravity of the Judges hath been to know their Commission, for *Tantum sibi est permissum, quantum commissum:*[1] and if the Commission be against Law, they ought not to sit by virtue of it.

3. That there was not any necessity that I should sit, who understood nothing of it, so long as the other Judges were there, the advice of whom had been had in this new Commission.

4. That I have endeavoured to inform my self of it, and have sent to the Rolls to have a Copy of it, but it was not enrolled.

5. None can sit by force of any Commission, until he hath took the Oath of Supremacy, according to the statute of 1 Eliz. And for this, if they will read the Commission so that we may hear it, and have a Copy to advise upon it, then I will either sit or shew cause to the contrary. But the Lord Treasurer would for divers reasons perswade me to sit, which I utterly denied.

---

1. [*Ed.:* Only so much is permitted as was committed to them:]

And to this the chief Justice, chief Baron, and some others of the Judges, seemed to incline; upon which the Lord Treasurer conferred in private with the Arch-bishop Bancroft, who said to him, that he had appointed divers causes of Heresie, Incest, and enormous Crimes to be heard upon this day, and for that he would proceed; but at last he was content that the Commission should be solemnly read, and so it was, which contained three great Skins of parchment, and contained divers points against the Laws and Statutes of England: and when this was read, all the Judges rejoyced that they did not sit by force of it: And then the Lords of the Council, Viz. The Arch-bishop, the Lord Treasurer, the Lord privy Seal, the Lord Admiral, the Lord Chamberlain, the Earl of Shrewsbury, the Earl of Worcester with the Bishops, took the Oath of Supremacy and Allegeance; and then we as Commissioners were required to take the Oath, which I refused until I had considered of it: But, as the Subject of the King, I and the other Judges also took the oaths of Supremacy and Allegeance.

Then the Lord Arch-bishop made an Oration in commendation of the care and providence of the King, for the peace and quiet of the Church; Also he commended the Commissioners, also the necessity of the Commission to proceed summarily in these days, wherein sins of detestable nature, and factions, and Schisms did abound, and protested to proceed sincerely by force of it; and then he caused to be called a most blasphemous Heretick, and after him another, who was brought thither by his appointment, to shew to the Lords and the Auditory the necessity of that Commission.

And after, the Arch-bishop came to the chief Justice and to me, and promised us, that we should have a Copy of the Commission, and then I should observe the diversity between the old Commission and this: and all the time that the long Commission was in reading, the Oath in taking, and the Oration made, I stood, and would not sit, as I was requested by the Arch-bishop and the Lords; and so by my example did all the rest of the Justices.

And the Arch-bishop said, that the King had commanded him to sit by vertue of this new Commission, in some open place, and at certain days: and for that cause he appointed the great Chamber at Lambeth in Winter, and the Hall in the Summer; and every Thursday in the Term time, at two of the Clock in the after-noon, and in the fore noon he would have a Sermon for the better informing of the Commissioners of their duty, in the true and sincere execution of their duties.

B. Commendams and the
King's Displeasure

Ed.: In a case concerning the powers of the King, or others, to grant a *commendam,* or temporary church office, the King sought to delay the court until he could appear. When Coke did not wait or consult, the King was displeased, but Coke stood his ground, promising "to do what should be fit for a judge to do." These notes were printed in the *Acts of the Privy Council, 1616.*

[303] | At Whitehall, the 6 of June, 1616.

Present: The Kinges Majestie, Lord Archbishop of Canterburie, Lord Chancellor, Lord Treasurer, Lord Privie Seale, Lord Stewarde, Lord Chamberlein, Lord Viscount Fenton, Lord Bishop of Winchester, Lord Zouch, Lord Knollis, Lord Wotton, Lord Stanhope, Mr. Vice-Chamberlein, Mr. Secretary Winwoode, Mr. Secretary Lake, Mr. Chancellor of the Exchecquer, Master of the Roles.

His Majestie, having this day given order for meeting of the Councell, and that all the Judges (being twelve in number) should bee sent for to bee present; when the Lordes were sett, and the Judges readie attendinge, his Majestie came himself in person to Councell, and opennd unto them the cause of that assembly; which was, that hee had called them together concerninge a question that had relacion to noe private person, but concerned God and the Kinge, the power of his Crowne, and the state of his Church, whereof hee was Protector; and that there was noe fitter place to handle it then at the head of his Councell Table; that there had ben a question pleaded and argued concerninge *commendams*,[1] the proceedinges wherein had either ben misreported, or mishandled; for his Majestie a yeare since had receaved advertizement concerning that case in twoe extreames: by some, that it did trench farr into his Prerogative Royall, in the generall power of graunting commendams; and by others, that the doubt rested only upon a special nature of a commendam, such as in respect of the incongruitie and exorbitant forme thereof might bee questioned, without impeachinge or weakeninge the generall power at all.

Whereupon his Majestie, willinge to knowe the true state thereof, comaunded the Lord Bishop of Winchester and Mr. Secretarie Winwoode to bee present at the next argument, and to reporte the state of the question and proceedinges unto his Majestie; but Mr. Secretary Winwoode, being absent by occasion, the Lord [Bishop] of Winchester only was present, and gave information to his Majestie of the particulars thereof; which his Majestie commaunded him to report to the Boarde. Whereupon the Lord [Bishop] of Winchester stoode up and reported: That Sergeant Chibborne (who argued the case against the commendams) had maintayned divers assertions and positions very prejudiciall to his Majesty's Prerogative Royall:

As first, that the translacion of bishopps was against the cannon lawe, and, for authoritie, vouched the cannons of the Councell of Sardis.

| That the Kinge had noe power to graunt commendams, but in case of [304] necessitie.

That there could bee noe necessitie, because there was noe neede of augmentacion of livinges, for noe man was bounde to keepe hospitallitie above his meanes.

Besydes manie other partes of his argument tending to the overthrowe of his Majesty's prerogative in cases of commendam.

The Lord [Bishop] of Winchester havinge made this reporte, his Majestie resumed his former narrative, lettinge the lordes knowe that after the Lord [Bishop] of Winchester had made unto his Majestie a reporte of that which passed at the argument of the case, like in substaunce to that which hee had now made, his Majestie, apprehendinge the matter to bee of soe hiegh a nature, commaunded his Attorney Generall to signifie his Majesty's pleasure to the Lord Chiefe Justice; that in regarde of his Majesty's other most waighty oc-

---

1. [*Ed.*: Commitment, an order granting temporary possession of a vacant ecclesiastical living or benefice, including its revenues until the office is permanently filled.]

casions, and for that his Majestie helde it necessary (upon the Lord [Bishop] of Winchester's reporte), that his Majestie bee first consulted with, before the Judges proceeded to argument; therefore the day appointed for the Judges' arguments should bee putt of, till they might speake with his Majestie. And this letter of his Majesty's Attorney was by his Majesty's comandment openly read, which followeth *in haec verba*.[2]

My Lord,

It is the Kinges expresse pleasure that, because his Majesty's times would not serve to conferr with your lordship and his Judges, touching the case of the commendams, at his last beinge in towne, in regarde of his Majestie's other most waightie occasions; and for that his Majestie holdeth it necessarie, upon the reporte which my Lord of Winchester (who was present at the last argument, by his Majesty's royall commandement) made to his Majestie that his Majestie bee first consulted with, ere there bee anie further proceedinge by argument of anie of the Judges, or otherwise; therefore that the day appointed for the further proceedinge of argument by the Judges in that case, bee putt of, till his Majesty's further pleasure bee knowne upon consultinge with him. And, to that ende, that your lordship forthwith signifie his commaundement to the rest of the Judges; whereof your lordship may not faile. And soe I leave your lordship to God's goodness.

Your lordship's lovinge freinde to comaunde.

Fr. Bacon.

This Thursday, at afternoone,
the 25th day of Aprill, 1616.

That upon this letter receaved, the Lord Chiefe Justice retorned worde to his Majesty's said Attorney by his servaunt, that it was fitt the rest of his bretheren should understaunde his Majesty's pleasure ymediately by letter from his said Attorney to the Judges of the severall Benches, and accordingly it was donn.

Whereupon all the said Judges assembled, and by their letter under their haundes certefyed his Majestie that they helde those letters (importing the significacion aforesaid) to bee contrary to lawe, and such as they could not yeild to the same by their oath; and that thereupon they had proceeded at

---

2. [*Ed.:* in these words.]

the day, I and did nowe certefie his Majesty thereof; which letter of the Judges   [305]
his Majestie alsoe commaunded to bee openly read, the tenor whereof followeth, *in haec verba*—

Most dread and most gracious Soveraigne.

It may please your most excellent Majestie to bee advertized that this letter
inclosed was delivered to mee, your Chiefe Justice, on Thursday last in
the afternoon, by a servaunt of your Majesty's Attorney Generall, and letters
of like effect were, on the day followinge, sent from him by his servaunt
to us, your Majesty's other Justices of every of your Courtes at Westminster.
Wee are and ever wilbe readie with all faithfull and true hartes, according
to our bounden duties to serve and obey your Majestie, and thinke ourselves
most happie to spende our lives and abillities to doe your Majestie faithfull
and true service. In this present case, mencioned in this letter, what in-
formacion hath ben made unto yow (whereupon Mr. Attorney doth ground
his letter), from the report of the Bishop of Winchester, wee knowe not.
This wee knowe, that the true substance of the case summarily is thus. It
consisteth principally upon the construccion of twoe Acts of Parliament,
the one of the 25 yeare of King Edward 3, and the other of the 25 yeare
of King Henry 8; whereof your Majesty's Judges, upon their oathes, and
according to their best knowledge and learninge, are bounde to deliver
the true understaundinge faithfully and uprightly. And the case is betweene
subjects for private interrest and inheritaunce, earnestly called on for justice
and expedition. Wee holde it our duties to informe your Majestie that our
oathe is in theis expresse wordes: That in case anie letters come unto us
contrary to lawe, that wee doe nothinge by such letters, but certefie your
Majestie thereof, and goe forth to doe the lawe, notwithstaundinge the
same letters. Wee have advisedly considered of the said letters of Mr. Attorney, and with one consent doe holde the same to bee contrary to lawe,
and that wee could not yeild to the same by our oath; assuredly persuadinge
ourselves that your Majestie, beinge truly informed that it staundeth not
with your royall and just pleasure to give way to them, and therefore know-
inge your Majesty's zeale to justice, and to bee most renowned therefore,
wee have, according to our oathes, and duties (at the day openly prefixed
the last tearme) proceeded, and thereof certefyed your Majestie, and shall
ever pray to the Almightie for your Majestie in all honor, health, and happiness longe to raigne over us.

Your Majesty's most humble and faithfull
subjects and servaunts,

Edw. Coke, Henry Hobart, Laur. Tanfeilde, P. Warburton, Geo. Snigge,
James Altham, Edw. Bromley, Jo. Croke, H. Winche, John Doddridge,
Augustine Nicolls, Rob. Houghton.
Serjants' Inne, 27 Aprill.

His Majestie, havinge considered of this letter, did by his princely letters
retorne aunsweare, reportinge himself to their owne knowledge and experience, what princely care hee had ever had, since his comeinge to the Crowne,
to have justice duly administred to his subjects with all possible expedicion,
[306] and I how farr hee was from crossinge or delayinge of justice, where the interrest
of anie private partie was questioned; but, on the other syde, expressinge himself that where the case concerned the hiegh powers and prerogatives of his
Crowne, hee would not endure to have them wounded through the sydes of
a private person, admonishinge them alsoe of a custome lately entertayned,
of a greater boldnes to dispute the hiegh pointes of his Majesty's prerogative,
in a popular and unlawfull libertie of argument, more then in former times,
and makeinge them perceave alsoe howe weake and impertinent the pretence
or allegacion of their oath was in a case of this nature, and howe well it might
have ben spared; with manie other waightie pointes in the said letter contayned; which letter alsoe, by his Majesty's commaundment, was publickely
read, and followeth *in haec verba:*—

> Trustie and well-beloved Councellor, and trustie and wel-beloved; wee greete
> yow well. Wee perceave by your letter that you conceave the commaun-
> dement given yow by our Attorney Generall, in our name, to have pro-
> ceeded upon wronge informacion. But if yee list to remember, what
> princely care wee have ever had, since our comeinge to this Crowne, to
> see justice duly administred to our subjects with all possible expedicion,
> and howe farr wee have ever benn from urginge the delay thereof in anie
> sorte, yee may easely persuade yourselves that it was noe smale reason which
> moved us to send yow that direccion. Yee might very well have spared your
> labor in informeinge us of the nature of your oath, for, although wee never
> studied the common lawe of Englaunde, yet are wee not ignoraunt of anie
> pointes which belonnge to a kinge to knowe. Wee are therefore to enforme
> yow hereby, that wee are farr from crossinge or delayinge anie thinge which
> may belonnge to the interrest of anie private partie in this case. But wee
> cannot bee contented to suffer the prerogative royall of our Crowne to be
> wounded, though the sydes of a private person. Wee have noe care at all
> which of the parties shall wynn his processe in this case, soe the right

prevaile, and that justice bee duly administered. But upon the other parte, wee have reason to foresee, that nothinge be donn in this case which may wound our prerogative in generall; and, therefore, soe that wee may be sure that nothinge shalbe debated amongst yow, which may concerne our generall power of givinge commendams, wee desire not the parties to have an hower's delay of justice. But, that our prerogative should not bee wounded in that regarde for all times hereafter, upon pretext of a private partie's interrest, wee sent yow that direccion; which wee accounte to be wounded aswell, if it bee publickly disputed upon, as if anie sentence were given against it. Wee are therefore to admonish yow that, since the prerogative of our Crowne hath ben more boldly dealte withall in Westminster Hall duringe the time of our raigne then ever it was before in the raignes of divers princes ymediatly precedinge us, that wee will noe longer endure that popular and unlawfull libertie; and, therefore, were wee justly moved to sende yow that direccion to | forbeare to meddle anie further in a case [307] of soe tender a nature, till wee had further thought upon it. Wee have cause inded to rejoyce of your zeale for the speedie execution of justice; but wee would bee gladd that all our good subjects might soe finde the fruites thereof, as that noe pleas before yow were of older date then this is. But as to your argument which yow found upon your oath, yow give our predecessors, who first founded that oath, a very uncharitable meetinge, in pervertinge their intention and zeale to justice, to make a weapon of it to use against their successors. For, although your oath bee, that yow shall not delay justice betwixt anie private parties, yet was it not meant that the Kinge should thereby receave harme, before hee bee forewarned thereof. Neither can yee denye but that every tearme yee will, out of your owne discretions, for reasons knowne unto yow, put of either the hearinge or determininge of an ordinary cause amongst private persons, till the next tearme followinge. Our pleasure therefore is, who are the heade and fountaine of justice under God, in our dominions, and wee, out of our absolute authoritie royall, doe commaunde yow, that yow forbeare to meedle anie further in this plea, till our comeinge to the towne, and that out of our owne mouth yow may heare our pleasure in this busines; which wee doe only out of the care wee have that our perogative may not receave an unwittinge and indirect blowe, and not to hinder justice to bee ministred to anie private parties; which noe importunitie shall persuade us to move yow in, like as only for avoydinge the unreasonnable importunitie of suitors in their owne particular, that oath was by our predecessors ordayned to be ministred unto yow. Soe wee hartely wish yow well to fare.

Postscript.—Yow shall upon the receipt of this our letter call our Attorney
Generall unto yow, who will informe yow of the particular pointes which
wee are unwillinge should bee publickly disputed in this case.

This letter beinge read, his Majestie resorted to take into his consideration
the partes of the Judges' letter, and other their proceedinges in that cause, and
the errors therein comitted and contayned: which errors his Majestie did sett
forth to bee both in matter and manner: in matter, as well by way of omission
as comission; for omission, that it was a faulte in the Judges that when they
hearde a Councellor at the barr presume to argue against his Majesty's prerogative (which in this case was in effect his supremacy), they did not interrupt
him, and reprove sharply that loose and bold course of disaffirmeinge and
impeachinge thinges of soe hiegh a nature, by discourse; especially since his
Majestie had observed, that ever since his comeinge to this Crowne the popular
sorte of lawiers have ben the men that most affrontedly in all Parlaments have
troden upon his prerogative; which beinge most contrary to their vocation of
anie men, since the lawe, nor lawyers, can never bee respected if the Kinge
bee not reverenced, it therefore best became the Judges of anie to cheque and
brydle such impudent lawyers, and in their severall Benches to disgrace them
that beare soe litle respect to the King's authoritie and prerogative. That his
Majestie had a doble prerogative, whereof the one was ordinary, and had relacion to his private interrest, which mought bee, and was, every day disputed
in Westminster Hall. The other was of a hiegher nature, referringe to his
supreame and imperiall power and soveragnitie, which ought not to bee dis-
puted or handled in vulgar argument; but that of late the Courtes of the |
Common Lawe were growne soe vaste and transcendent, as they did both
meddle with the King's prerogative, and had incroached upon all other Courtes
of Justice, as the High Commission, the Councells established in Wales and
Yorke, the Courte of Requests. Concerninge that which might be tearmed
Commission, his Majestie tooke exception to the Judges' letter, both in matter
and forme. For matter, his Majestie did plainely demonstrate that, whereas it
was contayned in the Judges' letter, that the significacion of his Majesty's
pleasure as aforesaid was contrary to lawe and not agreeable to the oath of a
Judge, that could not bee.

First, for that the puttinge of hearinge, or proceedinge upon, just and necessary cause is no denyinge or delay of justice, but a wisedome and maturitie
of proceedinge, and that there cannot bee a more just and necessary cause of

[308]

stay then the consultinge with the Kinge, when the cause concernes the Crowne, and that the Judges did dayly put of causes upon lighter occasions. And likewise his Majestie did desire to knowe of the Judges how his callinge them to consulte with him was contrary to lawe, which they never could aunsweare unto.

Secondly, that it was noe bare supposition or surmize that this case concerned the Kinges prerogative, for that it had ben directed and largly disputed at the barr, and the very disputinge thereof in a publicke audience is both daingerous and dishonorable to his Majestie.

Thirdly, that the manner of puttinge of which the Kinge required, was not infinite, nor for lounge time, but grounded upon his Majesty's waighty occasions, which were notorious; by reason whereof hee could not speake with the Judges before the argument, and that there was a certaine expectation of his Majesty's speedie retorne at Whitsuntide, and likewise that the case had ben soe lately argued, and could not receave judgment till Easter tearme next, as the Judges themselves afterwardes confessed.

And lastlie, because there was another just cause of absence for the twoe Cheife Justices, for that they ought to have assisted the Lord Chancellor the same day in a great cause of the Kinges, followed by the Lord Hunsdon against the Lord William Howarde in Chancerie; which cause of the Kinges (specially beinge soe waightie) ought to have had precedence before anie cause betweene partie and partie.

Also, whereas it was contayned in the Judges' letter that the case of the *commendams* was but a case of private interrest betweene partie and partie, his Majestie shewed plainely the contrary, not only by the argument of Serjaunt Chibborne, which was before his commaundement, but by the argument of the Judges themselves (namely Justice Nicholls), which was after; but especially since one of the parties is a Bishopp, who pleads for the commendam, only by the virtue of his Majesty's prerogative.

Also, whereas it was contayned in the Judges' letter that the parties called upon them earnestly for justice, his Majestie conceaves it to bee but pretence, urgeing them to prove that there I was anie sollicitation by the parties for expedicion, otherwise then in an ordinary course of attendaunce, which they could never prove. [309]

As for the forme of the letter, his Majestie noated that it was a newe thinge and very undecent, and unfitt for subjects to disobey the Kinges commaundement, but most of all to proceede in the meanetime, and to retorne unto him a bare certificate: whereas they ought to have concluded with the layinge downe and representinge of their reasons modestly unto his Majestie, why they should proceede, and soe to have submitted the same to his princely judgment, expectinge to knowe from him wheather they had given him satisfaccion.

After this his Majesty's declaration, all the Judges fell downe upon their knees, and acknowledged their error, for matter of forme, humbly cravinge his Majesty's gracious favour and pardon for the same.

But for the matter of the letter, the Lord Cheife Justice of the Kinges Bench entred into a defence thereof, the effect whereof was, that the stay required by his Majestie was a delay of justice, and, therefore, contrary to lawe and the Judges' oath; and that the Judges knewe well amongst themselves, that the case (as they meant to handle it) did not concerne his Majesty's prerogative of graunt of commendams, and that if the day had not helde by the not-comeinge of the Judges, the suite had ben discontinewed; which had ben a faylinge in justice, and that they could not adjourne it, because Mr. Attornei's letter mencioned noe day certaine, and that an adjornment must alwaies bee to a day certaine.

Unto which aunsweare of the Chiefe Justice, his Majestie did replye, that for the last conceipt, it was meere sophistrie, for that they might in their discretions have prefixed a convenient day, such as there might have ben time for them to consult with his Majestie before the same, and that his Majestie leafte that pointe of forme to themselves.

And for that other pointe, that they should take upon them peremptorily to discerne whether the case concerned the Kinges prerogative, without consultinge with his Majestie first, and informeinge his princely judgment, was a thing preposterous, for that they ought first to have made that appeare to his Majestie, and soe to have given him assurance thereof, upon consultacion with him.

And as for the mayne matter, that it should bee against the lawe, and against their oath, his Majestie sayde hee had sayed enough before; unto which the Lord Chiefe Justice in effect had made noe aunsweare, but only insisted upon the former opinion; and therefore the Kinge required the Lord Chancellor to deliver his opinion upon that pointe, whether the stay that had ben required by his Majestie were contrary to lawe, or against the Judges' oath.

The Lord Chancellor stoode up, and moved his Majestie that, because this question had relacion to matter of lawe, his Majestie would bee informed by his learned councell first, and they first to deliver their opinion, which his Majestie commaunded them to doe.

Thereupon his Majesty's Attorney Generall gave his opinion that the puttinge of the day in manner as was required by I his Majestie (to his understaundinge) was without all scruple noe delay of justice, nor dainger of the Judges' oath, insistinge upon some of the reasons which his Majestie had formerly opennd, and addinge that the letter hee had writt in his Majesty's name was noe imperious letter, as to say: That his Majestie, for certaine causes, or for causes knowne to himself, would have them put of the day, but plainely and fairely expressed the causes unto them; for that the Kinge conceaved, upon the Lord [Bishop] of Winchester's reporte, that the cause concerned him, and that his Majestie would willingly have spoken to them before, but by reason of his important busines could not, and therefore required a staye till they might conveniently speake with him, which they knewe could not bee lounge; and in the conclusion of his speech wished the Judges seriously to consider with themselves whether they were not in greater dainger of breach of their oath by their proceedinge, then they could have ben by their stay. For that it is parte of their oath to counsell his Majestie when they are called; and if they will proceede in a busines first, whereupon they are called to councell, and will councell him when the matter is past, it is more then a simple refusall to give him councell; and soe concluded his speech, and the rest of the learned councell consented to his opinion.

Whereupon the Lord Chiefe Justice of the King's Bench (aunsswearinge nothing to the matter) tooke exceptions that the Kinges councell learned should pleade or dispute with the Judges, for (hee sayde) they were to pleade before the Judges, and not to dispute with them. Whereunto the Kinges Attorney replyed, that hee found that exception strainge, for that the King's learned councell were by oath and office (and much more when they had the Kinges expresse commaundement), without feare of anie man's face, to proceede or declare against anie, the greatest peere or subject of the kingdome, and not only anie subject in particular, but any boddie of subjects, or persons, were the[y] Judges, or were they an upper or lower house of Parlament, in case that they exceede the limitts of their authoritie, or take anie thinge from his Majesty's royall power, or prerogative. And soe concluded that his challendge, and that in his Majesty's presence, was a wronge to their places, for which hee and his fellowes did appeale to his Majestie for reparacion. And thereupon his Majestie did affirme that it was their dutie soe to doe, and that

[310]

hee would mayntaine them therein, and tooke occasion afterwardes againe to speake of it. For when the Lord Chiefe Justice sayde hee would not dispute with his Majestie, the Kinge replyed, that the Judges would not dispute with him, nor his learned councell might not dispute with them; soe, whether they did well, or ill, it must not bee disputed.

After this the Lord Chancellor delivered his opinion, cleerely and plainely, that the stay which had beene by his Majestie required was not against lawe, nor any breach of a Judge's oath, and required that the oath itself might bee read out of the statute, which was donn by the Kinges Sollicitor, and all the wordes thereof waighed and considered.

[311] | Thereupon his Majestie and the Lordes thought good to aske the Judges severally their opinion; the question beinge put in this manner: Whether if at anie time in a case dependinge before the Judges, which his Majestie conceaved to concerne him, either in power or profitt, and thereupon required to consult with him, and that they should stay proceedings in the meanetime, they ought not to stay accordingly. They all (the Lord Chiefe Justice only excepted) yeilded that they would, and acknowledged it to bee their dutie soe to doe; only the Lord Chiefe Justice of the King's Bench sayd for aunsweare that when that case should bee, hee would doe that should bee fitt for a Judge to doe, and the Lord Chiefe Justice of the Common Pleas, who had assented with the rest, added, that hee would ever trust the justnes of his Majesty's comaundement.

After this was put to a pointe, his Majestie thought fitt, in respect of the further day of argument appointed the Saturday followeinge for the commendams, to knowe from his Judges what hee might expect from them concerninge the same. Whereupon the Lord of Canterburie breakeinge the case into some questions, his Majestie did require his Judges to deale plainely with him, whether they meant in their argument to touch the generall power of grauntinge commendams, yea or noe. Whereupon all his said Judges did promisse and assure his Majestie that, in the argument of the said case of commendams, they would speake nothinge which should weaken, or drawe into doubte, his Majesty's prerogative for the graunting of them, but intended particularly to insist upon the pointe of the laps, and other individuall pointes of this case, which they conceaved to bee of a forme differringe from all other commendams which have ben practized.

The Judges alsoe went further, and did promise his Majestie that they would not only abstaine from speakeinge anie thinge to weaken his Majesty's prerogative of commendams, but would directly and in plaine tearmes affirme the same, and correct the erronious and bold speeches which had ben used at the barr in derogation thereof.

Alsoe, all the Judges did in generall acknowledge and professe, with greate forwardnes that it was their dutie, if anie councellor at the barr presumed at anie time to call in question his Majesty's hiegh prerogatives and regallities, that they ought to reprehende them and silence them; and all promised soe to doe hereafter.

Lastly, the twoe Judges, which were then next to argue, Mr. Justice Dodridge and Mr. Justice Winche, openned themselves unto his Majestie thus farr, that they would insist chiefely upon the laps, and some pointes of uncertaintie, repugnancy and absurditie, beinge peculiar to this commendam, and that they would shewe their dislike of that which had ben sayde at the barr for the weakeninge of the generall power; and Mr. Justice Doddridge sayde that he would conclude for the Kinge that the Church was voyde, and in his Majesty's guifte; and alsoe sayde | that the Kinge might give a commendam to a Bishop, [312] either before or after his consecration, and that hee might either give it him duringe his life, or for a certaine number of yeares.

The Judges havinge thus farr submitted and declared themselves, his Majestie admonished them to keepe the boundes and lymitts of their severall Courtes, not to suffer his prerogative to bee wounded by rash and unadvised pleadinge before them, or by newe inventions of lawe. For as hee well knewe that the true and ancient common lawe is the most favourable for kinges of anie lawe in the worlde; soe hee advised them to apply themselves to the studie and practize of that ancient and best lawe, and not to extende the power of anie of their Courtes beyounde their due lymitts, followinge the president of the best ancient Judges, in the times of best Govermentes, and that then they might assure themselves that hee for his parte in the proteccion of them and expediting of justice, would walke in the stepps of the ancient and best kinges. And thereupon gave them leave to proceede in their argument.

When the Judges were removed, his Majestie, that had forborne to aske the votes and opinions of his councell before the Judges, because hee would not prejudicate the freedome of the Judges' opinions concerninge the point; whether the stay of proceedinges that had been by his Majestie required, could by anie construccion bee thought to bee within the compasse of the Judges' oath (which they had hearde reade unto them), did then put the question to his Councell, who all with one consent did give opinion that it was farr from anie colour or shadowe of such interpretacion, and that it was against common sence to thinke the contrary, especially since there is noe mention made in their oath of the delay of justice, but only that they shall not deny justice, nor bee moved by anie of the Kinges letters to doe any thinge contrary to lawe, or justice.

G. Cant., T. Ellesmere, Canc., T. Suffolke, E. Worcester, Lenox, Nottingham, Pembroke, W. Knollis, John Digbye, Raphe Winwoode, Tho. Lake, Fulk Grevill, Jul. Caesar, Fr. Bacon.

C. Coke's Hearing, June 26, 1616.

Ed.: Following the *commendams* argument, effectively staged by Francis Bacon, Coke's dismissal was but a matter of time. These notes were printed in the *Acts of the Privy Council, 1616.*

June 26.

It may please your most excellent Majestie.

The Lorde Chiefe Justice, presentinge himself on his knee at the Boarde, your Sollicitor signifyed: That hee was by your commaundement to charge him for certaine acts and speeches, wherein your Majestie was much unsatisfyed; which were in number three.

1. First, an act donn.

2. Secoundly, speeches of hiegh contempt utterred in a seate of justice.

3. Thirdly, uncomely and undutifull carryage in the presence of your Majestie, your Privie Councell, and your Judges.

Concerninge the first, which was the act. It was donn when hee was in place of trust, and concerned a statute of 12,000*li.* taken of Sir Christopher Hatton, to the use of Sir Edward Coke, when hee was your Majesty's Attorney-Generall; not to pay a debte of good value, due unto your Majestie, nor to accept of a discharge for the same, and for the better streingtheninge of that statute there was likewise a bond taken of 6,000*li.*, with suerties to the same effect; soe that Sir Christopher Hatton lay charged under the penaltie of 18,000*li.* not to pay the debte, to agree to noe surrender, discharge, or release, nor anie way to assent thereunto. That this offence was aggravated by denyall and protestacion made of late by the Lord Chiefe Justice, that hee was not privie to the condicion of the defeasaunce; whereas the statute was taken to his use, the defeasaunce by indenture, whereof Sir Christopher Hatton's part was founde, but the other parte was not founde. That he was privie to the peninge of it, inserted wordes with his owne haunde, and that Mr. Walter and Mr. Bridgman, his owne councell, were witnesses to it.

The secounde pointe was, wordes spoken in the Kinges Bench, the last day of Hillary tearme last, in a case of Glanvile and Allen, whereof your Sollicitor made a narrative relacion, and charged the Lord Chiefe Justice to have given too much harte and incoragement to that cause. That hee had too constauntly directed the jury, turned them thrice from the barr, threatenned to comitt them, examined them by the pole, and tolde them that they had ben tamperred withall. That hee had given warneinge to the councellors at the barr that, if [338] they sett their haundes to a Bill after judgement, hee would I foreclose them the Courte; and further in another case the same day sayde, that the Common Lawe of Englaunde would bee overthrowen, and that the light of the lawe would bee obscured, and that all this was confirmed by good wittnes.

The thirde and last pointe was, his undecent behaviour before your Majestie, your Councell, and your Judges; and that consisted of twoe partes. First, the exception hee tooke at your learned councell in your presence for speakinge by your commaundement.

The secound, that your Majestie havinge openned yourself in the case of *commendams,* and satisfyed the Judges, that your Majestie sendinge unto them had noe intent to delay justice; and question beinge putt to the rest of the Judges, whether they did hold it for a delay of justice, that your Majestie had sent in that cause, or if you shoulde send hereafter in a like case, wherein your Majesty's prerogative were interressed, the rest of the Judges submittinge themselves, hee alone dissented from all the rest.

This beinge the effect of your Sollicitor's charge, the Lord Chiefe Justice made aunsweare: That hee would, by their lordships' favours, beginn with the last, and sayde, that for the pointe of challendginge and takeinge exception at your Majesty's councell learned speakinge in the case of comendams by your Majesty's commaundement, hee acknowledged it for an error, and humbly submitted himself.

To the pointe, that upon the question asked the Judges touchinge stay of proceedinges, hee did deny, when all the rest of the Judges did yeild, his aunsweare was: that the question included a multitude of particulars, which suddenly occurringe to his minde, caused him to make that aunsweare, that when that time should bee, hee would doe that which should become an honest and just Judge.

For the bonde, he sayeth that that assuraunce was in hammeringe a yeare and a half. They were *elephantini libri;*[1] and nowe, twelve yeares beinge past, it was noe marvaile if his memorie were shorte, specially since about that time hee was imployed, first in the greate services of the priests' treason, and Cobham's treason, and the next yeare in the powder treason; and that, if anie thinge have slipped him in that multitude of businesses, lett theis services blott out his errors.

Secoundly, hee did use an argument *ab impossibili,*[2] which was, that the debte remayneinge at that time was 33,000*li.,* and that younge Mr. Hatton's meanes were very meane, not above 100 markes a yeare; and therefore impossible for him to redeeme it; and that, as soone as it came to a possibillitie, when hee first heard of Sir Robert Rich his offer, hee then submitted it, before such time as hee remembred the statute or defeasaunce.

Thirdly, *cui bono:*[3] Hee sayd hee never had anie profitt by it, but the presentacion to a benefice; and all the rest was his wive's.

Fowerthly, the Crowne was content with the installment, and hee did but take bondes to continewe it; and throughout all this, hee submitted himself to your Majestie and the Boarde, sayinge *Actus non facit reum, nisi mens sit rea.*[4]

| For his speeches in the Kinges Bench, etc., hee sayeth first, that whatsoever [339] was donn, was donn by common consent, and for those speeches, manie of them were spoken, and hee knewe by whom they were spoken, but not by himself: and then offerred fower consideracions.

1. That the commission (unto which nevertheles hee did in noe wise except) was *ad informandum non ad convincendum.*[5]

2. That there were but witnesses on one syde.

3. That the interrogatories might bee drawne too shorte.

4. That it was concerninge wordes spoken fower moneths agoe, which beinge spoken amongst manie might bee reported diversly, and thereupon produced a paper writen by himself, contayneinge (as hee sayeth) the true passages

---

1. [*Ed.:* elephantine books;]
2. [*Ed.:* of impossibility,]
3. [*Ed.:* to whose benefit?]
4. [*Ed.:* An act does not make someone guilty unless his mind is guilty.]
5. [*Ed.:* to inform, not to convict.]

of that day; which paper wee present to your Majestie herewithall, beinge, as hee sayd, sett downe by himself the next after, *sedato animo.*[6]

And touchinge the wordes: that the common lawe would bee overthrowen, and that the Judges would have but little to doe at Assizes, because the light of the lawe would bee obscured, hee confesseth the wordes, but sayth they were not spoken the same day, but another time in a cause of Sir Anthonie Mildmaies; and added, that hee will not maintaine the differrence betweene the twoe Courtes, nor bringe it into question; yet, if it were an error, hee may say *Erravimus cum patribus;*[7] and thereupon alleadged three examples: first, the articles against Cardinall Wolsey, 21 Henry 8, wherein the same wordes are used that such proceedinges in Chancery tended to the subversion of the common lawe; secoundly, the booke called the *Doctor and Student;* and thirdly, an opinion of the Judges in Throgmorton's case in Queen Elizabeth's time; addinge further that for the time to come there was noe dainger; for that the Judges, havinge receaved your Majesty's commaundement by your Attorney Generall, that noe Bills of that nature should hereafter bee receaved, hee and his bretheren have caused the same to bee entred as an order in the same Courte, which shalbe observed.

Which beinge the effect of his aunsweare, wee have thought good withall to add that before us, as well in speech as in action, hee behaved himself very modestly and submissively.

This certificate was made the 26 day of this present June.

. . .

[340] | At the Court at Greenewich, Sonday morneineinge (*sic*), the 30th of June, 1616.

Present: Lord Archbishop of Canterburie, Lord Treasurer, Lord Privie Seale, Lord Zouch, Lord Knollis, Lord Wotton, Mr. Vice-Chamberlein, Mr. Secretary Winwoode, Mr. Secretary Lake, Mr. Chancellor of the Exchecquer, Master of the Roles, Mr. Attorney Generall.

Sir Edward Coke, knight, Chiefe Justice of the King's Bench, presentinge himself this day at thes Boarde, upon his knees, Mr. Secretary Winwoode signifyed unto him that their lordships had made reporte to his Majestie of that which passed on Wednesday last at Whithall, where hee was charged by

---

6. [*Ed.:* in a calm frame of mind.]
7. [*Ed.:* we have erred with our fathers;]

his Majesty's Sollicitor with certaine thinges, wherein his Majesty was much unsatisfyed: which report contayned a true and just relacion, aswell of those thinges which were then objected against him, as of his aunsweares thereunto in particular, and that, rather to his advantage then otherwise; which beinge delivered in writinge, and in his princely judgement duly waighed and considered of, his Majestie was noe way satisfyed with his aunsweares to anie of those three pointes, wherewith he stood charged, vizt.: neither in that which hee made concerninge the bonde and defeasaunce upon the installment of a debte of Sir Christopher Hatton, late Lord Chancellor of Englaund; nor yet in that which hee maketh concerninge his speeches of hiegh contempt, utterred as he sate in the seate of justice, concerninge the overthrowe of the common law; nor lastly, in the aunsweare hee offereth to excuse his uncivill and indiscreete carryage before his Majestie, assisted with his Privie Councell and his Judges: but that the charge lyeth still upon him, notwithstandinge anie thinge contayned in his said aunsweares.

Nevertheles, such is his Majesty's clemencie and goodnes, as hee is pleased not to proceede heavely against him, but rather to looke upon the meritt of his former services; and accordingly hath decreed.

First: that hee bee sequestred from the Councell Table, untill his Majesty's pleasure be further knowne.

Secoundly: that hee doe forbeare to ryde this sommer's circuit as Justice of Assize.

Lastly: that duringe this vacacion, while hee hath time to live privately and dispose himself at home, hee take into his consideracion and review his bookes of Reportes, wherein (as his Majestie is informed) there bee manie exorbitaunt and extravagant opinions sett downe and published for positive and good lawe; and if, in the review and reading thereof, hee finde anie thinge fitt to be altred or amended, the correctinge thereof is leaft to his discretion. Amongst other thinges, his Majestie was not well pleased with the tytle of those bookes, | [341] wherein hee styled himself Lord Chiefe Justice of Englaunde, whereas hee could challendge noe more then Chiefe Justice of the Kinges Bench. And havinge corrected what in his discretion hee found meete in those Reportes, his Majesty's pleasure was, that hee should bringe the same privately to himself, that hee might consider thereof, as in his princely judgement should bee found expedient. Hereunto the Secretary advised him to conforme himself in all dutie and obeydience, as hee ought, whereby hee might hope that his Majestie in time would receave him againe to his gracious and princely favour.

Hereunto the Lord Chiefe Justice made aunsweare; that hee did in all humillitie prostrate himself to his Majesty's good pleasure: that hee acknowledged the decree to bee just, and proceeded rather from his Majesty's exceedinge mercie, then from his justice; gave humble thankes to their lordships for their favour and goodnes towards him, and hoped that his behaviour for the future should bee such as should deserve their lordships' favour.

My lordes havinge thus farr proceeded, the Lorde Treasurer told him that hee had one thinge more to lett him knowe, which belounged to the Erles Marshall's to take notice of, and was, that his coachman used of late to ryde bareheaded before him, which was more then hee could anie way challendge or assume to himself, and required him to forbeare it for the future. To which the Lord Chiefe Justice aunsweared: that the coachman did it for his owne ease, and not by his commaundement. And soe, with the like submission and acknowledgment of favour, departed.

D. Coke's Arrest after Parliament, 1621.

> *Ed.:* Through the Parliament of 1621, Coke's opposition to the King had grown. Eventually he opposed the King on matters not only of parliamentary privilege but also of foreign policy. James ordered the arrest of Coke, Selden, Prynne, and other members of the opposition, but ultimately no evidence was found against them. These notes were printed in the *Acts of the Privy Council, 1621–22.*

December 27, 1621.

I A letter to the Lieutennaunt of the Tower requireinge him to receave into [217] his custodie the person of Sir Edward Coke, knight, and to keepe him closse prisonner there untill further order, sufferinge him to make choice of twoe of his owne servaunts to wayte upon him soe as they be kept closse with him.

      Lord Archbishop, Lord Keeper, Lord Treasurer, Lord President, Lord
         Privy Seale, Lord Steward, Lord Marquis Hamilton, Earl Marshall,
         Lord Chamberlen, Earl of Kellie, Lord Viscount Falkland, Lord Carew,
         Lord Digbie, Lord Brooke, Mr. Treasurer, Mr. Secretary Calvert, Mr.
         Chancellor [of the Exchequer], Master of the Rolles.

. . .

December 27, 1621.

A warraunt to Sir Thomas Wilson, knight, requireing him to make his ymediate repare to Sir Edward Coke's house in Broad Streete, London, and to seale up all such locks and doores of anie roomes, chambers or studies in the said house, that hee should probably understaund or conceave to hold or contayne anie writings or papers belonginge to Sir Edward Coke and the same beinge soe sealed to charge and commaund the housekeeper or anie others who are put in trust therewith upon their allegeance that they suffer not the said doores to bee opened untill further order etc.

> Lord Archbishop, Lord Keeper, Lord Treasurer, Lord President, Lord Privy Seale, Lord Steward, Earl Marshall, Lord Chamberlen, Earl of Kellie, Lord Falkland, Lord Carew, Mr. Treasurer, Mr. Secretary Calvert.

The like warraunt to Francis Gall, esquire, one of the clerkes of the Signett to his Majestie, to seale up the doores of Sir Edward Coke's chambers in the Temple etc.

. . .

December 30, 1621.

A warraunt to Sir Robert Cotton, knight and barronet, Sir Thomas Wilson, knight, and John Dickenson, esquire, to repare to Sir Edward Coke's house in Broad Streete, London, and takeing unto you such of his servaunts as have the charge of the said house to make dilligent search for all such papers and writeings as doe anie way concerne his Majestie's service and the same to seale up and bringe forthwith unto us, to which purpose you are to breake of such seales as were lately sett upon the doores in the said house by order from this Board and in the presence of his said servaunts to open all such studies, clossetts, chests, trunkes, deskes or boxes, where you shall understaund or probably conceave anie such papers doe remaine, for which etc.

> Lord Archbishop, Lord Keeper, Lord President, Lord Privy Seale, Lord Steward, Lord Marquis Hamilton, Earl Marshall, Lord Chamberlen, Earl of Kellie, Lord Viscount Falkland, Lord Carew, Lord Digbie, Mr. Treasurer, Mr. Secretary Calvert, Mr. Chancellor [of the Exchequer].

Another of the same tenor to the same persons to make the like search in Sir Edward Coke's chambers in the Temple.

. . .

August 6, 1622.

[463] | Att the Court att Windsor, the 6th of August 1622.

His Majestie's pleasure was this day signified by Mr. Secretarie Calvert for the inlargement of Sir Edward Coke, knight, out of the Tower of London and his confinement to his house att Stocke in the county of Buckingham and within six miles compasse of the same until further order from his Majestie, provided that att what time his Majestie shalbe within the limittes of his confinement the said Sir Edward Coke doe not repaire to the Court without speciall licence from his Majestie, whereof this memoriall was commaunded to be entred in the register of Councell causes and a copie thereof sent unto the said Sir Edward Coke.

. . .

August 7, 1622.

Letters to the Lieutenant of the Tower.

That whereas his Majestie's pleasure was signified that Sir Edward Coke and Sir Robert Phillipps, knightes, and William Mallorey, esquire, should be discharged out of the Tower of London, the said Lieutenant should accordingly inlarge them etc.

Lord Steward, Lord Admirall, Earl Kellie, Lord Viscount Falkland, Mr. Treasurer, Mr. Secretary Calvart, Sir Edward Conway.

E. Sir Edward Coke's Case
The Sheriff's Oath, 1626

Ed.: As Coke became more obstreperous in parliment, Charles had him and four other opposition leaders appointed as sheriffs, who could not attend parliament but had to remain in their counties. This hearing followed. This report was first published in Croke's *Reports of Cases in Charles's Reign* at page 26.

Sir Edward Coke's Case

Sir Edward Coke, late Chief Justice of the Common Pleas, and afterwards of the King's Bench, and removed from his places, being made Sheriff of the county of Buckingham, had a *dedimus potestatem*[1] to take his oath annexed to a schedule; to which he took exceptions, for that there were more additions to the said oath than were in the ancient oath which is in the register, and afterwards confirmed and appointed by the statute of 18 Edw. 3. c. 4.: he therefore conceived there ought not to be such additions unless by Parliament. The additions were,

First, "that he should seek to suppress all errors and heresies commonly called lollories,[2] and should be assistant to the commissaries and Ordinary in church matters:" which part of the oath was added by reason of the statute of 5 Ric. 2. st. 2. c. 5. and 2 Hen. 4. c. 15. whereby it is appointed that the

---

1. [*Ed.:* Writ granting a privilege to one before court, such as the right of nonappearance.]

2. [*Ed.:* "Lollories," a corruption of "Lollardries," was an anti-clerical heresy popular in Richard's time, and which became the basis of English Protestantism.]

same should be taken by the sheriff, especially for those two causes. But he thereto certified, that those statutes are repealed by the 1 Edw. 6. c. 1. and 1 Eliz. c. 2. and therefore ought not to be taken.

The second addition was, "that he should return reasonable issues:" whereto he excepted, because it is appointed by the statute, and penalties imposed for not performing it; and it ought not to be upon oath.

The third addition was, "that he should return all juries of the nearest and sufficientest persons:" whereto he excepted, because that part of the oath is not appointed by any statute; and it is against common practice that he himself should return juries, it being commonly done by the under sheriff, who is also appointed by the statute to be sworn.

The fourth addition was, "that he should cause the Statute of Winton, and the statutes against rogues and vagabonds, to be put in execution:" whereto he excepted, because the Statute of Winton is altered, and the statutes against rogues and vagabonds are appointed to be executed by the justices of the peace, and not by the sheriff.

Upon these exceptions the Lord Keeper assembled all the justices to confer with them about the same. And as touching.

The first point, they conceived it was fit to be omitted out of the oath, because it is appointed by statutes which are repealed, and were intended against the religion now professed and established, which before was condemned for heresy, and is now held for the true religion.

For the second addition, they conceived it convenient and for the service of the King and subjects, and the greater part of them were of opinion, that an oath in this and the other points may be well enjoined by the King and order of State without Parliament, and it may be well imposed upon the sheriff to take, being for public benefit and execution of the laws.

For the third addition, it is not so strictly to be intended that he himself should return juries, but it ought to be intended according to the construction of law, that he himself, by himself or under-sheriff, should return juries; which is a sufficient performance; for the law saith, *qui per alium facit, per seipsum facit.*[3]

For the fourth addition, it rests upon the former reasons, that this oath

---

3. [*Ed.:* he who does something through another, does it himself.]

being appointed and continued divers years by direction of the State, although without the express authority of any statute law, yet may he well be continued for the public benefit in repressing such persons: and although authority be given to the justices of the peace to put those statutes in execution, yet it doth not take away the sheriff's right, who is the public conservator. And so they delivered their opinions to the Lord Keeper at his house at Reading.

VII

Appendix II:
The Epitaph of
Sir Edward Coke

The body of Sir Edward Coke lies entombed where he directed it to be, near his first wife, Bridget. His is a magnificent tomb on the north wall of the chancel within the sanctuary, near the high altar of St. Mary's Church at Tittleshall, Norfolk, England.

The monument, created by Nicholas Stone, includes a full-size effigy carved by Haydon. Besides the inscription of Coke's abbreviated motto, on the cornice, below his heraldric achievement, there are three inscribed panels, one in Latin and two in English.

DEO OPTIMO MAXIMO.

HÆ EXUVIÆ HVMANÆ EXPECTANT RESVRRECTIONEM PIORVM.

HIC SITVS EST.

NON PERITVRI NOMINIS, EDVARDVS COKE, EQVES AVRAT, LEGVM ANIMA, INTERPRES, ORACVLVM NON DVBIVM, ARCANORVM PROMI-CONDVS MYSTERIORVM, CVIVS FERÈ VNIVS BENEFICIO, IVRISPERITI NOSTRI SVNT IVRISPERITI.

ELOQVENTIÆ FLVMEN, TORRENS, FVLMEN, SVADÆ SACERDOS VNICVS.

DIVINVS HEROS.

PRO ROSTRIS ITA DIXIT, VT LITERIS INSVDASSE CREDERES, NON NISI HVMANIS ITA VIXIT VT NON NISI DIVINIS.

SACERRIMVS INTIMÆ PIETATIS INDAGATOR.

INTEGRITAS IPSA

VERÆ SEMPER CAVSÆ CONSTANTISSIMVS ASSERTOR NEC FAVORE NEC MVNERIBVS VIOLANDVS.

EXIMÌE MISERICORS

CHARIOR ERAT HVIC REVS QVAM SIBI.

CV   (MIRACVLI INSTAR EST) SICCOLVS SÆPÈ ILLE AVDIIT SENTENTIAM IN SE PROLATAM NVNQVAM HIC NISI MADIDOCVLVS PROTVLIT.

SCIENTIÆ OCEANVS

QVIQVE DVM VIXIT, BIBLIOTHECA VIVA, MORTVVS DICI MERVIT BIBLIOTECÆ PARENS.

DVODECIM LIBERORVM TREDECIM LIBRORVM PATER.

FACESSANT HINC MONVMENTA, FACESSANT MARMORA,

(NISI QVÒD PIOS FVISSE DENOTARINT POSTEROS)
IPSE SIBI SVVM EST MONVMENTVM,
MARMORE PERRENNIVS,
IPSE SIBI SVA EST ÆTERNITAS.[1]

1. [*Ed.:*

To God, the Highest and Greatest,
These Mortal Remains Await the Resurrection of the Faithful.
Here Lies
Edward Coke, Knight of Gold, of Imperishable Fame,
Spirit, Interpreter, and Inerrant Oracle of the Laws,
Discloser of its Secrets—Concealer of its Mysteries,
Thanks Almost Alone to Whose Good Office,
Our Lawyers Are Learned in the Law.
A River, Torrent, and Flood of Eloquence,
Singular Priest of Persuasion.
Divine Master.
In Courts, He Spoke
In Such a Way That One Would Believe Him To Have Studied Only the Secular,
But He Lived as One Who Had Studied Nothing but the Divine.
Most Devoted Investigator of Profound Faithfulness.
Integrity Itself,
Always the Most Constant Advocate of the Cause of Truth
Corrupted Neither by Favor Nor by Gifts
Exceptionally Merciful,
The Defendant was Dearer to Him than he was to Himself
(Which is a Miracle)
He Often Heard Sentence Pronounced Against Himself with Dry Eyes
Though Sentence Was Never Pronounced by this Man without Tears.
An Ocean of Knowledge
Who Alive, was a Living Library,
Deceased, Deserves the Name of Father of a Library.
Father of Twelve Children and Thirteen Books.
These Monuments May Crumble,
The Marble Decay,
(Except that they Show that his Children were Pious)
He Is His Own Monument to Himself.
More Lasting than Marble
He Himself Is His Own Immortality.

DEDICATED TO THE
MEMORY OF
SR. EDWARD COKE Knight, a late Reverend
IVDGE borne at MILEHAM in this County of NORF.
Excellent in all learning DIVINE & HVMANE, that for
HIS OWNE, this for HIS COVNTRIES good, Especially in
the knowledge & practise of the MVNICIPALL LAWES
of this KINGDOME,

A FAMOVS PLEADER, A SOVND COVNSELLER.

In HIS younger yeares RECORDER of the Cities of NORWICH
& LONDON, next SOLLICITOR generall to QVENE ELIZA:
and SPEAKER of the PARLIAMENT, in ye XXXV yeare of hir
Raigne. Afterwards ATTORNYE generall to the same
QVEENE, as also to her successor King IAMES.
To both, a faithfull servant, for their MA:ts for theire
safetyes. By Kinge IAMES constituted CHEIFE IVSTICE OF
both BENCHES successiuely. In both A IVST, in both AN
EXEMPLARY IVDGE. One of his MA:ties Most Honorable PRIVIE
COVNSELL. As also of COVNCELL to QVENE ANNE & CHEIFE
IVSTICE In Eire of all HIR Forrests, Chases, and Parkes.
RECORDER of ye Cittie of COVENTRYE, & HIGH STEWARD of
the Vniversity of CAMBRIDGE, whereof he was sometime

A MEMBER IN TRINITYE COLLEDGE.
HE HAD TWO WIVES,
By BRIDGET, HIS first WIFE (one of the Daughters &
Coheires of IOHN PASTON ESQ.) HE had Issue sevean
Sonnes and three Daughters.
And by the LADY ELIZABETH HIS second WIFE (one
of the Daughters of the R:T HON:BLE THOMAS late EARLE
of EXETER) HE had Issue two Daughters.

A CHAST HVSBAND: A PROVIDENT FATHER.

HE CROWNED HIS PIOVS LIFE, WITH AS PIOVS AND
CHRISTIAN DEPARTVRE AT STOKE POGES IN THE
COVNTY OF BVCKINGHAM ON WEDNESDAYE
THE THIRD DAY OF SEPTEMBER IN YE YEAR OF OVR
LORD MDCXXXIIII.

AND OF HIS AGE LXXXIII.
HIS LAST WORDES
THY KINGDOME COME, THY WILL BE DONE
LEARNE READER TO LIVE SO,
THAT THOV MAY'ST SO DYE.

Photograph courtesy of
Brian and Marjorie Gill

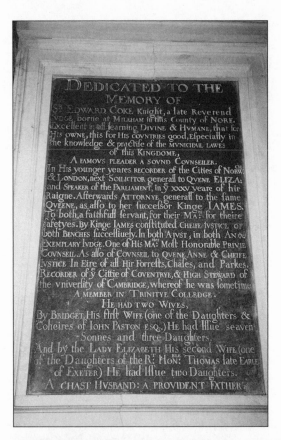

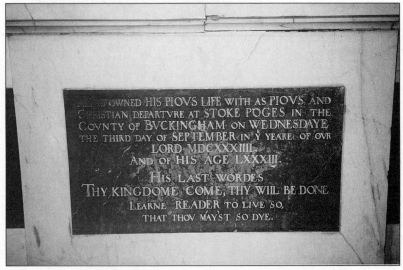

Selected Readings Concerning of the Life, Career, and Legacy of Sir Edward Coke[1]

I. Coke's Life and Career

Alward, Silas. "Coke: The Great Oracle of the Common Law." *The Canadian Law Times* 32 (1912): 929.

Aubrey, John. "Sir Edward Coke." In *"Brief Lives," Chiefly of Contemporaries, set down by John Aubrey, between the Years 1669 & 1696*, edited by Andrew Clark. Oxford: Clarendon Press, 1898. (Three lines relating to the false allegations of Lady Hatton's pregnancy at the time of her marriage to Coke have been suppressed in this edition.)

Birkenhead, Earl of [Frederick E. Smith]. "Sir Edward Coke." In *Fourteen English Judges*. New York: Cassell, 1926.

Barnes, Thomas G. "Notes from the Editors." Two Companion Pamphlets to *The First Part of the Institutes of the Laws of England*. Delran, N.J.: Legal Classics, 1995. (A facsimile reprint of the 18th edition of 1823.)

Bowen, Catherine Drinker. "Coke and the Carson Collection." In *Four Talks for Bibliophiles*. Philadelphia: Free Library of Philadelphia, 1958.

———. "Five against the Odds: How do Great Men Cope with Old Age? By Starting Over." 16 *Horizons* (1974): 78

———. *The Lion and the Throne: The Life and Times of Sir Edward Coke (1552–1634)*. Boston: Little, Brown & Co., 1957.

———. "The Lord of the Law." *American Heritage* 8 (1957): 4.

Boyer, Allen D. *Law, Liberty, and Parliament: Selected Essays on the Writings of Sir Edward Coke*. Indianapolis: Liberty Fund, 2004.

Burke, Edmund Plunkett, *Sir Edward Coke*. London: Baldwin and Cradock, 1833.

Campbell, Lord John. "Life of Sir Edward Coke." In *The Lives of the Chief Justices of England: From the Norman Conquest till the Death of Lord Mansfield*. London: John Murray, 1849–57.

Clark, Walter, *Coke, Blackstone, and the Common Law*. Rochester, N.Y.: The Lawyers Co-operative Publishing Co., 1918.

---

1. N.B.: Works are not repeated in each of the various categories to which they pertain.

Coke, Edward. *Vade Mecum*. In *Collectanea Topographica et Geneologica*. London: J. B. Nichols and Son, 1834–43. Taken by John Bruce from Coke's introductory leaves in his private manual. (The reader is cautioned to ignore dates Anno Domini in this edition which may have been mistakenly converted from regnal years. The manuscript is in the British Museum, Harleian MS. 6687, and is admirably described in John Baker's article "Coke's Note-Books," listed below in section H. 1. Further autobiographical notes by Coke are in the Holkham mss.)

Foss, Edward. "Edward Coke." In *The Judges of England: With Sketches of Their Lives, and Miscellaneous Notices Connected with the Courts at Westminster, from the Time of the Conquest*. London: Longman, Brown, Green, and Longmans, 1848–64.

Hahn, Edgar Aaron. *Edward Coke*. Rowfantia, no. 14. Cleveland: The Rowfant Club, 1949. Hill, Christopher. "Sir Edward Coke-Myth-Maker." In *Intellectual Origins of the English Revolution*. Oxford: Clarendon Press, 1965.

Holdsworth, Sir William. "The Influence of Sir Edward Coke on the Development of English Law." In *Essays in Legal History Read before the International Congress Held in London in 1913*, edited by Paul Vinogradoff. London, New York: Oxford University Press, 1913; In *A History of English Law*. 2d ed. Boston: Little, Brown, 1937.

———. "Sir Edward Coke." *Cambridge Law Journal* 5 (1935): 332.

———. *Some Makers of English Law*. Cambridge: Cambridge University Press, 1966.

Hostettler, John. *Sir Edward Coke: A Force for Freedom*. Chichester: Barry Rose, 1998.

James, Charles Warburton. *Chief Justice Coke, His Family & Descendants at Holkham*. London: Country Life Ltd.; New York: Charles Scribner's Sons, 1929.

Johnson, Cuthbert William. *The Life of Sir Edward Coke, Lord Chief Justice of England, with Memoirs of His Contemporaries*. London: Henry Colburn, 1837.

Jones, Martin David. "Sir Edward Coke and the Interpretation of Lawful Allegiance in Seventeenth Century England." *History of Political Thought* 7 (1986): 321.

Kippis, Andrew. *Biographia Britannica; Or, the Lives of the Most Eminent Persons Who Have Flourished in Great Britain and Ireland, from the Earliest Ages, Down to the Present Times: Collected from the Best Authorities, Printed and Manuscript, and Digested in the Manner of Mr. Bayle's Historical and Critical Dictionary*. London: W. and A. Strahan, for C. Bathurst, W. Strahan, etc., 1778–93.

"Letter . . . to sir Thomas Lake, relating to the proceedings of sir Edward Coke at Oatland and ii. Documents relating to sir Walter Raleigh's last voyage. Communicated to the Camden miscellany by S.R. Gardiner." *Camden Miscellany*. 5 (1864).

Lyon, Walter Hastings, and Herman Block. *Edward Coke, Oracle of the Law: Containing the Story of His Long Rivalry with Francis Bacon; Some Account of Their Times and Contemporaries; Famous Trials in Which Coke Participated; His Stand Against King James I to Maintain the Supremacy of the Common Law*. Boston: Houghton Mifflin Co., 1929.

MacKinnon, Sir Frank Douglas. *Record of a Tercentenary Commemoration of Sir Edward Coke (1551–1634).* London, 1934. Reprinted in "Sir Edward Coke: I. Inner Temple." *Law Quarterly Review* 51 (1935): 289; *Inner Temple Papers.* London: Stevens, 1948.

McDonnell, George P. "Sir Edward Coke." In *Dictionary of National Biography: From the Earliest Times to 1900.* Edited by Sir Leslie Stephen and Sir Sidney Lee. London: Oxford University Press, 1921–1922.

Record of Honor and Virtue: The Noble Memorial of the Right Honorable Sir Edward Coke, Knight, Sometimes Lord Chief Justice of England and Attorney General to Queen Elizabeth, Who Departed This Transitory Life at His Manor of Stoke in Buckinghamshire This September 1634. (Eulogy, dedicated to his daughter, Mrs. Anne Sadlier) (HLS MS 4125, Harvard Law School Library.)

Roscoe, Henry. *Eminent British Lawyers.* London: Longman, Rees, Orme, Brown, and Green, 1830.

Society for the Diffusion of Useful Knowledge. *Lives of Eminent Persons, Consisting of Galileo, Kepler, Newton, Mahomet, Wolsey, Sir E. Coke, Lord Somers, Caxton, Blake, Adam Smith, Niebuhr, Sir C. Wren, and Michael Angelo.* London: R. Baldwin, 1833.

Thorne, Samuel E. *Sir Edward Coke, 1552–1952.* The Selden Society Lecture, 1952. London: Brenard Quaritch, 1957.

———— *Essays in Legal History.* London: Hambledon Press, 1985.

Usher, Ronald G. "Sir Edward Coke." *St. Louis Law Review* 15 (1930): 325.

Windeyer, W. J. V. "Sir Edward Coke." In *Lectures on Legal History.* Sydney: Law Book of Australasia Pt. Ltd., 1949.

Woolrych, Humphry W. *The Life of the Right Honourable Sir Edward Coke, Knt., Lord Chief Justice of the King's Bench.* London: J. & W. T. Clarke, 1826.

Wrangham, Francis. "Sir Edward Coke." In *The British Plutarch Containing the Lives of the Most Eminent Divines, Patriots, Statesmen, Warriors, Philosophers, Poets, and Artists, of Great Britain and Ireland from the Accession of Henry VIII to the Present Time.* 6 vols. London: J. Mawman, and Baldwin, Cradock, and Joy, 1816.

II. Topical Commentaries

A. Coke's Tools
1. Language

Boyer, Allen D. "Sir Edward Coke, Ciceronianus: Classical Rhetoric and the Common Law Tradition." *International Journal for the Semiotics of Law/Revue Internationale de Sémiotique Juridique* 10 (1997): 3.

Disraeli, Isaac. "Of Coke's Style, and His Conduct." In *Curiosities of Literature.* New York: J. Widdleton, 1872.

Hornstein, L. H. "Some Chaucer Allusions by Sir Edward Coke." *Modern Language Notes* 60 (1945): 483.

Howell, W. S. *Rhetoric and Logic in England 1500–1700*. Princeton: Princeton University Press, 1956.

Shoeck, R. J. "Rhetoric and Law in Fifteenth-Century England." *Studies in Philology* 50 (1953): 110.

2. Books

Abbot, L. W. *Law Reporting in England, 1485–1585*. London: Athlone Press, 1973.

Hassal, W. O., ed. *A Catalogue of the Library of Sir Edward Coke*. Preface by Samuel Thorne. New Haven: Yale University Press, 1950.

James, C. W. "Some Notes on the Library of Printed Books at Holkham." *Transactions of the Bibliographical Society*, n.s., 11 (1931): 435.

———. "Some Notes upon the Manuscript Library at Holkham." *The Library*, 4th ser., 2 (1922): 213.

Lewis, Clive S. [C. S.] *English Literature in the Sixteenth Century Excluding Drama*. Oxford: Clarendon Press, 1954.

Stebbings, Chantal, ed. *Law Reporting in England*. London: Hambledon Press, 1995.

Topulos, Katherine. "A Common Lawyer's Bookshelf Recreated: An Annotated Bibliography of a Collection of Sixteenth-Century English Law Books." *Law Library Journal* 84 (1992): 641.

3. History

Fussner, F. Smith. *The Historical Revolution: English Historical Writing and Thought, 1580–1640*. London: Routledge and Paul, 1962.

Goodrich, Peter. "Doctor Duxbury's Cure: Or, a Note on Legal Historiography." *Cardozo Law Review* 15 (1994): 1567.

———. "Poor Illiterate Reason: History, Nationalism and Common Law." *Social & Legal Studies* 1 (1992): 7.

Ross, Richard J. "The Memorial Culture of Early Modern English Lawyers: Memory as Keyword, Shelter, and Identity, 1560–1640." *Yale Journal of Law & the Humanities* 10 (1998): 229.

Woolf, D. R. *The Idea of History in Early Stuart England: Erudition, Ideology, and "The Light of Truth" from the Accession of James I to the Civil War*. Toronto: University of Toronto Press, 1990.

4. Law

Aumann, Francis Robert. "Lord Coke: The Compleat Student of the Common Law." *Kentucky Law Journal* 17 (1930): 64.

Jamieson, David F. "Custom, Reason and Legislation in the Thought of Sir Edward Coke." Ph.D. diss., University of Utah, 1978.

McQuade, J. Stanley. "Medieval 'Ratio' and Modern Formal Studies: A Reconsideration of Coke's Dictum That Law Is the Perfection of Reason." *American Journal of Jurisprudence* 38 (1993): 359.

Singer, Barbara A. "The Reason of the Common Law." *University of Miami Law Review* 37 (1983): 797.

Thorne, Samuel E. "Courts of Record and Sir Edward Coke." *University of Toronto Law Journal* 2 (1937): 24.

———. *Essays in Legal History.* London: Hambledon Press, 1985.

B. Judges and the Common Law

Baker, J. H. "The Structure of a Court." In *The Legal Profession and the Common Law: Historical Essays.* London: Hambledon Press, 1986.

Berman, Harold. "The Origins of Historical Jurisprudence: Coke, Selden, and Hale." *Yale Law Journal* 103 (1994): 1651.

Cantor, Norman F. *Imagining the Law.* New York: Harper Collins, 1997.

Clark, Walter. "Coke, Blackstone, and the Common Law." *Case and Comment* 24 (1918): 861.

Coquillette, Daniel R. *The Anglo-American Legal Heritage: Introductory Materials.* Durham, North Carolina: Carolina Academic Press, 1999.

Francis, Clinton W. "The Structure of Judicial Administration and the Development of Contract Law in Seventeenth-Century England." *Columbia Law Review* 83 (1983): 35.

Glen, Garrard. "Edward Coke and Law Restatement." *Virginia Law Review* 17 (1931): 447.

Goedecke, W. Robert. "Edward Coke, Francis Bacon, and the Foundations of Law." In *Change and the Law.* Tallahassee: Florida State University Press, 1969.

Goldberg, Ronnie Lee. "Sir Edward Coke and the Common Law." Ph.D. diss., University of Chicago, 1978.

Gray, Charles. "Reason, Authority, and Imagination: The Jurisprudence of Sir Edward Coke." In *Culture and Politics from Puritanism to the Enlightenment,* edited by Perez Zagorin. Berkeley: University of California Press, 1980.

Hale, Sir Matthew. Introduction to *The History of the Common Law of England,* by Charles M. Gray. Chicago: University of Chicago Press, 1971.

Holdsworth, William S. "The Influence of Coke on the Development of English Law." In *Essays in Legal History,* edited by Paul Vinogradoff. Oxford: Oxford University Press, 1914.

Ives, E. W. "Social Change and the Law." In *The English Revolution, 1600–1660.* New York: Barnes & Noble, 1969.

Kenyon, J. P. "The Judiciary." In *The Stuart Constitution, 1603–1688: Documents and Commentary.* Cambridge: Cambridge University Press, 1966.

Lewis, John Underwood. "Sir Edward Coke (1552–1633): His Theory of 'Artificial Reason' as a Context for Modern Basic Legal Theory." *Law Quarterly Review* 84 (1968): 330.

Milsom, S. F. C. *Historical Foundations of the Common Law.* London: Butterworths, 1969.

Powell, Jim. "An Independent Judiciary." In *The Triumph of Liberty: A 2,000-year History Told Through the Lives of Freedom's Greatest Champions.* New York: Free Press, 2000.

Prest, Wilfrid R. *The Inns of Court under Elizabeth I and the Early Stuarts, 1590–1640.* London: Longman, 1972.

———. *The Rise of the Barristers: A Social History of the English Bar, 1590–1640.* Oxford: Clarendon Press, 1991.

Simpson, A. W. B. *The History of the Common Law of Contract: The Rise of the Action of Assumpsit.* Oxford: Clarendon Press, 1975.

———. *A History of the Land Law.* 2d ed. Oxford: Clarendon Press, 1986.

Stumpf, Samuel Enoch. "Sir Edward Coke: Advocate of the Supremacy of the Law." *Vanderbilt Studies in the Humanities* 1 (1951): 34.

Thorne, Samuel E. "Tudor Social Transformation and Legal Change." *New York University Law Review* 26 (1951): 10.

———. *Essays in Legal History.* London: Hambledon Press, 1985.

C. Competition with Other Benches

Baker, John H. "The Common Lawyers and the Chancery: 1616." *Irish Jurist,* n.s. 4 (1969): 368.

———. *The Legal Profession and the Common Law: Historical Essays.* London: Hambledon Press, 1986.

Cumming, Charles S. "The English High Court of Admiralty." *The Maritime Lawyer* 17 (1992): 209.

De Smith, S. A. "The Prerogative Writs." *Cambridge Law Journal* 11 (1951): 40.

Fortier, Mark. "Equity and Ideas: Coke, Ellesmere, and James I." *Renaissance Quarterly* 51 (1998): 1255.

Gray, Charles M. "The Boundaries of the Equitable Function." *American Journal of Legal History* 20 (1976): 192.

———. "Prohibitions and the Privilege Against Self-Incrimination." In *Tudor Rule and Revolution: Essays for G. R. Elton from His American Friends,* edited by DeLloyd J. Guth and John W. McKenna. Cambridge: Cambridge University Press, 1982.

———. *The Writ of Prohibition: Jurisdiction in Early Modern English Law.* New York: Oceana Publications, 1994.

Greene, Douglas G. "The Court of the Marshalsea in Late Tudor and Stuart England." *American Journal of Legal History* (1976): 267.

Harrington, Matthew P. "The Legacy of the Colonial Vice-Admiralty Courts (Part I)." *Journal of Maritime Law & Commerce* 26 (1995): 581.

Jones, W. J. *The Elizabethan Court of Chancery.* Oxford: Clarendon Press, 1967.

Levy, Leonard W. "Origins of the Fifth Amendment and Its Critics." *Cardozo Law Review* 19 (1997): 821.

MaGuire, M. H. "The Attack of the Common Lawyers on the Oath Ex Officio." In *Essays in Honor of C. H. McIlwaind.* Cambridge: Harvard University Press, 1936.

Usher, Roland G. *The Rise and Fall of the High Commission.* Oxford: Oxford University Press, 1968.

D. Administrative Law and Management of the Bench and Bar

Cohen, Maxwell. "Some Considerations on the Origins of Habeas Corpus." *Canadian Bar Review* 16 (1938): 92.

———. "Habeas Corpus cum Causa—The Emergence of the Modern Writ." *Canadian Bar Review* 18 (1940): 10.

De Smith, S. A. "Wrongs and Remedies in Administrative Law." *Modern Law Review* 15 (1952): 189.

Henderson, Edith G. *Foundations of English Administrative Law: Certiorari and Mandamus in the Seventeenth Century.* Cambridge: Ames Foundations, 1963.

Milsom, S. F. C. "The Origins and Early History of Judicial Review in England." Ph.D. diss. University of Cambridge, 1957.

Pollack, Malla. "Purveyance and Power, or Over-Priced Free Lunch: The Intellectual Property Clause as an Ally of the Takings Clause in the Public's Control of Government." *Southwestern University Law Review* 30 (2000): 1.

Rose, Jonathan. "The Legal Profession in Medieval England: A History of Regulation." *Syracuse Law Review* 48 (1998): 1.

Schwartz Bernard. *Lions over the Throne: The Judicial Revolution in English Administrative Law.* New York: New York University Press, 1987.

Winfield, Percy Henry. *The History of Conspiracy and Abuse of Legal Procedure.* Cambridge: Cambridge University Press, 1921.

E. Judicial Review

Boudin, Louis B. "Lord Coke and the American Doctrine of Judicial Power." *New York University Law Review* 6 (1928–29): 233.

Boyer, Allen Dillard. "Undersanding, Authority, and Will: Sir Edward Coke and the Elizabethan Origins of Judicial Review." *Boston College Law Review* 39 (1997): 43.

Easterbrook Frank. "Substance and Due Process." *Supreme Court Review* (1982): 85.

Hamburger, Philip A. "Revolution and Judicial Review: Chief Justice Holt's Opinion in *City of London v. Wood*." *Columbia Law Review* 94 (1994): 2091.

Jaffe Louis L., and Edith G. Henderson. "Judicial Review and the Rule of Law: Historical Origins." *Law Quarterly Review* 72 (1956): 345.

Lloyd, Aaron. "Lord Cooke's Fundamental Rights, and the Institution of Substantive Judicial Review." *Auckland University Law Review* 8 (1999): 1172.

Nelson, William E. *Marbury v. Madison: The Origins and Legacy of Judicial Review.* Lawrence: University Press of Kansas, 2000.

Orth, John V. "Did Sir Edward Coke Mean What He Said?" *Constitutional Commentary* 33 (1999): 16.

F. Judicial Independence

Black, Barbara A. "Massachusetts and the Judges: Judicial Independence in Perspective." *Law & History Review* 3 (1985): 101.

Cox, Archibald. "The Independence of the Judiciary: History And Purposes." *University of Dayton Law Review* 21 (1996): 565.

Hoffman, Jonathan M. "By the Course of the Law: The Origins of the Open Courts Clause of State Constitutions." *Oregon Law Review* 74 (1995): 1279.

Lederman, William R. "The Independence of the Judiciary." Parts 1, 2. *Canadian Bar Review* 34 (1956): 769, 1139.

Lemmings, David. "The Independence of the Judiciary in Eighteenth-Century England." In *The Life of the Law: Proceedings of the Tenth British Legal History Conference,* edited by Peter Birks, 126. London: Hambledon Press, 1993.

Noonan, John T. "The John Dewey Memorial Lecture: Education, Intelligence, and Character in Judges." *Minnesota Law Review* 71 (1987): 1119.

Redish, Martin H., and Lawrence C. Marshall. "Adjudicatory Independence and the Values of Procedural Due Process." *Yale Law Journal* 95 (1986): 455.

Riggs, Burkeley N., and Tamera D. Westerberg. "Judicial Independence: An Historical Perspective." *Denver University Law Review* 74 (1997): 337.

Roth, Philip J. "The Dangerous Erosion of Judicial Immunity." *Brief* 18 (1989): 26.

Ziskind, Martha A. "Judicial Tenure in the American Constitution: English and American Precedents." *Supreme Court Review* (1969): 135.

G. The English Constitution

Allen, J. W. *English Political Thought, 1603–1660.* 2 vols. London: Methuen & Co. Ltd., 1938.

Beaute, Jean. *Un Grand Juriste Anglais, Sir Edward Coke, 1552–1634: Ses Idées Politiques et Constitutionnelles: Ou, Aux Origines De La Democratie Occidentale Moderne.* Paris: Presses Universitaires de France, 1975.

Burgess, Glenn. *The Politics of the Ancient Constitution: An Introduction to English*

Political Thought, 1603–1642. University Park: Pennsylvania State University Press, 1992.

———. "The Political Thought of Edward Coke." In *Absolute Monarchy and the Stuart Constitution.* New Haven: Yale University Press, 1996.

Eusden, John Dykstra. *Puritans, Lawyers, and Politics.* New Haven: Yale University Press, 1958.

Freidrich, Carl J. "Common Law against Natural Law: James I, Edward Coke, and Francis Bacon." In *The Philosophy of Law in Historical Perspective.* Chicago: University of Chicago Press, 1957.

Hill, Christopher. *The Century of Revolution, 1603–1714.* Edinburgh: T. Nelson, 1961.

Jones, William J. "The Crown and the Courts in England, 1603–1625." In *The Reign of James VI and I,* edited by Alan G. R. Smith. London: St. Martin's Press, 1973.

Kelley, Donald R. "Elizabethan Political Thought." In *The Varieties of British Political Thought, 1500–1800,* edited by J. G. A. Pocock. Cambridge: Cambridge University Press, 1993.

Klein, William. "The Ancient Constitution Revisited." In *Political Discourse in Early Modern Britain,* edited by Nicholas Phillipson and Quentin Skinner. Cambridge: Cambridge: Cambridge University Press, 1993.

Maitland, Frederic William. *The Constitutional History of England.* Cambridge: Cambridge University Press, 1908.

Montague, F. C. *The Political History of England from the Accession of James I to the Restoration (1603–1660).* 2d ed. New York: Longmans, Green & Co., 1911.

Ogilvie, Sir Charles. *King's Government and the Common Law, 1471–1641.* Oxford: Blackwell, 1958.

Pocock, J. G. A. *The Ancient Constitution and the Feudal Law: A Study of English Historical Thought in the Seventeenth Century.* Cambridge: Cambridge University Press, 1957 (new ed. 1987).

Russell, Conrad. "Divine Rights in the Early Seventeenth Century." In *Public Duty and Private Conscience in Seventeenth Century England: Essays Presented to G. E. Aylmer,* edited by John Morrill, Paul Slack, and Daniel Woolf. Oxford: Clarendon Press, 1993.

Sourzh, Gerald. "Constitution: Changing Meanings of the Term from the Early Seventeenth to the Late Eighteenth Century." In *Conceptual Change and the Constitution,* edited by Terence Ball and J. G. A. Pocock. Lawrence: University Press of Kansas, 1988.

Tanner, J. R. "Constitutional Questions in the Parliaments of James I." In *English Constitutional Conflicts of the Seventeenth Century, 1603–1689.* Cambridge: Cambridge University Press, 1928.

Wormuth, Francis D. *The Royal Prerogative, 1603–1649: A Study in English Political and Constitutional Ideas.* Ithaca, N.Y.: Cornell University Press, 1939.

H. Coke's Writings and Cases

Bridgman, Richard Whalley. *A Short View of Legal Bibliography: Containing Some Critical Observations on the Authority of the Reporters and Other Law Writers; Collected from the Best Authorities* . . . London: W. Reed, 1807.

Gest, John Marshall. "The Writings of Sir Edward Coke." *Yale Law Journal* 18 (1909): 504.

———. *The Lawyer in Literature.* Boston: Boston Book Co., 1913.

Gray, Charles M. *Copyhold, Equity, and the Common Law.* Harvard Historical Monographs, vol. 53. Cambridge: Harvard University Press, 1963.

Hicks, Frederick Charles. *Men and Books Famous in the Law.* Rochester, N.Y.: The Lawyers Co-operative Publishing Co., 1921.

Holdsworth, W. S. *Sources and Literature of English Law.* Oxford: Clarendon Press, 1928.

Ross, Richard J. "The Commoning of the Common Law: The Renaissance Debate over Printing English Law, 1520–1640." *University of Pennsylvania Law Review* 146 (1998): 323.

Siegel, Stephen A. "The Aristotelian Basis of English Law, 1450–1800." *New York University Law Review* 56 (1981): 18.

1. *The Reports,* Generally

Baker, J. H. "Coke's Notebooks and the Sources of His Reports." *Cambridge Law Journal* 30 (1972): 59.

———. *The Legal Profession and the Common Law: Historical Essays.* London: Hambledon Press, 1986.

Dawson, John P. "The Named Reporters (1535–1790)." In *Oracles of the Law.* Ann Arbor: University of Michigan Law School, 1968.

Jenkins, David. *Eight Centuries of Reports; Or, Eight Hundred Cases Solemnly Adjudged in the Exchequer Chamber, Or, upon Writs of Error.* 4th ed. Edited by Charles Francis Morrell. Translated by Theodore Barlow. London: H. Sweet & Sons, 1885.

Plucknett, T. F. T. "The Genesis of Coke's Reports." In *Studies in English Legal History* 15 (1985): 190. (First published in *Cornell Law Review* 17 (1942): 190.)

Sheppard, Steve, "Introduction to the 1826 Edition." In Edward Coke, *The Reports of Sir Edward Coke in Thirteen Parts.* Union, N.J.: Lawbook Exchange, 2002 (reprint of 1826 edition).

Veerder, Van Vechten. "The English Reports, 1292–1865." *Harvard Law Review* 15 (1901): 11.

Worrall, John, ed. *The Reports of Sir Edward Coke, Kt., in Verse. Wherein the Name of Each Case, and the Principal Points, Are Contained in Two Lines. To Which Are Added, References in the Margin to All the Editions of the Said Reports; and Two Tables, One of the Names of the Cases, and the Other of the Principal Matters.* London: H.

Lintot, 1742. Third edition, edited by J. Wesley Miller, published by William S. Hein, 1999. (It is not certain, but it is possible that the original verse renderings, likely enlarged in this edition, are the poetry written by Coke for his children, as recorded in the Lambeth mss inventory of items seized from Coke's servant Pepys. This theory is propounded by Lord Campbell. Campbell *Lives of the Chief Justices* I:336 n. The verses are bad enough, and Coke's ambivalence toward rhyming poets was strong enough, that it might be true. J. Wesley Miller, the recent editor of the *Reports in Verse,* hypothesizes authorship by poet Giles Jacob (1688–1744).)

2. Particular Cases

William Aldred's Case (9 Reports 57b), p. 308

Coquillette, Daniel R. "Mosses from an Old Manse: Another Look at Some Historic Property Cases about the Environment." *Cornell Law Review* 64 (1979): 761.

Smith, George P. "Nuisance Law: The Morphogenesis of an Historical Revisionist Theory of Contemporary Economic Jurisprudence." *Nebraska Law Review* 74 (1995): 658.

Christianson v. Snohomish Health Dist., 946 P. 2d 768 (Wash. 1997).

Prawner v. Battle Creek Co-op Creamery, 113 N. W. 2d 518 (Neb. 1962).

James Bagg's Case (11 Reports 93a), p. 404

Gilmore, Michael S. "Standing Law in Idaho: A Constitutional Wrong Turn." *Idaho Law Review* 31 (1995): 509.

Case of the Bankrupts (2 Reports 25a), p. 45

Weisberg, Robert. "Commercial Morality, the Merchant Character, and the History of the Voidable Preference." *Stanford Law Review* 39 (1986): 3.

(Bates's Case) Customs, Subsidies, and Impositions (12 Reports 33), p. 441

Elkins, Jeremy. "Constitutions and 'Survivor Stories': Declarations of Rights." *University of Chicago Law School Roundtable* 3 (1996): 243.

Oakley, Francis. "Jacobean Political Theology: The Absolute and Ordinary Powers of the King." *Journal of the History of Ideas* 29 (1968): 323.

Doctor Bonham's Case (8 Co. Rep. 114), p. 264

Berger, Raoul. "Doctor Bonham's Case: Statutory Construction or Constitutional Theory?" *University of Pennsylvania Law Review* 117 (1969): 521.

Cascarelli, Joseph C. "Is Judicial Review Grounded in and Limited by Natural Law?" *Cumberland Law Review* 30 (2000): 373.

Cook, Harold J. "Against Common Right and Reason: The Royal College of Physicians *versus* Doctor Thomas Bonham." *American Journal of Legal History* 29 (1985): 301.

Gray, Charles M. "Bonham's Case Reviewed." *Proceedings of the American Philosophical Society* 116 (1972): 35.

Grey, Thomas C. "Origins of the Unwritten Constitution: Fundamental Law in American Revolutionary Thought." *Stanford Law Review* 30 (1978): 843.

Michael, Helen K. "The Role of Natural Law in Early American Constitutionalism: Did the Founders Contemplate Judicial Enforcement of 'Unwritten' Individual Rights?" *North Carolina Law Review* 69 (1991): 421.

Plucknett, Theodore. "Bonham's Case and Judicial Review." *Harvard Law Review* 40 (1926): 30.

Smith, George P. "Dr. Bonham's Case and the Modern Significance of Lord Coke's Influence." *Washington Law Review* 41 (1966): 297.

Thorne, S. E. "Dr. Bonham's Case." *Law Quarterly Review* 54 (1938): 543.

California v. Green, 399 U.S. 149 (1970) (White, J., majority) (Harlan, J., concurring).

Collins v. Dixie Transport, Inc., 543 So. 2d 160 (Miss. 1989).

Dutton v. Evans, 400 U.S. 74 (1970).

McGowan v. Mississippi State Oil & Gas Bd., 604 So. 2d 312 (Miss. 1992).

Calvin's Case, (7 Reports 1), p. 166

Bogen, David S. "The Individual Liberties Within the Body of the Constitution: A Symposium: The Privileges and Immunities Clause of Article IV." *Case Western Reserve Law Review* 37 (1987): 794.

Carey, George W. "Liberty and the Fifth Amendment: Original Intent." *Benchmark* 4 (1990): 301.

Flaherty, Martin Stephen. "Note: The Empire Strikes Back: *Annesley v. Sherlock* and the Triumph of Imperial Parliamentary Supremacy." *Columbia Law Review* 87 (1987): 593.

Heyman, Steven J. "Constitutional Perspectives: The First Duty of Government: Protection, Liberty, and the Fourteenth Amendment." *Duke Law Journal* 41 (1991): 507.

Houston, Michael Robert W. "Note: Birthright Citizenship in the United Kingdom and the United States: A Comparative Analysis of the Common Law Basis for Granting Citizenship to Children Born of Illegal Immigrants." *Vanderbilt Journal of Transnational Law* 33 (2000): 693.

Jones, David Martin. "Sir Edward Coke and the Interpretation of Lawful Allegiance in Seventeenth Century England." *History of Political Thought* 7 (1986): 321.

Kettner, James H. *The Development of American Citizenship, 1608–1870.* Chapel Hill: University of North Carolina Press, 1978.

McHugh, P. G. "The Common-Law Status of Colonies and Aboriginal 'Rights': How Lawyers and Historians Treat the Past." *Saskatchewan Law Review* 61 (1998): 393.

O'Melinn, Liam Seamus. "Note: The American Revolution and Constitutionalism in the Seventeenth-Century West Indies." *Columbia Law Review* 95 (1995): 104.

Price, Polly J. "Natural Law and Birthright Citizenship in Calvin's Case." *Yale Journal of Law and the Humanities* 9 (1997): 73.

Wheeler, Harvey. "Calvin's Case (1608) and the McIlwain-Schuyler Debate." *American Historical Review* 61 (1956): 587.

Wilson, James. "Considerations on the Nature and Extent of the Legislative Authority of the British Parliament." In James Wilson, *The Works of James Wilson.* Edited by Robert McCloskey, vol. 2, p. 726. Cambridge: Harvard University Press, 1967.

Wroth, L. Kinvin. "Symposium—Law and Civil Society: Part II: Traditional Forms of Sub-Federal Institutions: Article: Notes for a Comparative Study of the Origins of Federalism in the United States and Canada." *Arizona Journal of International and Comparative Law* 15 (1998): 93.

Miller v. U.S., 357 U.S. 301 (1958) (Clark, J., dissenting).

Schneider v. Rusk, 377 U.S. 163 (1964) (Clark, J., dissenting).

U.S. v. Wong Kim Ark., 169 U.S. 649 (1898).

Archbishop of Canterbury's Case (2 Reports 46a), p. 49

Foy, H. Miles. "Some Reflections on Legislation, Adjudication, and Implied Private Actions in the State and Federal Courts." *Cornell Law Review* 71 (1986): 501.

Chudleigh's Case (1 Reports 113b).

Reid, Charles J., Jr. "The Seventeenth-Century Revolution in the English Land Law." *Cleveland State Law Review* 43 (1995): 221.

Cutler v. Dixon (4 Reports 14b), p. 111

Hayden, Paul T. "Reconsidering the Litigator's Absolute Privilege to Defame." *Ohio State Law Journal* 54 (1993): 985.

Schnapper, Eric. "'Libelous' Petitions for Redress of Grievances—Bad Historiography Makes Worse Law." *Iowa Law Review* 74 (1989): 74.

Pierson v. Ray, 386 U.S. 547 (1967).

Murphy v. AA. Matthews, a Div. of CRS Group Engineers, Inc., 841 S.W. 2d 671 (Mo. 1992).

Bruce v. Byrne-Stevens & Associates Engineers, Inc., 776 P. 2d 666 (Wash. 1989).

Floyd and Baker (12 Reports 23), p. 427

State Attorney v. Parrotino, 628 So. 2d 1097 (Fla. 1993).

Fuller's Case (12 Reports 41), p. 454

Herman, Lawrence. "The Unexplored Relationship Between the Privilege Against Compulsory Self-Incrimination and the Involuntary Confession Rule (Part I)." *Ohio State Law Journal* 53 (1992): 101.

O'Reilly, Gregory W. "England Limits the Right to Silence and Moves Towards an Inquisitorial System of Justice." *Journal of Criminal Law and Criminology* 85 (1994): 402.

Randall, Charles H. "Sir Edward Coke and the Privilege Against Self-Incrimination." *South Carolina Law Quarterly* 8 (1955): 417.

Usher, Roland G. "Nicholas Fuller: A Forgotten Exponent of English Liberty." *The American Historical Review* 12 (1907): 743.

Heydon's Case (3 Reports 7a), p. 78

Larue, L. H. "Special Issue on Legislation: Statutory and Constitutional Interpretation: Statutory Interpretation: Lord Coke Revisited." *University of Pittsburgh Law Review* 48 (1987): 733.

Sinclair, M. B. W. "Statutory Reasoning." *Drake Law Review* 46 (1997): 299.

Strauss, Peter L. "The Courts and the Congress: Should Judges Disdain Political History?" *Columbia Law Review* 98 (1998): 242.

Thorne, S. E. "The Equity of a Statute and Heydon's Case." *University of Illinois Law Review* 31 (1936): 202.

Board of Sup'rs of King and Queen County v. King Land Corp., 380 S.E. 2d 895 (Va. 1989).

Conley v. Sousa, 554 S.W. 2d 87 (Ky. 1977).

Northern X-Ray Co., Inc. v. State By and Through Hanson, 542 N.W. 2d 733 (N.D. 1996).

Pierson v. Ray, 386 U.S. 547 (1967) (Douglas, J., dissenting).

Stattner v. City of Caldwell, 727 P. 2d 1142 (Idaho 1986).

Truesdale v. South Carolina Highway Dept., 213 S.E. 2d 740 (S.C. 1975).

Case of the Isle of Ely (10 Reports 141a), p. 378

Bosselman, Fred P. "Limitations Inherent in the Title to Wetlands at Common Law." *Stanford Environmental Law Journal* 15 (1996): 247.

Case *De Libellis Famosa* (5 Reports 125), p. 145

Mayton, William T. "Seditious Libel and the Lost Guarantee of a Freedom of Expression." *Columbia Law Review* 84 (1984): 91.

Post, Robert C. "Symposium: New Perspectives in the Law of Defamation: The Social Foundations of Defamation Law: Reputation and the Constitution." *California Law Review* 74 (1986): 691.

Lutrell's Case (4 Reports 86a).
Bernards v. Link, 248 P. 2d 341 (Or. 1952).

MacKalley's Case (9 Reports 61b), p. 314
Ker v. State of California, 374 U.S. 23 (1963) (Brennan, J., dissenting).

Marshalsea (10 Reports 68b), p. 314
Noto, Thomas J. "*Pulliam v. Allen:* Delineating the Immunity of Judges from Prospective Relief." *Catholic University Law Review* 34 (1985): 829.
Wladis, John D. "Common Law and Uncommon Events: The Development of the Doctrine of Impossibility of Performance in English Contract Law." *Georgetown Law Journal* 75 (1987): 1575.
Burnham v. Superior Court of California, County of Marin, 495 U.S. 604 (1990).
Pulliam v. Allen, 466 U.S. 522 (1984) (Powell, J., dissenting).
Office of State Attorney, Fourth Judicial Circuit of Florida v. Parrotino, 628 So. 2d 1097 (Fla. 1993).

Case of the Monopolies (11 Reports 84b), p. 394
Corré, Jacob I. "The Argument, Decision, and Reports of Darcy v. Allen." *Emory Law Journal* 45 (1996): 1261.
Davies, D. Seaborne. "Further Light on the Case of Monopolies." *Law Quarterly Review* 48 (1932): 394.
Miller, Sidney T. "The Case of the Monopolies—Some of Its Results and Suggestions." *Michigan Law Review* 6 (1907): 1.
Sears, Roebuck & Co. v. Stiffel Co., 376 U.S. 225 (1964).
U.S. v. Line Material Co., 333 U.S. 287 (1948).

Pinnel's Case (5 Reports 117), p. 144
Teeven, Kevin M. "Development of Reform of the Preexisting Duty Rule and Its Persistent Survival." *Alabama Law Review* 47 (1996): 387.

Premunire (12 Reports 37), p. 447
Raack, David W. "A History of Injunctions in England Before 1700." *Indiana Law Journal* 61 (1986): 539.
Thorne, Samuel E. "Praemunire and Sir Edward Coke." *Huntington Library Quarterly* 462 (1938): 85.

The King's Prerogative in Saltpetre (12 Reports 12).
Novak, William J. "Common Regulation: Legal Origins of State Power in America." *Hastings Law Journal* 45 (1994): 1061.

Proclamations (12 Reports 74), p. 486

Cope, Esther. "Sir Edward Coke and the Proclamations." *American Journal of Legal History* 15 (1971): 215.

McConnell, Michael W. "Tradition and Constitutionalism Before the Constitution." *University of Illinois Law Review* (1998): 173.

Sir Stephen Proctor's Case (12 Reports 118), p. 494

Barnes, Thomas G. "A Cheshire Seductress, Precedent, and a 'Sore Blow' to Star Chamber." In *On the Laws and Customs of England: Essays in Honor of Samuel E. Thorne,* edited by Morris S. Arnold, et al. Chapel Hill: University of North Carolina Press, 1981.

Prohibitions del Roy (12 Reports 63), p. 478

State ex. rel. Village of Los Ranchos de Albuquerque v. City of Albuquerque, 889 P. 2d 185 (N.M. 1994).

Cincinnati & M.V.R. Co. v. Village of Roseville, 81 N.E. 178 (Ohio 1907).

Rooke's Case (5 Reports 99), p. 141

Wade, Sir William. *Administrative Law.* 6th ed. Oxford: Clarendon Press, 1988.

Lonner v. Ricks, 212 S.W. 2d 552 (Ark. 1948).

Countess of Rutland's Case (5 Reports 25b).

Powell, H. Jefferson. "The Original Understanding of Original Intent." *Harvard Law Review* 98 (1985): 885.

Semayne's Case (5 Reports 91), p. 135.

Cuddihy, William J. "The Fourth Amendment: Origins and Original Meaning, 602–1791." Ph.D. diss. Claremont Graduate School, 1957.

Cuddihy, William, and B. Carmon Hardy. "A Man's House Was Not His Castle: Origins of the Fourth Amendment to the United States Constitution." *William and Mary Quarterly,* 3rd. Ser., 37 (1980): 371.

Davies, Thomas Y. "Recovering the Original Fourth Amendment." *Michigan Law Review* 98 (1999): 547.

Goddard, Jennifer M. "Note: The Destruction of Evidence Exception to the Knock and Announce Rule: A Call for Protection of Fourth Amendment Rights." *Boston University Law Review* 75 (1995): 449.

Sklansky, David A. "The Fourth Amendment and Common Law." *Columbia Law Review* 100 (2000): 1739

Witten, Todd. "Note: *Wilson v. Arkansas:* Thirty Years After the Supreme Court Addresses the Knock and Announce Issue." *Akron Law Review* 29 (1996): 447.

Com. v. Carlton, 701 A. 2d 148 (Pa. 1997).

Green v. U.S., 355 U.S. 184 (1957) (Scalia, J., concurring).

Johnson v. Com., 189 S.E. 2d 678 (Va. 1972).

Lee v. State, 489 So. 2d 1382 (Miss. 1986).

Miller v. U.S., 357 U.S. 301 (1958).

Payton v. New York, 445 U.S. 573 (1980).

State v. Attaway, 870 P. 2d 103 (N.M. 1994).

State v. Dixon, 924 P. 2d 181 (Haw. 1996).

State v. Ford, 801 P. 2d 754 (Or. 1990).

State v. Thompson, 571 A. 2d 266 (N.H. 1990).

Steagald v. U.S., 451 U.S. 204 (1981).

Wilson v. Arkansas, 514 U.S. 927 (1995).

Shelley's Case (1 Reports 88b), p. 6

Orth, John V. "Observation: Requiem for the Rule in Shelley's Case." *North Carolina Law Review* 67 (1989): 681.

Reppy, William A. "Judicial Overkill in Applying the Rule in Shelley's Case." *Notre Dame Law Review* 73 (1997): 83.

Simpson, A. W. B. "Politics and Law in Elizabethan England, Shelley's Case (1581)." In *Leading Cases in the Common Law.* Oxford: Clarendon Press, 1995.

Countess of Shrewsbury's Case (12 Reports 94).

Dutton v. Evans, 400 U.S. 74 (1970).

Blair v. United States, 250 U.S. 273, 279 (1919).

Moss Point Lumber Co. v. Board of Sup'rs of Harrison County, 42 So. 290 (Miss. 1906).

Slade's Case (4 Reports 91a), p. 116

Baker, J. H. "New Light on Slade's Case." *Cambridge Law Journal* 29 (1971): 51.

Lucke, H. K. "Slade's Case and the Origin of the Common Counts." Parts 1–3. *Law Quarterly Review* 81, 82 (1965–1966): 422, 539, 81.

Ricks, Val D. "In Defense of Mutuality of Obligation: Why 'Both Should Be Bound, or Neither.'" *Nebraska Law Review* 78 (1999):491.

Simpson, A. W. B. *A History of the Common Law of Contract: The Rise of the Action of Assumpsit.* Oxford: Oxford University Press, 1975.

———. "The Place of Slade's Case in the History of Contract." *Law Quarterly Review* 74 (1958): 381.

Holt v. Feigenbaum, 419 N.E. 2d 332 (N.Y. 1981).

Town of Westport v. Bossert Corp., 335 A. 2d 297 (Conn. 1973).

In re Traub's Estate, 92 N.W. 2d 480 (Mich. 1958).

Spencer's Case (5 Reports 16).

French, Susan F. "Toward a Modern Law of Servitudes: Reweaving the Ancient Strands." *Southern California Law Review* 55 (1982): 55.

Reichman, Uriel. "Symposium Issue: Article: Toward a Unified Concept of Servitudes." *Southern California Law Review* 55 (1982): 1179.

Sutton's Hospital (10 Reports 1), p. 347

Yeazell, Stephen C. *Digging for the Missing Link: From Medieval Group Litigation to the Modern Class Action.* New Haven and London: Yale University Press, 1987.

Sierra Club v. Morton, 405 U.S. 727 (1972) (Douglas, J., dissenting).

Case of Swans (7 Reports 15), p. 232

Wise, Steven M. "The Legal Thinghood of Nonhuman Animals." *Boston College Environmental Affairs Law Review* 23 (1996): 471.

Twyne's Case (3 Reports 80b).

Clark, Robert. "The Duties of the Corporate Debtor to Its Creditors." *Harvard Law Review* 90 (1977): 505.

Vaux's Case (4 Reports 44a), p. 112

U.S. v. Scott, 437 U.S. 82 (1978).

Green v. U.S., 355 U.S. 184 (1957) (Frankfurter, J., dissenting).

Vynior's Case (4 Reports 81).

von Mehren, Robert. "From Vynior's Case to Mitsubushi: The Future of Arbitration and Public Law." *Brooklyn International Law Journal* (1986): 585.

3. Particular Trials

Sir Walter Raleigh's Case.

Coote, Stephen. *A Play of Passion: The Life of Sir Walter Raleigh.* London: Macmillan, 1993.

Graham, Kenneth W. "The Right of Confrontation and the Hearsay Rule: Sir Walter Raleigh Loses Another One." *Criminal Law Bulletin* 8 (1972): 99.

Raleigh, Sir Walter, *The Works of Sir Walter Raleigh, Kt., Now First Collected: To Which Are Prefixed the Lives of the Author.* Edited by William Oldys and Thomas Birch. 8 vols. Oxford: The University Press, 1829.

State v. Lanam, 459 N.W. 2d 656 (Minn. 1990) (Kelley, J., dissenting).

State v. Smith, 323 S.E. 2d 316 (N.C. 1984) (Martin, J., dissenting).

State v. Faafiti, 513 P. 2d 697 (Haw. 1973).

State v. Bailey, 110 S.E. 2d 165 (N.C. 1961).

Essex's Case.

Hammer, Paul E. J. *The Polarisation of Elizabethan Politics: The Political Career of Robert Devereux, 2nd Earl of Essex, 1585–1597.* Cambridge: Cambridge University Press, 1999.

Strachey, Lytton. *Elizabeth and Essex: A Tragic History.* New York: Harcourt Brace, 1996.

The Gunpowder Plot.

Caraman, Philip. *Henry Garnet, 1555–1606 and the Gunpowder Plot.* New York: Farrar, Strauss, & Giroux, 1964.

Fraser, Antonia. *Faith and Treason: The Story of the Gunpowder Plot.* New York: Doubleday, 1996.

Nicholls, Mark. *Investigating the Gunpowder Plot.* New York: University of Manchester Press, 1991 (distributed by St. Martin's Press).

Ross, Williamson H. *The Gunpowder Plot.* London: Faber and Faber, 1951.

Somerset's Case (Overbury murders).

Amos, Andrew. *Great Oyer of Poisoning: The Trial of the Earl of Somerset for the Poisoning of Sir Thomas Overbury, in the Tower of London, and Various Matters Connected Therewith, etc.* London: R. Bentley, 1846.

McElwee, William. *The Murder of Sir Thomas Overbury.* London: Faber and Faber, 1952.

"Truth Brought to Light by Time." In Walter Scott, ed., *A Collection of Scarce and Valuable Tracts, on the Most Interesting and Entertaining Subjects: But Chiefly Such as Relate to the History and Constitution of These Kingdoms. (Somers Tracts).* 2d ed. rev., 13 vol., London: T. Cadell, W. Davies, 1809–15.

White, Beatrice. *Cast of Ravens: The Strange Case of Sir Thomas Overbury.* New York: George Braziller, Inc., 1965.

Articuli Cleri.

Clanton, Bradley S. "Standing and the English Prerogative Writs: The Original Understanding." *Brooklyn Law Review* 63 (1997): 1001.

Peacham's Case.

Patterson, D. L. Jr., "Chief Justice Jeffreys and the Law of Treason," *Political Science Quarterly* 20 (1905): 493.

Stewart, Jay. "Servants of Monarchs and Lords: The Advisory Role of Early English Judges." *American Journal of Legal History* 38 (April 1994): 117.

4. *The Institutes,* Generally

Atkinson, W. A. "The Printing of Coke's Institutes." *Law Times* 162 (1926): 435.

Sheppard, Steve. "Casebooks, Commentaries, and Curmudgeons: An Introductory History of Law in the Lecture Hall." *Iowa Law Review* 78 (1997): 547.

Simpson, A. W. B. "The Rise and Fall of the Legal Treatise: Legal Principles and the Forms of Legal Literature." *University of Chicago Law Review* 48 (1981): 632.

5. Particular Doctrines in *The Institutes*

Abram, Suzanne L. "Note: Problems of Contemporaneous Construction in State Constitutional Interpretation." *Brandeis Law Journal* 38 (2000): 613.

Arnold, Richard S. "Trial by Jury: The Constitutional Right to a Jury of Twelve in Civil Trials." *Hofstra Law Review* 22 (1993): 1.

Burkhart, Ann M. "Freeing Mortgages of Merger." *Vanderbilt Law Review* 40 (1987): 283.

Bush, Jonathan A. "'You're Gonna Miss Me When I'm Gone': Early Modern Common Law Discourse and the Case of the Jews." *Wisconsin Law Review* (1993): 1225.

Christie, George C. "The Uneasy Place of Principle in Tort Law." *SMU Law Review* 49 (1996): 525.

Dripps, Donald A. "The Constitutional Status of the Reasonable Doubt Rule." *California Law Review* 75 (1987): 1665.

Fisher, George. "The Jury's Rise as Lie Detector." *Yale Law Journal* 107 (1997): 575.

Gardner, Martin R. "The Mens Rea Enigma: Observations on the Role of Motive in the Criminal Law Past and Present." *Utah Law Review* (1993): 635.

Hafetz, Jonathan L. "Note: The Untold Story of Noncriminal Habeas Corpus and the 1996 Immigration Acts." *Yale Law Journal* 107 (1998): 2509.

Harrison, Jack B. "How Open Is Open? The Development of the Public Access Doctrine Under State Open Court Provisions." *University of Cincinnati Law Review* 60 (1992): 1307.

Lindgren, James. "Blackmail: Morals: The Theory, History, and Practice of the Bribery-Extortion Distinction." *University of Pennsylvania Law Review* 141 (1993): 1695.

———. "The Elusive Distinction Between Bribery and Extortion: From the Common Law to the Hobbs Act." *UCLA Law Review* 35 (1988): 815.

Oldham, James C. "The Origins of the Special Jury." *University of Chicago Law Review* 50 (1983): 137.

Orth, John V. "Taking from A and Giving to B: Substantive Due Process and the Case of the Shifting Paradigm." *Constitutional Commentary* 14 (1997): 337.

Stephen, Sir James Fitzjames. *A History of the Criminal Law of England.* 3 vols. London: MacMillan & Co., 1883.

Tomkovicz, James J. "The Endurance of the Felony-Murder Rule: A Study of the Forces That Shape Our Criminal Law." *Washington & Lee Law Review* 51 (1994): 1429.

Wang, Janice Sue. "Comment: State Constitutional Remedy Provisions and Article I, Section 10 of the Washington State Constitution: The Possibility of Greater Judicial Protection of Established Tort Causes of Action and Remedies." *Washington Law Review* 64 (1989): 203.

I. Coke's Service in Parliament

Christianson, Paul. "Political Thought in Early Stuart England." *Historical Journal* 30 (1987): 960.

Cust, Richard. "Charles I, the Privy Council, and the Forced Loan." *Journal of British Studies* 24 (1985): 208.

———. *The Forced Loan and English Politics, 1626–1628.* Oxford: Oxford University Press, 1987.

Flemion, J. S. "The Struggle for the Petition of Right in the House of Lords: The Study of an Opposition Victory." *Journal of Modern History* 45 (1973): 193.

Foster, Elizabeth Read. "The Procedure of the House of Commons Against Patents and Monopolies, 1621–1624." In *Conflict in Stuart England: Essays in Honor of Wallace Notestein,* edited by A. W. Aiken and B. D. Henning. New York: Archon Books, 1960.

———, ed. *Proceedings in Parliament 1610.* New Haven: Yale University Press, 1966.

Hexter, J. H. "Power Struggle, Parliament, and Liberty in Early Stuart England." *Journal of Modern History* 50 (1978): 1.

Hinton, R. W. K. "The Decline of Parliamentary Government under Elizabeth I and the Early Stuarts." *Cambridge Historical Journal* 13 (1957): 116.

Hirst, Derek. "Elections and the Privileges of the House of Commons in the Early Seventeenth Century: Confrontation or Compromise?" *Historical Journal* 18 (1975): 851.

———. *The Representative of the People?: Voters and Voting in England Under the Early Stuarts.* Cambridge: Cambridge University Press, 1975.

Hulme, Harold. "The Winning of Freedom of Speech by the House of Commons." *The American Historical Review* 61 (1956): 825.

Jansson, Maija, and William B. Bidwell. *Proceedings in Parliament 1625.* New Haven: Yale University Press, 1987.

Johnson, Robert C., Mary Frear Keeler, Maija Jansson Cole, and William B. Bidwell, eds. *Commons Debates 1628.* Yale Center for Parliamentary History. New Haven: Yale University Press, 1977.

Judson, Margaret Atwood. *The Crisis of the Constitution: An Essay in Constitutional and Political Thought in England, 1603–1645.* New Brunswick: Rutgers University Press, 1949.

Lake, Peter. "Anti-Popery: The Structure of a Prejudice." In *Conflict in Early Stuart England: Studies in Religion and Politics, 1603–1642,* edited by Richard Cust and Ann Hughes. London: Longman, 1989.

Merz, Ruth. "Sir Edward Coke in the Parliament of 1621." Master's thesis, Washington University, 1942.

Mitchell, Williams M. *The Rise of the Revolutionary Party in the English House of Commons, 1603–1629.* New York: Columbia University Press, 1957.

Notestein, Wallace, Frances Helen Relf, and Hartley Simpson. *Commons Debates, 1621.* New Haven: Yale University Press, 1935.

Pocock, J. G. A. "The Commons Debates of 1628." *Journal of the History of Ideas* 39 (1978): 329.

Ruigh, Robert E. *The Parliament of 1624: Politics and Foreign Policy.* Harvard Historical Studies, vol. 87. Cambridge: Harvard University Press, 1971.

Russell, Conrad. *Parliaments and English Politics, 1621–1629.* Oxford: Clarendon Press, 1979.

———. "Parliamentary History in Perspective, 1604–1629." In *Unrevolutionary England, 1603–1642.* London: Hambledon Press, 1990.

White, Steven D. *Sir Edward Coke and "The Grievances of the Commonwealth," 1621–1628.* Chapel Hill: University of North Carolina Press, 1979.

Willson, David Harris. *The Privy Councillors in the House of Commons, 1604–1629.* Minneapolis: University of Minnesota Press, 1940.

Zaller, Robert. *The Parliament of 1621: A Study in Constitutional Conflict.* Berkeley: University of California Press, 1971.

J. Coke's Views on Parliament and Statutes

Baade, Hans W. "The Casus Omissus: A Pre-History of Statutory Analogy." *Syracuse Journal of International Law and Commerce* 20 (1994): 45.

McIlwain, Charles H. *The High Court of Parliament and Its Supremacy.* New Haven: Yale University Press, 1910.

McKay, R. A. "Coke—Parliamentary Supremacy or the Supremacy of the Law?" *Michigan Law Review* 22 (1924): 215.

K. Impeachments

Cecil, Henry. *Tipping the Scales.* London: Hutchinson, 1964.

Hurstfield, Joel. *Freedom, Corruption and Government in Elizabethan England.* Cambridge: Harvard University Press, 1973.

Marcus, Richard L. "English Common Law: Studies in the Sources: The Tudor Treason Trials: Some Observations on the Emergence of Forensic Themes." *University of Illinois Law Review* (1984): 675.

Noonan, John T. *Bribes: The Intellectual History of a Moral Idea.* New York: Macmillan, 1984.

Powell, Damian X. "Why Was Sir Francis Bacon Impeached? The Common Lawyers and the Chancery Revisited: 1621." *History* 81 (1996): 511.

Roberts, Clayton. *The Growth of Responsible Government in Stuart England.* Cambridge: Cambridge University Press, 1966.

Smith, Lacey Baldwin. *Treason in Tudor England: Politics and Paranoia.* Princeton: Princeton University Press, 1986.

Snapp, Harry F. "The Impeachment of Roger Maynwaring." *Huntington Library Quarterly* 30 (1966–67): 217.

Tite, Colin G. C. *Impeachment and Parliamentary Judicature in Early Stuart England.* London: Athlone Press, 1974.

L. Magna Carta

Ashley, Maurice. *Magna Carta in the Seventeenth Century.* Charlottesville: University Press of Virginia, 1965.

Blackstone, William. *The Great Charter and Charter of the Forest, with Other Authentic Instruments, to Which Is Affixed an Introductory Discourse Containing the History of the Charters.* Oxford: Clarendon Press, 1759. Reprinted in—. *Tracts, Chiefly Relating to the Antiquities and Laws of England.* 3d ed. Oxford: Clarendon Press, 1781.

Butterfield, Sir Herbert. *The Englishman and His History.* Cambridge: The University Press, 1944.

———. *Magna Carta in the Historiography of the Sixteenth and Seventeenth Centuries.* Reading: University of Reading, 1969.

———. *The Whig Interpretation of History.* New York: W. W. Norton, 1965.

Ely, James W., Jr. "The Oxymoron Reconsidered: Myth and Reality in the Origins of Substantive Due Process." *Constitutional Commentary* 16 (1999): 315.

Goodhart, Arthur L. *Law of the Land.* Charlottesville: University of Virginia Press, 1966.

Hazeltine, H. D. "The Influence of Magna Carta on American Constitutional Development." In *Magna Carta Commemoration Essays,* edited by Henry Elliot Malden. London: Royal Historical Society, 1917.

Helmholz, R. H. "Magna Carta and the *ius commune.*" *University of Chicago Law Review* 66 (1999): 297.

Holt, J. C. *Magna Carta.* 2d ed. Cambridge: Cambridge University Press, 1992.

Howard, A. E. Dick. *The Road from Runnymede: Magna Carta and Constitutionalism in America.* Charlottesville: University Press of Virginia, 1968.

Jennings, Sir Ivor. *Magna Carta and Its Influence in the World Today.* London: Central Office of Information, 1965.

Johnson, Samuel. *A History and Defence of Magna Charta: Containing a Copy of the Original Charter at Large, with an English Translation; the Manner of Its Being Obtained from King John, with Its Preservation and Final Establishment in the Succeeding Reigns. With an Introductory Discourse, Containing a Short Account of the Rise and Progress of National Freedom, from the Invasion of Caesar to the Present Times.* London: J. Bell, 1769.

McKencie, W. S. *Magna Carta.* Glasgow: Malehose & Sons, 1914.

Pallister, Anne. *Magna Carta: The Heritage of Liberty.* New York: Oxford University Press, 1971.

Radin, Max. "The Myth of Magna Carta." *Harvard Law Review* 60 (1947): 1060.

Sandoz, Ellis, ed. *The Roots of Liberty: Magna Carta, the Ancient Constitution, and the Anglo-American Tradition of Rule of Law.* Columbia: University of Missouri Press, 1993. (Including essays by Ellis Sandoz, J. C. Holt, Christopher W. Brooks, Paul Christianson, John Phillip Reid, and Corrine Comstock Weston.)

Swindler, William F. *Magna Carta.* New York: Grosset and Dunlap, 1968.

Thompson, Faith. *Magna Carta: Its Role in the Making of the English Constitution, 1300–1629.* Minneapolis: University of Minnesota Press, 1948.

Thorne, Samuel, William H. Dunham, Philip B. Kurland, and Sir Ivor Jennings. *The Great Charter: Four Essays on Magna Carta and the History of Our Liberty.* New York: Pantheon, 1965.

M. The Petition of Right

Boynton, Lindsay. "Martial Law and the Petition of Right." *English Historical Review* 74 (1959): 23.

Creasy, Sir Edward Shepherd. *The Textbook of the Constitution: Magna Charta, the Petition of Right, and the Bill of Rights.* London: Richard Bentley, 1848.

Forster, John. *Sir John Eliot: A Biography 1590–1632.* London: Longman, Roberts, & Green, 1864.

Foster, Elizabeth Read. "Printing the Petition of Right." *Huntington Library Quarterly* 28 (1974): 81.

Guy, J. A. "The Origins of the Petition of Right Reconsidered." *Historical Journal* 25 (1982): 289.

Mosse, George Lachmann. *The Struggle for Sovereignty in England, from the Reign of Queen Elizabeth to the Petition of Right.* East Lansing: Michigan State College Press, 1950.

Popofsky, Linda. "Habeas Corpus and 'Liberty of the Subject': Legal Arguments for the Petition of Right in the Parliament of 1628." *The Historian* 41 (1979): 257.

Reeve, L. J. "The Legal Status of the Petition of Right." *Historical Journal* 29 (1986): 257.

Relf, Frances Helen. "The Petition of Right: Bibliographical Notes for the Parliament of 1628." Ph.D. diss., University of Minnesota, 1917.

Schnapper, Eric. "The Parliament of Wonders (Review essay of Johnson, Kealer, Cole, and Bidwell, eds., *Commons Debates 1628*)." *Columbia Law Review* 84 (1984): 1665.

Thompson, Christopher. "The Origins of the Politics of the Parliamentary Middle Group, 1625–1629." *Transactions of the Royal Historical Society,* 5th ser., 22 (1972).

Young, Michael B. "The Origins of the Petition of Right Reconsidered Further." *Historical Journal* 27 (1984): 449.

N. Economics

Anderson, Gary M., and Robert D. Tollison. "Barristers and Barriers: Sir Edward Coke and the Regulation of Trade." *Cato Journal* 13 (1993): 49.

McCormack, Wayne. "Economic Substantive Due Process and the Right of Livelihood." *Kentucky Law Journal* 82 (1994): 397.

MacPherson, C. B. *The Political Theory of Possessive Individualism: Hobbes to Locke.* Oxford: Clarendon Press, 1962.

Malamet, Barbara. "The 'Economic Liberalism' of Sir Edward Coke." *Yale Law Journal* 76 (1967): 1321.

Reid, Charles J. "The Seventeenth-Century Revolution in the English Land Law." *Cleveland State Law Review* 43 (1995): 221.

Siegan, Bernard H. "*Propter Honoris Respectum:* Separation of Powers & Economic Liberties." *Notre Dame Law Review* 70 (1995): 415.

Wagner, Donald O. "Coke and the Rise of Economic Liberalism." *Economic History Review* 6 (1935): 30.

———. "The Common Law and Free Enterprise: An Early Case of Monopoly." *Economic History Review* 7, no. 1 (1937): 217.

O. Liberty

Carlyle, Alexander James. *Political Liberty.* Oxford: Clarendon Press, 1941.

Hayek, Friedrich. *The Constitution of Liberty.* Chicago: University of Chicago Press, 1978.

Hinton, R. W. K. "Government and Liberty under James I." *Cambridge Historical Journal* 11 (1955): 48.

Palmer, Ben W. "Edward Coke: Champion of Liberty." *American Bar Association Journal* 32 (1946): 135.

P. Legacy in England

Berman, Harold J., and Charles J. Reid. "The Transformation of English Legal Science: From Hale to Blackstone." *Emory Law Journal* 45 (1996): 437.

Care, Henry. *English Liberties: Or, The Free-born Subject's Inheritance.* London: G. Larkin, 1680(?).

Coquillette, Daniel R. "Ideology and Incorporation III: Reason Regulated—The Post-Restoration English Civilians, 1653–1735." *Boston University Law Review* 67 (1987): 289.

Gough, J. W. "Sir Edward Coke." In *Fundamental Law in English History.* Oxford: Oxford University Press, 1955.

Hale, Sir Matthew. *The History and Analysis of the Common Law of England: Written by a Learned Hand.* London: J. Nutt, 1713.

Haller, William. *Liberty and Reformation in the Puritan Revolution.* New York: Columbia University Press, 1955.

Hanson, Donald W. *From Kingdom to Commonwealth: The Development of Civic Consciousness in English Political Thought.* Cambridge: Harvard University Press, 1970.

Jones, William J. *Politics and the Bench: The Judges and the Origins of the English Civil War.* London: Allen and Unwin, 1971.

Keeton, George W. *Shakespeare's Legal and Political Background.* New York: Barnes & Noble, 1968. (See chapter four.)

Landon, Michael. *The Triumph of the Lawyers: 1678–1689.* Tuscaloosa: University of Alabama Press, 1970.

Levack, Brian P. "Possession, Witchcraft, and the Law in Jacobean England." *Washington and Lee Law Review* 52 (1995): 1613.

Malcolm, Joyce Lee. "Introduction." In *The Struggle for Sovereignty: Eighteenth-Century English Political Tracts.* Indianapolis: Liberty Fund, 1999. (See also entries throughout.)

Pocock, J. G. A. "Burke and the Ancient Constitution: A Problem in the History of Ideas" in Pocock, *Politics, Language and Time: Essays on Political Thought and History.* Chicago: University of Chicago Press, 1989.

Pollard, A. F. *The Evolution of Parliament.* London: Longman, Green & Co., 1920.

Pollock, Sir Frederic. *The Expansion of the Common Law.* London: Stevens and Sons, 1904.

Stephenson, Carl, and Frederick George Marcham. *Sources of English Constitutional History: A Selection of Documents from A.D. 600 to the Present.* New York: Harper & Row, 1937.

Stone, Lawrence. *The Causes of the English Revolution, 1529–1642.* New York: Harper & Row, 1972.

Taswell, Langmead, and Thomas Pitt. *English Constitutional History from the Teutonic Conquest to the Present Time.* 10th ed. London: Sweet & Maxwell, 1946.

Wood, Thomas. *Institutes of the Laws of England.* London: E. and R. Nutt and R. Gosling, 1720.

———. "Some Thoughts Concerning the Study of the Laws of England in the Two Universities." In Michael H. Hoeflich, ed., *The Gladsome Light of Jurisprudence: Learning the Law in England and the United States in the 18th and 19th Centuries.* New York: Greenwood Press, 1988.

Q. Legacy in the United States

Baade, Hans W. "'Original Intention': Raoul Berger's Fake Antique." *North Carolina Law Review* 70 (1992): 1523.

Baker, Fred A. *The Fundamental Law of American Constitutions.* Washington, D.C.: J. Byrne & Co., 1916.

Berger, Raoul. "The Founders' Views—According to Jefferson Powell." *Texas Law*

Review 67 (1989): 1033. (See "Powell" under the Countess of Rutland's Case, II.H.2, above.)

———. "Perspectives on Natural Law: Natural Law and Judicial Review: Reflections of an Earthbound Lawyer." *University of Cincinnati Law Review* 61 (1992): 5.

———. "Response: Original Intent: The Rage of Hans Baade." *North Carolina Law Review* 71 (1993): 1151.

Bilder, Mary Sarah, "The Lost Lawyers: Early American Legal Literates and Trans-atlantic Culture." *Yale Journal of Law and the Humanities* 11 (1999): 47.

———. "The Origin of the Appeal in America." *Hastings Law Journal* 48 (1997): 913.

Billings, Warren M. "Justices, Books, Laws, and Courts in Seventeenth-Century Virginia." *Law Library Journal* 85 (1993): 277.

Black, Barbara Aronstein. "The Constitution of the Empire: The Case for the Colonists." *University of Pennsylvania Law Review* 124 (1975–76): 1157.

———. "A Bicentennial Celebration of the Constitution: The Third Circuit Judicial Conference in Philadelphia: Retrospective View. An Astonishing Political Innovation: The Origins of Judicial Review." *University of Pittsburgh Law Review* 49 (1988): 691.

Clark, J. C. D. *The Language of Liberty 1660–1732: Political Discourse and Social Dynamics in the Anglo-American World.* Cambridge: Cambridge University Press, 1994.

Colburn, Trevor. *The Lamp of Experience: Whig History and the Intellectual Origins of the American Revolution.* Indianapolis: Liberty Fund, 1998.

Coquillette, Daniel R. "First Flower—The Earliest American Law Reports and the Extraordinary Josiah Quincy Jr. (1744–1775)." *Suffolk University Law Review* 30 (1996): 1.

———. "Legal Ideology and Incorporation IV: The Nature of Civilian Influence on Modern Anglo-American Commercial Law." *Boston University Law Review* 67 (1987): 877.

Corwin, Edward S. *The Doctrine of Judicial Review: Its Legal and Historical Basis and Other Essays.* Princeton: Princeton University Press, 1914.

———. "The Establishment of Judicial Review, I." *Michigan Law Review* 11 (1910): 102.

———. "The Establishment of Judicial Review, II." *Michigan Law Review* 9 (1911): 283.

———. "The 'Higher Law' Background of American Constitutional Law." Parts 1, 2. *Harvard Law Review* 42 (1928): 149, 365.

———. *The "Higher Law" Background of American Constitutional Law.* Ithaca, N.Y.: Great Seal Books, 1955.

———. *Liberty Against Government: The Rise, Flowering and Decline of a Famous Juridical Concept.* Baton Rouge: Louisiana State University Press, 1948.

Curtis, Michael Kent. "Historical Linguistics, Inkblots, and Life after Death: The Privileges or Immunities of Citizens of the United States." *North Carolina Law Review* 78 (2000): 1071.

Dalzell, George W. *Benefit of Clergy in America and Related Matters.* Winston-Salem, N. C.: John F. Blair, 1955.

Ely, James W. Jr. "Comment: Comments on Clinton: Reconsidering the Role of Natural Law in John Marshall's Jurisprudence." *John Marshall Law Review* 33 (2000): 1141.

Flint, George Lee, Jr. "Secured Transactions History: The Fraudulent Myth." *New Mexico Law Review* 29 (1999): 363.

Geller, Lawrence D., and Peter J. Gomes. *The Books of the Pilgrims.* New York: Garland Publishing, 1975.

Greene, Jack P. *Peripheries and Center: Constitutional Development in the Extended Polities of the British Empire and the United States 1607–1788.* New York: W. W. Norton, 1986.

Grey, Thomas C. "Origins of the Unwritten Constitution: Fundamental Law and American Revolutionary Thought." *Stanford Law Review* 30 (1978): 843.

Haines, Charles G. *The Revival of Natural Law Concepts: A Study of the Establishment and of the Interpretation of Limits on Legislatures with Special Reference to the Development of Certain Phases of American Constitutional Law.* Harvard Studies in Jurisprudence, vol. 4. New York: Russell & Russell, 1965.

Haskins, George Lee. *Law and Authority in Early Massachusetts; A Study in Tradition and Design.* New York, Macmillian, 1960.

Healy, Michael P. "*Communis Opinio* and the Methods of Statutory Interpretation: Interpreting Law or Changing Law." *William and Mary Law Review* 43 (2001) 539.

Hill, Alfred. "The Political Dimension of Constitutional Adjudication." *Southern California Law Review* 63 (1990): 1237.

Koch, William C. "Reopening Tennessee's Open Courts Clause: A Historical Reconsideration of Article I, Section 17 of the Tennessee Constitution." *Memphis State University Law Review* 27 (1997): 333.

Kurland, Philip B. "Magna Carta and Constitutionalism in the United States: The Myth and the Noble Lie." In *The Great Charter: Four Essays on Magna Carta and the History of Our Liberty,* edited by Samuel Thorne, William H. Dunham, Philip B. Kurland, and Sir Ivor Jennings. New York: Pantheon, 1965.

Lawson, Gary, and Guy Seidman. "Downsizing the Right to Petition." *Northwestern University Law Review* 93 (1999): 739.

Lovejoy, David. *The Glorious Revolution in America.* New York: Harper Torchbooks, 1974.

McCarthy, Finbarr. "Participatory Government and Communal Property: Two Radical Concepts in the Virginia Charter of 1606." *University of Richmond Law Review* 29 (1995): 327

McConnell, Michael W. "Tradition and Constitutionalism Before the Constitution." *University of Illinois Law Review* (1998): 173.

McDowell, Gary L. "Coke, Corwin, and the Constitution: The 'Higher Law Background' Reconsidered." *The Review of Politics* 55 (1993): 393.

McIlwain, Charles H. *The American Revolution.* New York: Macmillan Co., 1923.

McManus, Edgar J. *Law and Liberty in Early New England: Criminal Justice and Due Process, 1620–1692.* Amherst: University of Massachusetts Press, 1993.

Mandell, Joshua R. "Comment: Trees That Fall in the Forest: the Precedential Effect of Unpublished Opinions." *Loyola of Los Angeles Law Review* 34 (2000): 1255.

Manning, John F. "Textualism and the Equity of the Statute." *Columbia Law Review* 101 (2001): 1.

Massey, Calvin R. "Symposium: Perspective on Natural Law: The Natural Law Component of The Ninth Amendment," *University of Cincinnati Law Review* 61 (1992): 49.

Morris, Richard B. "Massachusetts and the Common Law." *American Historical Review* 31 (1926): 443.

Mullett, Charles F. "Coke and the American Revolution." *Economica* 12 (1932): 457.

———. *Fundamental Law and the American Revolution, 1760–1776.* New York: Columbia University Press, 1933.

———. "The Eighteenth-Century Background of John Marshall's Constitutional Jurisprudence." *Michigan Law Review* 76 (1978): 893.

Notestein, Wallace. *The English People on the Eve of Colonization, 1603–1630.* New York: Harper, 1954.

Penn, William. *English Liberties: Or, The Freeborn Subject's Inheritance.* London: G. Larkin or J. Howe, 1682. (Sometimes attributed to Henry Care.)

———. *The Excellent Privilege of Liberty & Property Being the Birth-Right of the Free-Born Subjects of England.* Philadelphia: William Bradford, 1687.

Pope, Herbert. "The Fundamental Law and the Power of the Courts." *Harvard Law Review* 27 (1913): 45.

Pound, Roscoe. "Common Law and Legislation." *Harvard Law Review* 21 (1907): 386.

———. *The Formative Era of American Law.* Boston: Little, Brown, 1938.

Reid, John Philip. *The Briefs of the American Revolution: Constitutional Arguments Between Thomas Hutchinson, Governor of Massachusetts Bay, and James Bowdoin for the Council and John Adams for the House of Representatives.* New York: New York University Press, 1981.

———. *The Concept of Liberty in the Age of the American Revolution.* Chicago: University of Chicago Press, 1988.

————. *Constitutional History of the American Revolution*. 4 vols. Madison: University of Wisconsin Press, 1986–1995. (1 vol. abridgment, 1995.)

Reinsch, Paul S. "The English Common Law in the Early American Colonies." In *Select Essays in Anglo-American Legal History*, edited by American Association of Law Schools. Boston: Little, Brown & Co., 1907.

Riggs, Robert E. "Substantive Due Process in 1791." *Wisconsin Law Review* (1990): 941.

Roesler, Shannon M. "Comment: The Kansas Remedy by Due Course of Law Provision: Defining a Right to a Remedy." *Kansas Law Review* 47 (1999): 655.

Rossiter, Clinton. *Seedtime of the Republic: The Origin of the American Tradition of Political Liberty*. New York: Harcourt, Brace, 1953.

Schwartz, Paul, Barbara Kern, and R. B. Bernstein. *Thomas Jefferson and Bolling v. Bolling: Law and Legal Profession in Pre-Revolutionary America*. San Marino, Calif.: Huntington Library, 1999.

Schweber, Howard. "The 'Science' of Legal Science: The Model of the Natural Sciences in Nineteenth-Century American Legal Education." *Law and History Review* 17 (1999): 421.

Scott, Arthur P. "The Constitutional Aspects of the 'Parson's Cause.'" *Political Science Quarterly* 31 (1916): 558.

Sheppard, Steve, ed. *The History of Legal Education in the United States: Commentaries and Primary Sources*. Pasadena: Salem Press, 1998.

Sherry, Suzanna. "The Founders' Unwritten Constitution." *University of Chicago Law Review* 54 (1987): 1127.

————. "Symposium: Perspective on Natural Law: Natural Law in the States." *University of Cincinnati Law Review* 61 (1992): 171.

Stoner, James R. *Common Law and Liberal Theory: Coke, Hobbes, and the Origins of American Constitutionalism*. Lawrence: University of Kansas Press, 1992.

Whitman, James Q. "Why Did the Revolutionary Lawyers Confuse Custom and Reason?" *University of Chicago Law Review* 58 (1991): 1321.

Wright, Benjamin Fletcher. *American Interpretations of Natural Law: A Study in the History of Political Thought*. London: Russell & Russell, 1962.

Zweiben, Beverly. *How Blackstone Lost the Colonies: English Law, Colonial Lawyers and the American Revolution*. New York: Garland Publishing, 1990.

Anastasoff v. U. S., 223 F. 3d 898 (8th Cir., 2000) (Arnold, C. J.).

R. Legacy Elsewhere.

Aja Espil, Jorge A. *En Los Orígenes De La Tratadística Constitucional*. Buenos Aires: Abeledo-Perrot, 1968.

Clark, David. "Legal History: The Icon of Liberty: The Status and Role of Magna

Carta in Australian and New Zealand Law." *Melbourne University Law Review* 24 (2000): 866.

Parent, Hugues. "Histoire de l'acte Volontaire En Droit Penal Anglais et Canadien." *McGill Law Journal* 45 (2000): 975.

III. Selected Commentaries on Related Matters

A. Coke's Monarchs and Their Governance
Trevelyan, George Macaulay. *England Under the Stuarts.* London: Methuen & Co., 1949.

1. Elizabeth I
Erickson, Carolly. *The First Elizabeth.* New York: St. Martin's Press, 1997.

Neale, Sir John Ernest. *The Elizabethan House of Commons.* New Haven: Yale University Press, 1950.

———. *Elizabeth I and Her Parliaments, 1584–1601.* New York: St. Martin's Press, 1958.

Nichols, John. *The Progresses and Public Processions of Queen Elizabeth.* London: J. Nichols and Son, 1823.

2. James VI and I
James I. "The Trew Law of Free Monarchies (The 1598 Text)." In *The Political Works of James I.* 1616. Reprint. Edited by Charles H. McIlwain. Cambridge: Harvard University Press, 1918. And in James VI and I. *Political Writings.* Edited by Johann B. Sommerville. Cambridge: Cambridge University Press, 1994.

Nichols, J. B., ed. *The Progresses, Processions, and Magnificent Festivities of King James the First, His Royal Consort, Family, and Court.* London: J. B. Nichols, 1828.

Parent, Hugues. "Histoire de l'Acte Volontaire en Droit Penal Anglais et Canadien." *McGill Law Journal* 45 (2000): 975.

Smith, Alan G. R., ed. *The Reign of James VI and I.* New York: St. Martin's Press, 1973.

Usher, Roland G. "James I and Sir Edward Coke." *English History Review* 18 (1903): 664.

Willson, David Harris. *King James VI and I.* London: Jonathan Cape, 1956.

3. Charles I
Reeve, L. J. *Charles I and the Road to Personal Rule.* Cambridge: Cambridge University Press, 1989.

Sharpe, Kevin. *The Personal Rule of Charles I.* New Haven: Yale University Press, 1993.

B. Rivals, Allies, and Sponsors

1. Sir Francis Bacon

Burch, Charles Nelson. "The Rivals [Coke and Bacon]." *Virginia Law Review* 14 (1928): 507.

Coquillette, Daniel R. *Francis Bacon.* Stanford: Stanford University Press, 1992.

Du Maurier, Dame Daphne. *The Winding Stair: Sir Francis Bacon, His Rise and Fall.* London: Gollancz, 1976.

Jardine, Lisa, and Alan Stewart. *Hostage to Fortune: The Troubled Life of Francis Bacon.* New York: Farrar, Straus & Giroux, 1999.

Marwil, Jonathan L. *The Trials of Counsel: Francis Bacon in 1621.* Detroit: Wayne State University Press, 1976.

Matthews, Nieves. *Francis Bacon: The History of a Character Assassination.* New Haven: Yale University Press, 1999.

Peltonen, Makku, ed. *The Cambridge Companion to Bacon.* Cambridge: Cambridge University Press, 1996.

Spedding, James. *An Account of the Life of Francis Bacon, Extracted from the Edition of His Occasional Writings.* New York: Houghton Mifflin, 1878.

———. Robert Ellis, and Douglas Heath, eds. *The Works of Francis Bacon.* 14 vols. London: Longman, 1857–1874.

Vickers, Brian, ed. *Essential Articles for the Study of Francis Bacon.* The Essential Article Series. Hamden, Conn.: Archon Books, 1968.

Zagorin, Perez. *Francis Bacon.* Princeton: Princeton University Press, 1999.

2. Thomas Egerton, Baron Ellesmere

Dawson, John P. "Coke and Ellesmere Disinterred: The Attack on the Chancery in 1616." *University of Illinois Law Review* 36 (1936): 127.

Jones, W. J. "Ellesmere and Politics, 1603–1617." In *Early Stuart Studies: Essays in Honor of David Harris Willson,* edited by Howard S. Reinmuth. Minneapolis: University of Minnesota Press, 1970.

Knafla, Louis A. *Law and Politics in Jacobean England: The Tracts of Lord Chancellor Ellesmere.* Cambridge: Cambridge University Press, 1977.

Plucknett, T. F. T. "Ellesmere on Statutes." *Law Quarterly Review* 60 (1944): 242.

3. William Cecil, Lord Burghley

Cecil, William. *The Execution of Justice in England.* Edited by Robert M. Kingdon. Folger Shakespeare Library. Ithaca, N.Y.: Cornell University Press, 1965.

Dennis, George Ravenscroft. *The Cecil Family.* Boston: Houghton Mifflin, 1914.

Graves, Michael A. R. *Burghley: William Cecil, Lord Burghley.* New York: Longman, 1998.

Hickes, Sir Michael. *The "Anonymous Life" of William Cecil, Lord Burghley.* Edited by Alan G. R. Smith. Lewiston, N.Y.: E. Mellen Press, 1990.

Read, Conyers. *Lord Burghley and Queen Elizabeth.* New York: Alfred A. Knopf, 1960.

4. Robert Cecil, Earl of Salisbury

Cecil, Algernon. *A Life of Robert Cecil, First Earl of Salisbury.* London: J. Murray, 1915.

Handover, P. M. *The Second Cecil: The Rise to Power, 1563–1604, of Sir Robert Cecil, Later First Earl of Salisbury.* London: Eyre & Spottiswoode, 1959.

Haynes, Alan Robert. *Cecil, Earl of Salisbury, 1563–1612: Servant of Two Sovereigns.* London: P. Owen, 1989.

5. John Selden

Berkowitz, David Sandler. *John Selden's Formative Years: Politics and Society in Early Seventeenth-Century England.* Washington, D.C.: Folger Shakespeare Library, 1988.

Christianson, Paul. *Discourse on History, Law, and Governance in the Public Career of John Selden, 1610–1635.* Toronto: University of Toronto Press, 1996.

———. "The Five Knights' Case, and Discretionary Imprisonment in Early Stuart England." *Criminal Justice History* 6 (1985): 65.

———. "Young John Selden and the Ancient Constitution, ca. 1610–18." *Proceedings of the American Philosophical Society* 128 (1984): 271.

Selden, John. *Opera Omnia, tam Edita quem Inedita. Collegit ac Recensuit Vita Auctoris, Praefationes Indices Adjecit.* Edited by David Wilkins. 6 vols. London: J. Walthoe [and others], 1726.

6. Sir John Davies

Klemp, P. J. *Fulke Greville and Sir John Davies: A Reference Guide.* Boston: G. K. Hall, 1985.

Pawlisch, Hans S. "Sir John Davies, the Ancient Constitution, and Civil Law." *History Journal* 23 (1980): 689.

Sanderson, James L. *Sir John Davies.* Boston: Twayne Publishers, 1975.

7. Sir Christopher Hatton

Brooks, Eric St. John. *Sir Christopher Hatton: Queen Elizabeth's Favourite.* London: J. Cape, 1946.

Vines, Alice Gilmore. *Neither Fire Nor Steel: Sir Christopher Hatton.* Chicago: Nelson-Hall, 1978.

8. Lady Elizabeth Hatton

Disraeli, Isaac. "Domestic History of Sir Edward Coke." In *Curiosities of Literature.* New York: J. Widdleton, 1872. (Contains transcripts of a defense of Lady Hatton that may be the work of Francis Bacon.)

Norsworthy, Laura. *The Lady of Bleeding Heart Yard: Lady Elizabeth Hatton, 1578–1646.* New York: Harcourt, Brace & Co., 1936.

Turner, Jesse. "Concerning Divers Notable Stirs Between Sir Edward Coke and His Lady." *American Law Review* 51 (1917): 883.

9. Roger Williams

Carpenter, Edmund James. *Roger Williams: A Study of the Life, Times and Character of a Political Pioneer.* New York: Grafton Press, 1909. Reprint. Freeport, N.Y.: Books for Libraries Press, 1972.

Covey, Cyclone. *The Gentle Radical: A Biography of Roger Williams.* New York: Macmillan, 1966.

Eberle, Edward J. "Roger Williams' Gift: Religious Freedom in America." *Roger Williams University Law Review* 4 (1999): 425.

Felker, Christopher D. "Roger Williams' Uses of Legal Discourse: Testing Authority in Early New England." *The New England Quarterly* 63 (1990): 624.

Hall, Timothy D. *Separating Church and State: Roger Williams and Religious Liberty.* Bloomington: University of Illinois Press, 1998.

Miller, Perry. *Roger Williams: His Contribution to the American Tradition.* Indianapolis: Bobbs-Merrill, 1953.

Williams, Roger. *The Correspondence of Roger Williams.* Edited by Glenn W. LaFantasie. Hanover: Brown University Press, 1988.

10. Coke's Heirs

Coke, Roger. *A Detection of the Court and State of England During the Four Last Reigns, and the Inter-Regnum: Consisting of Private Memoirs, &c., with Observations and Reflections: Also an Appendix Discovering the Present State of the Nation. in Two Volumes* London, 1694.

———. *A Survey of the Politicks of Mr. Thomas White, Thomas Hobbs, and Hugo Grotius Also, Elements of Power & Subjection, Or, the Causes of Humane, Christian, and Legal Society.* London: Printed for G. Bedell and T. Collins, 1662.

———. *A Supplement to the First Edition of the Detection of the Court and State of England During the Four Last Reigns and the Inter-regnum: Containing Many Secrets Never Before Made Publick: as Also a More Impartial Account of the Civil Wars in England than Has Yet Been Given.* London: Printed for Andrew Bell, 1696.

———. *Justice Vindicated from the False Focus Put upon it by Thomas White, Gent., Thomas Hobbs, and Hugo Grotius. And Also Elements of Power & Subjection Wherein Is Demonstrated the Cause of All Humane, Christian and Legal Society,* London: G. Bedell and T. Collins, 1660.

Longueville, Thomas. *The Curious Case of Lady Purbeck; A Scandal of the XVIIth*

Century. London: Longmans, Green, & Co., 1909. (The story of Coke's daughter Frances.)

Stirling, A. M. W. *Coke of Norfolk, and His Friends: The Life of Thomas William Coke*. London: J. Lane, 1912.

C. Selected Early Criticism

Brooke, Sir Robert. *The Reading of M. Robert Brook, Serjeant of the Law, and Recorder of London, upon the Stat. of Magna Charta, Chap. 16*. London: M. Flesher and R. Young, 1641.

Egerton, Thomas (Baron Ellesmere and Viscount Brackley). *The Lord Chancellor Egerton's Observations on the Lord Coke's Reports: Particularly in the Debate of Causes Relating to the Right of the Church; the Power of the King's Prerogative; the Jurisdiction of Courts; Or, the Interest of the Subject*. London: B. Lintott, 1710(?). Reprinted in Knafla, *Law and Politics in Jacobean England*, listed above in section III.B.2.

Fulbecke, William. *A Parallele or Conference of the Civil Law, the Canon Law, and the Common Law of this Realme of England*. London: Company of Stationers, 1618.

Hobart, Sir Henry. *The Reports of that Reverend and Learned Judge, The Right Honorable Sr. Henry Hobart Knight and Baronet, Lord Chief Justice of His Majesty's Court of Common Pleas; and Chancellor of both Their Highnesses Henry and Charles, Princes of Wales, 1603–1625*. 5th ed. Edited by Edward Chilton. London: E. and R. Nut and R. Gosling, 1724. (Chief Justice Hobart's ruling in the 1614 case, *Day v. Savage*, holds, "Because even an Act of Parliament, made against natural equity, as to make a man Judge in his own case, is void in itself, for *Jura natura sunt immutabilia*, and they are *leges legum*.")

Hobbes, Thomas. *Dialogue Between a Philosopher and a Student of the Common Law of England*. Edited by Joseph Cropsey. Chicago: University of Chicago Press, 1971.

De Vere, Edward (Earl of Oxford). "Some Notes and Observations upon the Statute of Magna Charta, Chapter 29, and Other Statutes Concerning the Proceedings in the Chancery . . . , 1615–1616." MS. 1031, Manuscript in Harvard Law School Department of Special Collections, Cambridge.

Parsons, Robert. *An Answere To The Fifth Part Of Reportes Lately set forth by Syr Edward Cooke, Knight, the Kinges Attorney Generall. Concerning The Ancient & Moderne Municipall lawes of England, which do Apperteyne to Spirituall Power & Iurisdiction. By Occasion Whereof, & of the Principall Question set downe in the Sequent page, there is laid forth an Evident, Plaine & Perspicuous. Demonstration of the Continuance of Catholicke Religion in England, from our first Kinges christened, Unto these dayes*. St. Omer, France: English College Press, 1606.

———. *A Quiet and Sober Reckoning With M. Thomas Morton Somewhat Set in Choler by His Aduersary P. R.: Concerning Certaine Imputations of Wilfull Falsities Obiected to the Said T. m. in a Treatise of P. R. Intituled of Mitigation, Some Part Wherof He*

Hath Lately Attempted to Answere in a Large Preamble to a More Ample Reioynder Promised by Him. But Here in the Meane Space the Said Imputations Are Iustified, and Confirmed, & with Much Increase of New Untruthes on His Part Returned Upon Him Againe: So as Finally the Reckoning Being Made, the Verdict of the Angell, Interpreted by Daniel, Is Verified of Him. There Is Also Adioyned a Peece of a Reckoning with Syr. Edward Cooke, Now L. Chief Iustice of the Comon Pleas, about a Nihil Dicit, & Some Other Points Uttered by Him in Two Late Preambles, to His Sixt and Seauenth Partes of Reports. St. Omer, France: English College Press, 1609.

Prynne, William. *Brief Animadversions On, Amendments Of, & Additional Explanatory Records To, the Fourth Part of the Institutes of the Lawes of England, Concerning the Jurisdiction of Courts: Compiled by the Late Famous Lawyer, Sir Edward Cooke, Knight, Wherein the Misquotations, Mistakes of Records, Antiquities Cited in Them Are Rectified, Some Doubtful Passages Explained, Many Defective Omissions of Usefull Records Supplyed . . . : the Transcripts of Which Records out of The Originals, Are at Large Inserted, Many Others Chronologically and Briefly Quoted: with Several Tables Thereunto. . . .* London: Thomas Ratcliffe and Thomas Daniel, 1669.

———. *Irenarches redivivus, Or, A briefe collection of sundry usefull and necessary statutes and petitions in Parliament (not hitherto published in print, but extant onely in the Parliament Rolls) concerning the necessity, utility, institution, qualification, jurisdiction, office, commission, oath, and against the causlesse, clandestine dis-commissioning of Justices of Peac fit to be publikely known and observed in these reforming times.: With some short deductions and a touch of the antiquity and institution of assertors and justices of peace in other forraign kingdomes. / Together with a full refutation of Sir Edward Cooks assertion, and the commonly received erronious opinion, of a difference between ordinances and Acts of Parliament in former age here cleerly manifested to be then but one and the same in all respects, and in point of the threefold assent. Published for the common good, by William Prynne of Lincolns-Inne.* London: for Michael Spark at the Bible in Green-Arbor, 1648.

Zouch, Richard. *The Jurisdiction of the Admiralty of England Asserted, Against Sr. Edward Coke's Articuli Admiralitatis, in XXII Chapter of His Jurisdiction of Courts.* London: F. Tyton and T. Dring, 1663.

IV. Noteworthy Mentions

Allen, Carleton Kemp. *Law in the Making.* 7th ed. Oxford: Clarendon Press, 1964.

Baker, J. H. *An Introduction to English Legal History.* 3d ed. London: Butterworths, 1990.

Bendix, Reinhard. *Kings or People: Power and the Mandate to Rule.* Berkeley: University of California Press, 1978.

Friedrich, Carl Joachim. *The Philosophy of Law in Historical Perspective.* 2d. ed. Chicago: University of Chicago Press, 1958.

Gardiner, Samuel R. *History of England from the Accession of James I to the Outbreak of the Civil War, 1603–1642.* 10 vols. London: Longmans, Green & Co., 1884.

Helgerson, Richard. *Forms of Nationhood: Elizabethan Writings of England.* Chicago: University of Chicago Press, 1992.

Hill, Christopher. *Society and Puritanism in Pre-Revolutionary England.* New York: Schocken Books, 1964.

Hirst, Derek. *Authority and Conflict: England, 1603–1625.* Cambridge: Harvard University Press, 1986.

Kantorowicz, Ernst H. *The King's Two Bodies: A Study in Medieval Political Theology.* Princeton: Princeton University Press, 1957.

McWhirter, Darien A. *The Legal 100: A Ranking of the Individuals Who Have Most Influenced the Law.* Secaucus, N.J.: The Citadel Press, 1998.

Plucknett, Theodore F. T. *A Concise History of the Common Law.* Rochester, N.Y.: Lawyers Co-operative Publishing Company, 1929.

Pound, Roscoe, and Theodore F. T. Plucknett. *Readings on the History and System of the Common Law.* Rochester: Lawyers Co-operative Publishing Company, 1927.

Radin, Max. *Handbook of Anglo-American Legal History.* St. Paul: West Publishing Co., 1936.

Schwartz, Bernard. *The American Heritage History of Law in America.* New York: McGraw Hill, 1974.

Smith, Alan G. R. *The Emergence of a Nation State: The Commonwealth of England 1529–1660.* London: Longman Group, 1984.

Sommerville, J. P. *Politics and Ideology in England, 1603–1640.* Harlow: Longmans, 1986.

Thatcher, Rt. Hon. Baroness Margaret. *The Rule of Law in a Dangerous World.* Washington, D.C.: National Legal Center for the Public Interest, 1994.

Turner, Edward Raymond. *The Privy Council of England in the Seventeenth and Eighteenth Centuries, 1603–1784.* Baltimore: The Johns Hopkins Press, 1927.

Wootton, David, ed. *Divine Right and Democracy: An Anthology of Political Writing in Stuart England.* London: Penguin, 1986.

Wormser, Rene A. *The Story of the Law and the Men Who Made It—From the Earliest Times to the Present.* New York: Simon & Schuster, 1962.

Table of Regnal Years[1]

Rulers in England Prior to the Conquest

Kings of Kent

Hencgest	c. 455–488
Oeric (Oisc)	c. 488–512
Eormenric	c. 512–560
Æthelberht I	c. 560 or 585–616
Eadbald	616–640
Earconberht	640–664
Ecgberht I	664–673
Hlothhere	673–685
Eadric	685–686
Oswine	689–690
Swæfheard & Wihtred	690–692
Wihtred	692–725

Kings of West Kent

Eadberht I	725–748
Eardwulf	748–762
Sigered	762–c. 764
Ecgberht II	c. 764

Kings of East Kent

Æthelberht II	725–762
Eadberht II	762–c. 764

1. Dates are drawn from C. R. Cheney, *A Handbook of Dates For Students of British History*, (rev. M. Jones) Cambridge: Cambridge University Press, 2000; E. B. Fryde et al., eds. *Handbook of British Chronology*, Cambridge: Cambridge University Press, 1996.

| Eanmund | c. 764 |
| Heahberht | 765 |

Kings of Kent

Æthelbald (Mercia)	716–757
Offa (Mercia)	757–776
Ecgberht II	c. 779
Ealhmund	c. 784
Offa (Mercia) (again)	c. 784 or 785–796
Eadberht Præn	796–798
Cuthred	798–807
Baldred	821–825

Then ruled by Wessex.

Kings of Northumbria

Kings of Deira

Ælle	c. 560–588 or 590
Æthelric (of Bernicia)	588 or 590–593
Edwin	616–633
Osric	633–634
Oswald	634–642
Oswine	642 or 643–651
Oswiu	651–670

Then ruled by Scandinavian York.

Kings of Bernicia

Ida	c. 547–559 or 560
Glappa	559 or 560
Adda	560–568
Æthelric	568–572
Theodric	572–579
Frithuwald	579–585
Hussa	585–592
Æthelfrith	592–616
Eanfrith	633 or 634–634
Oswald	634–642
Oswiu	642–670

Then ruled by Northumbria.

Kings of the Northumbrians

Ecgfrith	670–685
Aldfrith	686–705
Eadwulf	705 or 706
Osred I	706–716
Coenred (Cenred)	716–718
Osric ?	718–729
Ceolwulf	729–737
Eadberht	737–758
Oswulf	758–759
Æthelwald Moll	759–765
Alhred	765–774
Æthelred I	774–778 or 779
Ælfwald I	778 or 779–788
Osred II	778–790
Æthelred I (again)	790–796
Osbald	796
Eardwulf	796–806
Ælfwald II	806–808
Eardwulf (again)	808–810
Eanrad (Eanred)	810–840 or 841
Æthelred II	840 or 841–844
Rædwulf	844
Æthelred II (again)	844–848 or 849
Osberht	848 or 849–862 or 863
Ælle	862 or 863–867
Osberht (again)	867
Ecgberht I	867–872
Ricsige	873–876
Ecgberht II	876–878
Eadwulf of Bamburgh	878–913
Aldred	913–927

Then ruled by Scandinavian York.

Rulers of the Scandinavian Kingdom of York

Halfdan I	875 or 876–877
Guthfrith	883–895
Sigfrith (Sievert, Sigfred)	895

Cnut (Knutr)	c. 895 or 901–unknown
Æthelwold	c. 899–c. 903
Halfdan II	unknown–910
Eowils (Ecwils)	910
Ragnald I (Ragnall I)	c. 914–920
Sihtric II Caech (Sigtryggr Caech)	c. 920–927
Olaf I (Anlaf I, Olafr I) Cuaran (Guthfrithsson)	927 ?
Guthfrith II	927
Athelstan, k. of English	927–939
Olaf II Guthfrithson	939–941
Olaf I Cuaran (again)	941–944
Ragnald II Guthfrithson	943–944
(Edmund, k. of English	944–946)
(Eadred, k. of English	946–947)
Eric Bloodaxe	947–948
Eadred	948–950
Olaf I Cuaran (again)	c. 949–952
Eric Bloodaxe (again)	952–954

Then ruled by Wessex.

Kings of Mercia

Cearl	c. 600
Penda	626 or 623–655
Wulfhere	c. 658–675
Æthelred	675–704
Coenred	704–c. 709
Ceolred	709–716
Æthelbald	716–757
Beornred	757
Offa	757–796
Ecgfrith	796
Coenwulf (Cenwulf)	796–821
Coelwulf I	821–823
Beornwulf	823–825
Ludeca	825–827
Wiglaf	827–840

Berhtwulf	840–852
Burgred	852–873 or 874
Ceolwulf II	874–879
Æthelred (Ealdorman) (Anglo-Saxon)	c. 880–911
Æthelflæd (Anglo-Saxon)	911–918
Ælfwyn (Anglo-Saxon)	918

Then ruled by Wessex.

Rulers of the Hwicce (Worcester)

Eanhere	c. 660s
Eanfrith	c. 660s
Osric	c. 670s–680s
Oshere	c. 690s–716
Æthelheard	after 709
Æthelweard	after 706–716
Æthelric	c. 736
Eanberht	c. 755–759
Uhtred	c. 755–777 or 779
Ealdred (Aldred)	c. 755–778

Then ruled partly by Wessex, partly by Angles, then by Mercia.

Kings of Lindsey

Aldfrith, son of Eata	c. 786–796

Usually subject to Northumbria.

Kings of the East Angles

Rædwald	c. 616 to 627
Earpwald	c. 616 to 627 or 628
Richberht	627 or 628
Sigeberht	630 or 631
Ecgric	c. 630
Anna	before 654
Æthelhere	654
Æthelwald	before 664
Aldwulf	663 or 664–713

Ælfwald	713–749
Hun, Beonna, & Æthelberht I	after 749
Æthelberht II	after 794
Eadwald	c. 800
Æthelstan (Guthrum) (Scandinavian)	c. 830 to 845
Æthelweard	c. 845 to 855
Edmund	c. 855–869
Æthelred	c. 875
Oswald	c. 875

Then ruled by Scandinavians, then Wessex from 917.

Scandinavian Kings of East Anglia

Guthrum (Æthelstan)	c. 879 or 880–890
Eohric	before 902

Kings of the South Saxons (Sussex)

Ælle	c. 477–after 491
Æthelwalh	c. 674–682
Nothhelm (Nunna)	c. 692–714
Watt	c. 692–700
Æthelstan	c. 714
Æthelberht	c. 714 to 733–747 to 770
Oswald ?	before 772
Osmund ?	c. 760–770 to 772
Oslac	c. 760–780
Ealdwulf	c. 760–790 to 798
Ælfwald	c. 760–772

Then ruled by others, then by Wessex.

Kings of the East Saxons (Essex)

Sæberht (Saba)	c. 604–616 or 617
Seaxred	c. 616 or 617–c. 617
Sæweard	c. 616 or 617–c. 617
Sigeberht I (parvus)	c. 616 or 617–before? 635
Sigeberht II (sanctus)	c. before? 653 to before 664

Swithelm	c. 653 to 664–c. 664
Swithfrith ?	c. 664
Sigehere	c. 664–690
Sebbi	c. 664–c. 694
Sigeheard	c. 694–c. 705
Swæfred	c. 694–d. 704
Offa	c. 694? to 709–709
Swæfberht	c. 709–738
Selered	c. 738–746
Swithred	c. 746
Sigeric I	before 798
Sigered	c. 798–c. 823
Sigeric II ?	c. 825

Then ruled by Wessex.

Kings of the West Saxons (Wessex)

Cerdic	519–534
Cynric	534–560
Ceawlin	560–593
Ceol	591–597
Ceolwulf	597–611
Cynegils	611–642
Cenwealh	642–672
Seaxburh (queen)	672–674
Æscwine	674–676
Centwine	676–685
Cædwalla	685–688
Ine	688–726
Æthelheard	726–740
Cuthred	740–756
Sigeberht	756–757
Cynewulf	757–786
Beorhtric	786–802
Ecgberht	802–839
Æthelwulf	839–858
Æthelberht	858–865
Æthelred I	865–871
Alfred the Great	after 871–899

Edward the Elder	after 899–924
Ælfwerd (Wessex)	924
Æthelstan	after 924–939

A Note on Arthur, King of the Britons

Coke believed some of the legends of King Arthur as the historical truth, as did his contemporaries such as Camden. In the ninth *Reports*, he notes Arthur's reign as in 516, describing the scope of *The Mirrour* but perhaps relying on histories of William of Malmesbury or Geoffrey de Monmouth, which he owned. Malory's *Le Morte D'Arthur* had been printed by Caxton in 1485, but Coke did not list it in his library. For more on the origins of the Arthurian legends, see Thomas Malory, *Le Morte Darthur: The Winchester Manuscript,* Helen Cooper, ed., Oxford: Oxford University Press, 1998.

Kings of the English, 927–1066

Æthelstan	927–939
Edmund I	939–946
Eadred	946–955
Eadwig	955–959
Edgar I	959–July 975
Edward I the Martyr	975–978
Æthelred II the Unready	978–1013
Swein (Swegn) Forkbeard	1013–1014
Æthelred II (again)	1014–1016
Edmund II Ironside	1016
Cnut	1016–1035
Harthacnut & Harold	1035–1037
Harold I Harefoot	1037–1040
Harthacnut	1040–1042
Edward II the Confessor	1042–1066
Harold II Godwinesson	1066
Edgar II the Ætheling	not crowned

Then ruled by Normans.

Regnal Years, from the Conquest to 1154

William I of Normandy (the Conqueror)

Regnal Year	Begins A.D.
1 Wil. 1	Dec. 25, 1066
2 Wil. 1	Dec. 25, 1067
3 Wil. 1	Dec. 25, 1068
4 Wil. 1	Dec. 25, 1069
5 Wil. 1	Dec. 25, 1070
6 Wil. 1	Dec. 25, 1071
7 Wil. 1	Dec. 25, 1072
8 Wil. 1	Dec. 25, 1073
9 Wil. 1	Dec. 25, 1074
10 Wil. 1	Dec. 25, 1075
11 Wil. 1	Dec. 25, 1076
12 Wil. 1	Dec. 25, 1077
13 Wil. 1	Dec. 25, 1078
14 Wil. 1	Dec. 25, 1079
15 Wil. 1	Dec. 25, 1080
16 Wil. 1	Dec. 25, 1081
17 Wil. 1	Dec. 25, 1082
18 Wil. 1	Dec. 25, 1083
19 Wil. 1	Dec. 25, 1084
20 Wil. 1	Dec. 25, 1085
21 Wil. 1	Dec. 25, 1086

William II (Rufus)

Regnal Year	Begins A.D.
1 Wil. 2	Sep. 26, 1087
2 Wil. 2	Sep. 26, 1088
3 Wil. 2	Sep. 26, 1089
4 Wil. 2	Sep. 26, 1090
5 Wil. 2	Sep. 26, 1091
6 Wil. 2	Sep. 26, 1092
7 Wil. 2	Sep. 26, 1093
8 Wil. 2	Sep. 26, 1094
9 Wil. 2	Sep. 26, 1095

10 Wil. 2	Sep. 26, 1096
11 Wil. 2	Sep. 26, 1097
12 Wil. 2	Sep. 26, 1098
13 Wil. 2	Sep. 26, 1099

Henry I

Regnal Year	Begins A.D.
1 Hen. 1	Aug. 5, 1100
2 Hen. 1	Aug. 5, 1101
3 Hen. 1	Aug. 5, 1102
4 Hen. 1	Aug. 5, 1103
5 Hen. 1	Aug. 5, 1104
6 Hen. 1	Aug. 5, 1105
7 Hen. 1	Aug. 5, 1106
8 Hen. 1	Aug. 5, 1107
9 Hen. 1	Aug. 5, 1108
10 Hen. 1	Aug. 5, 1109
11 Hen. 1	Aug. 5, 1110
12 Hen. 1	Aug. 5, 1111
13 Hen. 1	Aug. 5, 1112
14 Hen. 1	Aug. 5, 1113
15 Hen. 1	Aug. 5, 1114
16 Hen. 1	Aug. 5, 1115
17 Hen. 1	Aug. 5, 1116
18 Hen. 1	Aug. 5, 1117
19 Hen. 1	Aug. 5, 1118
20 Hen. 1	Aug. 5, 1119
21 Hen. 1	Aug. 5, 1120
22 Hen. 1	Aug. 5, 1121
23 Hen. 1	Aug. 5, 1122
24 Hen. 1	Aug. 5, 1123
25 Hen. 1	Aug. 5, 1124
26 Hen. 1	Aug. 5, 1125
27 Hen. 1	Aug. 5, 1126
28 Hen. 1	Aug. 5, 1127
29 Hen. 1	Aug. 5, 1128
30 Hen. 1	Aug. 5, 1129
31 Hen. 1	Aug. 5, 1130
32 Hen. 1	Aug. 5, 1131

33 Hen. 1	Aug. 5, 1132
34 Hen. 1	Aug. 5, 1133
35 Hen. 1	Aug. 5, 1134
36 Hen. 1	Aug. 5, 1135

Stephen

Regnal Year	Begins A.D.
1 Steph.	Dec. 22, 1135
2 Steph.	Dec. 22, 1136
3 Steph.	Dec. 22, 1137
4 Steph.	Dec. 22, 1138
5 Steph.	Dec. 22, 1139
6 Steph.	Dec. 22, 1140
7 Steph.	Dec. 22, 1141
8 Steph.	Dec. 22, 1142
9 Steph.	Dec. 22, 1143
10 Steph.	Dec. 22, 1144
11 Steph.	Dec. 22, 1145
12 Steph.	Dec. 22, 1146
13 Steph.	Dec. 22, 1147
14 Steph.	Dec. 22, 1148
15 Steph.	Dec. 22, 1149
16 Steph.	Dec. 22, 1150
17 Steph.	Dec. 22, 1151
18 Steph.	Dec. 22, 1152
19 Steph.	Dec. 22, 1153

Regnal Years, from their Regularization, Commencing 1154, to 1648

Henry II

Regnal Year	Begins A.D.
1 Hen. 2	Dec. 19, 1154
2 Hen. 2	Dec. 19, 1155
3 Hen. 2	Dec. 19, 1156
4 Hen. 2	Dec. 19, 1157

5 Hen. 2	Dec. 19, 1158
6 Hen. 2	Dec. 19, 1159
7 Hen. 2	Dec. 19, 1160
8 Hen. 2	Dec. 19, 1161
9 Hen. 2	Dec. 19, 1162
10 Hen. 2	Dec. 19, 1163
11 Hen. 2	Dec. 19, 1164
12 Hen. 2	Dec. 19, 1165
13 Hen. 2	Dec. 19, 1166
14 Hen. 2	Dec. 19, 1167
15 Hen. 2	Dec. 19, 1168
16 Hen. 2	Dec. 19, 1169
17 Hen. 2	Dec. 19, 1170
18 Hen. 2	Dec. 19, 1171
19 Hen. 2	Dec. 19, 1172
20 Hen. 2	Dec. 19, 1173
21 Hen. 2	Dec. 19, 1174
22 Hen. 2	Dec. 19, 1175
23 Hen. 2	Dec. 19, 1176
24 Hen. 2	Dec. 19, 1177
25 Hen. 2	Dec. 19, 1178
26 Hen. 2	Dec. 19, 1179
27 Hen. 2	Dec. 19, 1180
28 Hen. 2	Dec. 19, 1181
29 Hen. 2	Dec. 19, 1182
30 Hen. 2	Dec. 19, 1183
31 Hen. 2	Dec. 19, 1184
32 Hen. 2	Dec. 19, 1185
33 Hen. 2	Dec. 19, 1186
34 Hen. 2	Dec. 19, 1187
35 Hen. 2	Dec. 19, 1188

Richard I

Regnal Year	Begins A.D.
1 Ric. 1	Sep. 3, 1189
2 Ric. 1	Sep. 3, 1190
3 Ric. 1	Sep. 3, 1191

4 Ric. 1	Sep. 3, 1192
5 Ric. 1	Sep. 3, 1193
6 Ric. 1	Sep. 3, 1194
7 Ric. 1	Sep. 3, 1195
8 Ric. 1	Sep. 3, 1196
9 Ric. 1	Sep. 3, 1197
10 Ric. 1	Sep. 3, 1198

John

Regnal Year	Begins A.D.
1 John	May 27, 1199
2 John	May 18, 1200
3 John	May 3, 1201
4 John	May 23, 1202
5 John	May 15, 1203
6 John	June 3, 1204
7 John	May 19, 1205
8 John	May 11, 1206
9 John	May 31, 1207
10 John	May 15, 1208
11 John	May 7, 1209
12 John	May 27, 1210
13 John	May 12, 1211
14 John	May 3, 1212
15 John	May 23, 1213
16 John	May 8, 1214
17 John	May 28, 1215
18 John	May 19, 1216

Henry III

Regnal Year	Begins A.D.
1 Hen. 3	Oct. 28, 1216
2 Hen. 3	Oct. 28, 1217
3 Hen. 3	Oct. 28, 1218
4 Hen. 3	Oct. 28, 1219

5 Hen. 3	Oct. 28, 1220
6 Hen. 3	Oct. 28, 1221
7 Hen. 3	Oct. 28, 1222
8 Hen. 3	Oct. 28, 1223
9 Hen. 3	Oct. 28, 1224
10 Hen. 3	Oct. 28, 1225
11 Hen. 3	Oct. 28, 1226
12 Hen. 3	Oct. 28, 1227
13 Hen. 3	Oct. 28, 1228
14 Hen. 3	Oct. 28, 1229
15 Hen. 3	Oct. 28, 1230
16 Hen. 3	Oct. 28, 1231
17 Hen. 3	Oct. 28, 1232
18 Hen. 3	Oct. 28, 1233
19 Hen. 3	Oct. 28, 1234
20 Hen. 3	Oct. 28, 1235
21 Hen. 3	Oct. 28, 1236
22 Hen. 3	Oct. 28, 1237
23 Hen. 3	Oct. 28, 1238
24 Hen. 3	Oct. 28, 1239
25 Hen. 3	Oct. 28, 1240
26 Hen. 3	Oct. 28, 1241
27 Hen. 3	Oct. 28, 1242
28 Hen. 3	Oct. 28, 1243
29 Hen. 3	Oct. 28, 1244
30 Hen. 3	Oct. 28, 1245
31 Hen. 3	Oct. 28, 1246
32 Hen. 3	Oct. 28, 1247
33 Hen. 3	Oct. 28, 1248
34 Hen. 3	Oct. 28, 1249
35 Hen. 3	Oct. 28, 1250
36 Hen. 3	Oct. 28, 1251
37 Hen. 3	Oct. 28, 1252
38 Hen. 3	Oct. 28, 1253
39 Hen. 3	Oct. 28, 1254
40 Hen. 3	Oct. 28, 1255
41 Hen. 3	Oct. 28, 1256
42 Hen. 3	Oct. 28, 1257
43 Hen. 3	Oct. 28, 1258

44 Hen. 3	Oct. 28, 1259
45 Hen. 3	Oct. 28, 1260
46 Hen. 3	Oct. 28, 1261
47 Hen. 3	Oct. 28, 1262
48 Hen. 3	Oct. 28, 1263
49 Hen. 3	Oct. 28, 1264
50 Hen. 3	Oct. 28, 1265
51 Hen. 3	Oct. 28, 1266
52 Hen. 3	Oct. 28, 1267
53 Hen. 3	Oct. 28, 1268
54 Hen. 3	Oct. 28, 1269
55 Hen. 3	Oct. 28, 1270
56 Hen. 3	Oct. 28, 1271
57 Hen. 3	Oct. 28, 1272

Edward I

Regnal Year	Begins A.D.
1 Edw. 1	Nov. 20, 1272
2 Edw. 1	Nov. 20, 1273
3 Edw. 1	Nov. 20, 1274
4 Edw. 1	Nov. 20, 1275
5 Edw. 1	Nov. 20, 1276
6 Edw. 1	Nov. 20, 1277
7 Edw. 1	Nov. 20, 1278
8 Edw. 1	Nov. 20, 1279
9 Edw. 1	Nov. 20, 1280
10 Edw. 1	Nov. 20, 1281
11 Edw. 1	Nov. 20, 1282
12 Edw. 1	Nov. 20, 1283
13 Edw. 1	Nov. 20, 1284
14 Edw. 1	Nov. 20, 1285
15 Edw. 1	Nov. 20, 1286
16 Edw. 1	Nov. 20, 1287
17 Edw. 1	Nov. 20, 1288
18 Edw. 1	Nov. 20, 1289
19 Edw. 1	Nov. 20, 1290
20 Edw. 1	Nov. 20, 1291

21 Edw. 1	Nov. 20, 1292
22 Edw. 1	Nov. 20, 1293
23 Edw. 1	Nov. 20, 1294
24 Edw. 1	Nov. 20, 1295
25 Edw. 1	Nov. 20, 1296
26 Edw. 1	Nov. 20, 1297
27 Edw. 1	Nov. 20, 1298
28 Edw. 1	Nov. 20, 1299
29 Edw. 1	Nov. 20, 1300
30 Edw. 1	Nov. 20, 1301
31 Edw. 1	Nov. 20, 1302
32 Edw. 1	Nov. 20, 1303
33 Edw. 1	Nov. 20, 1304
34 Edw. 1	Nov. 20, 1305
35 Edw. 1	Nov. 20, 1306

Edward II

Regnal Year	Begins A.D.
1 Edw. 2	July 8, 1307
2 Edw. 2	July 8, 1308
3 Edw. 2	July 8, 1309
4 Edw. 2	July 8, 1310
5 Edw. 2	July 8, 1311
6 Edw. 2	July 8, 1312
7 Edw. 2	July 8, 1313
8 Edw. 2	July 8, 1314
9 Edw. 2	July 8, 1315
10 Edw. 2	July 8, 1316
11 Edw. 2	July 8, 1317
12 Edw. 2	July 8, 1318
13 Edw. 2	July 8, 1319
14 Edw. 2	July 8, 1320
15 Edw. 2	July 8, 1321
16 Edw. 2	July 8, 1322
17 Edw. 2	July 8, 1323
18 Edw. 2	July 8, 1324
19 Edw. 2	July 8, 1325
20 Edw. 2	July 8, 1326

Edward III

Regnal Year	Begins A.D.
1 Edw. 3	Jan. 25, 1327
2 Edw. 3	Jan. 25, 1328
3 Edw. 3	Jan. 25, 1329
4 Edw. 3	Jan. 25, 1330
5 Edw. 3	Jan. 25, 1331
6 Edw. 3	Jan. 25, 1332
7 Edw. 3	Jan. 25, 1333
8 Edw. 3	Jan. 25, 1334
9 Edw. 3	Jan. 25, 1335
10 Edw. 3	Jan. 25, 1336
11 Edw. 3	Jan. 25, 1337
12 Edw. 3	Jan. 25, 1338
13 Edw. 3	Jan. 25, 1339
14 Edw. 3	Jan. 25, 1340
15 Edw. 3	Jan. 25, 1341
16 Edw. 3	Jan. 25, 1342
17 Edw. 3	Jan. 25, 1343
18 Edw. 3	Jan. 25, 1344
19 Edw. 3	Jan. 25, 1345
20 Edw. 3	Jan. 25, 1346
21 Edw. 3	Jan. 25, 1347
22 Edw. 3	Jan. 25, 1348
23 Edw. 3	Jan. 25, 1349
24 Edw. 3	Jan. 25, 1350
25 Edw. 3	Jan. 25, 1351
26 Edw. 3	Jan. 25, 1352
27 Edw. 3	Jan. 25, 1353
28 Edw. 3	Jan. 25, 1354
29 Edw. 3	Jan. 25, 1355
30 Edw. 3	Jan. 25, 1356
31 Edw. 3	Jan. 25, 1357
32 Edw. 3	Jan. 25, 1358
33 Edw. 3	Jan. 25, 1359
34 Edw. 3	Jan. 25, 1360
35 Edw. 3	Jan. 25, 1361
36 Edw. 3	Jan. 25, 1362

37 Edw. 3	Jan. 25, 1363
38 Edw. 3	Jan. 25, 1364
39 Edw. 3	Jan. 25, 1365
40 Edw. 3	Jan. 25, 1366
41 Edw. 3	Jan. 25, 1367
42 Edw. 3	Jan. 25, 1368
43 Edw. 3	Jan. 25, 1369
44 Edw. 3	Jan. 25, 1370
45 Edw. 3	Jan. 25, 1371
46 Edw. 3	Jan. 25, 1372
47 Edw. 3	Jan. 25, 1373
48 Edw. 3	Jan. 25, 1374
49 Edw. 3	Jan. 25, 1375
50 Edw. 3	Jan. 25, 1376
51 Edw. 3	Jan. 25, 1377

Richard II

Regnal Year	Begins A.D.
1 Ric. 2	June 22, 1377
2 Ric. 2	June 22, 1378
3 Ric. 2	June 22, 1379
4 Ric. 2	June 22, 1380
5 Ric. 2	June 22, 1381
6 Ric. 2	June 22, 1382
7 Ric. 2	June 22, 1383
8 Ric. 2	June 22, 1384
9 Ric. 2	June 22, 1385
10 Ric. 2	June 22, 1386
11 Ric. 2	June 22, 1387
12 Ric. 2	June 22, 1388
13 Ric. 2	June 22, 1389
14 Ric. 2	June 22, 1390
15 Ric. 2	June 22, 1391
16 Ric. 2	June 22, 1392
17 Ric. 2	June 22, 1393
18 Ric. 2	June 22, 1394
19 Ric. 2	June 22, 1395
20 Ric. 2	June 22, 1396
21 Ric. 2	June 22, 1397

22 Ric. 2	June 22, 1398
23 Ric. 2	June 22, 1399

Henry IV

Regnal Year	Begins A.D.
1 Hen. 4	Sep. 30, 1399
2 Hen. 4	Sep. 30, 1400
3 Hen. 4	Sep. 30, 1401
4 Hen. 4	Sep. 30, 1402
5 Hen. 4	Sep. 30, 1403
6 Hen. 4	Sep. 30, 1404
7 Hen. 4	Sep. 30, 1405
8 Hen. 4	Sep. 30, 1406
9 Hen. 4	Sep. 30, 1407
10 Hen. 4	Sep. 30, 1408
11 Hen. 4	Sep. 30, 1409
12 Hen. 4	Sep. 30, 1410
13 Hen. 4	Sep. 30, 1411
14 Hen. 4	Sep. 30, 1412

Henry V

Regnal Year	Begins A.D.
1 Hen. 5	March 21, 1413
2 Hen. 5	March 21, 1414
3 Hen. 5	March 21, 1415
4 Hen. 5	March 21, 1416
5 Hen. 5	March 21, 1417
6 Hen. 5	March 21, 1418
7 Hen. 5	March 21, 1419
8 Hen. 5	March 21, 1420
9 Hen. 5	March 21, 1421
10 Hen. 5	March 21, 1422

Henry VI

Regnal Year	Begins A.D.
1 Hen. 6	Sep. 1, 1422
2 Hen. 6	Sep. 1, 1423

3 Hen. 6	Sep. 1, 1424
4 Hen. 6	Sep. 1, 1425
5 Hen. 6	Sep. 1, 1426
6 Hen. 6	Sep. 1, 1427
7 Hen. 6	Sep. 1, 1428
8 Hen. 6	Sep. 1, 1429
9 Hen. 6	Sep. 1, 1430
10 Hen. 6	Sep. 1, 1431
11 Hen. 6	Sep. 1, 1432
12 Hen. 6	Sep. 1, 1433
13 Hen. 6	Sep. 1, 1434
14 Hen. 6	Sep. 1, 1435
15 Hen. 6	Sep. 1, 1436
16 Hen. 6	Sep. 1, 1437
17 Hen. 6	Sep. 1, 1438
18 Hen. 6	Sep. 1, 1439
19 Hen. 6	Sep. 1, 1440
20 Hen. 6	Sep. 1, 1441
21 Hen. 6	Sep. 1, 1442
22 Hen. 6	Sep. 1, 1443
23 Hen. 6	Sep. 1, 1444
24 Hen. 6	Sep. 1, 1445
25 Hen. 6	Sep. 1, 1446
26 Hen. 6	Sep. 1, 1447
27 Hen. 6	Sep. 1, 1448
28 Hen. 6	Sep. 1, 1449
29 Hen. 6	Sep. 1, 1450
30 Hen. 6	Sep. 1, 1451
31 Hen. 6	Sep. 1, 1452
32 Hen. 6	Sep. 1, 1453
33 Hen. 6	Sep. 1, 1454
34 Hen. 6	Sep. 1, 1455
35 Hen. 6	Sep. 1, 1456
36 Hen. 6	Sep. 1, 1457
37 Hen. 6	Sep. 1, 1458
38 Hen. 6	Sep. 1, 1459
39 Hen. 6	Sep. 1, 1460

following his restoration:

| 49 Hen. 6 | Sep.–Oct. 1470 |

Edward IV

Regnal Year	Begins A.D.
1 Edw. 4	March 4, 1461
2 Edw. 4	March 4, 1462
3 Edw. 4	March 4, 1463
4 Edw. 4	March 4, 1464
5 Edw. 4	March 4, 1465
6 Edw. 4	March 4, 1466
7 Edw. 4	March 4, 1467
8 Edw. 4	March 4, 1468
9 Edw. 4	March 4, 1469
10 Edw. 4	March 4, 1470
11 Edw. 4	March 4, 1471
12 Edw. 4	March 4, 1472
13 Edw. 4	March 4, 1473
14 Edw. 4	March 4, 1474
15 Edw. 4	March 4, 1475
16 Edw. 4	March 4, 1476
17 Edw. 4	March 4, 1477
18 Edw. 4	March 4, 1478
19 Edw. 4	March 4, 1479
20 Edw. 4	March 4, 1480
21 Edw. 4	March 4, 1481
22 Edw. 4	March 4, 1482
23 Edw. 4	March 4, 1483

Edward V

Regnal Year	Begins A.D.
1 Edw. 5	April 9, 1483

Richard III

Regnal Year	Begins A.D.
1 Ric. 3	June 26, 1483
2 Ric. 3	June 26, 1484
3 Ric. 3	June 26, 1485

Henry VII

Regnal Year	Begins A.D.
1 Hen. 7	Aug. 21, 1485
2 Hen. 7	Aug. 22, 1486
3 Hen. 7	Aug. 22, 1487
4 Hen. 7	Aug. 22, 1488
5 Hen. 7	Aug. 22, 1489
6 Hen. 7	Aug. 22, 1490
7 Hen. 7	Aug. 22, 1491
8 Hen. 7	Aug. 22, 1492
9 Hen. 7	Aug. 22, 1493
10 Hen. 7	Aug. 22, 1494
11 Hen. 7	Aug. 22, 1495
12 Hen. 7	Aug. 22, 1496
13 Hen. 7	Aug. 22, 1497
14 Hen. 7	Aug. 22, 1498
15 Hen. 7	Aug. 22, 1499
16 Hen. 7	Aug. 22, 1500
17 Hen. 7	Aug. 22, 1501
18 Hen. 7	Aug. 22, 1502
19 Hen. 7	Aug. 22, 1503
20 Hen. 7	Aug. 22, 1504
21 Hen. 7	Aug. 22, 1505
22 Hen. 7	Aug. 22, 1506
23 Hen. 7	Aug. 22, 1507
24 Hen. 7	Aug. 22, 1508

Henry VIII

Regnal Year	Begins A.D.
1 Hen. 8	Apr. 22, 1509
2 Hen. 8	Apr. 22, 1510
3 Hen. 8	Apr. 22, 1511
4 Hen. 8	Apr. 22, 1512
5 Hen. 8	Apr. 22, 1513
6 Hen. 8	Apr. 22, 1514
7 Hen. 8	Apr. 22, 1515
8 Hen. 8	Apr. 22, 1516

9 Hen. 8	Apr. 22, 1517
10 Hen. 8	Apr. 22, 1518
11 Hen. 8	Apr. 22, 1519
12 Hen. 8	Apr. 22, 1520
13 Hen. 8	Apr. 22, 1521
14 Hen. 8	Apr. 22, 1522
15 Hen. 8	Apr. 22, 1523
16 Hen. 8	Apr. 22, 1524
17 Hen. 8	Apr. 22, 1525
18 Hen. 8	Apr. 22, 1526
19 Hen. 8	Apr. 22, 1527
20 Hen. 8	Apr. 22, 1528
21 Hen. 8	Apr. 22, 1529
22 Hen. 8	Apr. 22, 1530
23 Hen. 8	Apr. 22, 1531
24 Hen. 8	Apr. 22, 1532
25 Hen. 8	Apr. 22, 1533
26 Hen. 8	Apr. 22, 1534
27 Hen. 8	Apr. 22, 1535
28 Hen. 8	Apr. 22, 1536
29 Hen. 8	Apr. 22, 1537
30 Hen. 8	Apr. 22, 1538
31 Hen. 8	Apr. 22, 1539
32 Hen. 8	Apr. 22, 1540
33 Hen. 8	Apr. 22, 1541
34 Hen. 8	Apr. 22, 1542
35 Hen. 8	Apr. 22, 1543
36 Hen. 8	Apr. 22, 1544
37 Hen. 8	Apr. 22, 1545
38 Hen. 8	Apr. 22, 1546

Edward VI

Regnal Year	Begins A.D.
1 Edw. 7	Jan. 28, 1547
2 Edw. 7	Jan. 28, 1548
3 Edw. 7	Jan. 28, 1549
4 Edw. 7	Jan. 28, 1550
5 Edw. 7	Jan. 28, 1551

6 Edw. 7	Jan. 28, 1552
7 Edw. 7	Jan. 28, 1553

Jane

Regnal Year	Begins A.D.
1 Jane	July 6, 1553

Mary

Regnal Year	Begins A.D.
1 Mar.	July 19, 1553
2 Mar.	July 6, 1554

Philip and Mary

Regnal Year	Begins A.D.
1&2 P.&M.	July 25, 1554
1&3 P.&M.	July 6, 1555
2&3 P.&M.	July 25, 1555
2&4 P.&M.	July 6, 1556
3&4 P.&M.	July 25, 1556
3&5 P.&M.	July 6, 1557
4&5 P.&M.	July 25, 1557
4&6 P.&M.	July 6, 1558
5&6 P.&M.	July 25, 1558

Elizabeth I

Regnal Year	Begins A.D.
1 Eliz. 1	Nov. 17, 1558
2 Eliz. 1	Nov. 17, 1559
3 Eliz. 1	Nov. 17, 1560
4 Eliz. 1	Nov. 17, 1561
5 Eliz. 1	Nov. 17, 1562
6 Eliz. 1	Nov. 17, 1563
7 Eliz. 1	Nov. 17, 1564
8 Eliz. 1	Nov. 17, 1565
9 Eliz. 1	Nov. 17, 1566
10 Eliz. 1	Nov. 17, 1567

11 Eliz. 1	Nov. 17, 1568
12 Eliz. 1	Nov. 17, 1569
13 Eliz. 1	Nov. 17, 1570
14 Eliz. 1	Nov. 17, 1571
15 Eliz. 1	Nov. 17, 1572
16 Eliz. 1	Nov. 17, 1573
17 Eliz. 1	Nov. 17, 1574
18 Eliz. 1	Nov. 17, 1575
19 Eliz. 1	Nov. 17, 1576
20 Eliz. 1	Nov. 17, 1577
21 Eliz. 1	Nov. 17, 1578
22 Eliz. 1	Nov. 17, 1579
23 Eliz. 1	Nov. 17, 1580
24 Eliz. 1	Nov. 17, 1581
25 Eliz. 1	Nov. 17, 1582
26 Eliz. 1	Nov. 17, 1583
27 Eliz. 1	Nov. 17, 1584
28 Eliz. 1	Nov. 17, 1585
29 Eliz. 1	Nov. 17, 1586
30 Eliz. 1	Nov. 17, 1587
31 Eliz. 1	Nov. 17, 1588
32 Eliz. 1	Nov. 17, 1589
33 Eliz. 1	Nov. 17, 1590
34 Eliz. 1	Nov. 17, 1591
35 Eliz. 1	Nov. 17, 1592
36 Eliz. 1	Nov. 17, 1593
37 Eliz. 1	Nov. 17, 1594
38 Eliz. 1	Nov. 17, 1595
39 Eliz. 1	Nov. 17, 1596
40 Eliz. 1	Nov. 17, 1597
41 Eliz. 1	Nov. 17, 1598
42 Eliz. 1	Nov. 17, 1599
43 Eliz. 1	Nov. 17, 1600
44 Eliz. 1	Nov. 17, 1601
45 Eliz. 1	Nov. 17, 1602

James I

Regnal Year	Begins A.D.
1 Jac. 1	March 24, 1603
2 Jac. 1	March 24, 1604

3 Jac. 1	March 24, 1605
4 Jac. 1	March 24, 1606
5 Jac. 1	March 24, 1607
6 Jac. 1	March 24, 1608
7 Jac. 1	March 24, 1609
8 Jac. 1	March 24, 1610
9 Jac. 1	March 24, 1611
10 Jac. 1	March 24, 1612
11 Jac. 1	March 24, 1613
12 Jac. 1	March 24, 1614
13 Jac. 1	March 24, 1615
14 Jac. 1	March 24, 1616
15 Jac. 1	March 24, 1617
16 Jac. 1	March 24, 1618
17 Jac. 1	March 24, 1619
18 Jac. 1	March 24, 1620
19 Jac. 1	March 24, 1621
20 Jac. 1	March 24, 1622
21 Jac. 1	March 24, 1623
22 Jac. 1	March 24, 1624
23 Jac. 1	March 24, 1625

Charles I

Regnal Year	Begins A.D.
1 Caro. 1	March 27, 1625
2 Caro. 1	March 27, 1626
3 Caro. 1	March 27, 1627
4 Caro. 1	March 27, 1628
5 Caro. 1	March 27, 1629
6 Caro. 1	March 27, 1630
7 Caro. 1	March 27, 1631
8 Caro. 1	March 27, 1632
9 Caro. 1	March 27, 1633
10 Caro. 1	March 27, 1634
11 Caro. 1	March 27, 1635
12 Caro. 1	March 27, 1636
13 Caro. 1	March 27, 1637
14 Caro. 1	March 27, 1638

15 Caro. 1	March 27, 1639
16 Caro. 1	March 27, 1640
17 Caro. 1	March 27, 1641
18 Caro. 1	March 27, 1642
19 Caro. 1	March 27, 1643
20 Caro. 1	March 27, 1644
21 Caro. 1	March 27, 1645
22 Caro. 1	March 27, 1646
23 Caro. 1	March 27, 1647
24 Caro. 1	March 27, 1648

Index

Littleton, Sir William, 581, 582

lives, no liability in acts to save, 477–78

loans
commission of, 1236
knights' loans, Charles I's exaction of. *See* The Five Knights' Case; Petition of Right

local ligeance, 177, 179–80, 183–88

Locke, John, xxx, lxv, lxviii

Lockton, John, 999

Lofield and Clun's Case, 334

logic as used by Littleton, 583

Lollards, 465–71, 1036, 1332

London
assassination of Duke of Buckingham, celebration of, lxiv
the Chamberlain of London's Case, 131–33
College of Physicians' right to control practice of medicine in (Dr. Bonham's Case), l, lvi, lxix, 264–83, 1351–52
Common Council, 1266
Essex's attempt to rally people of, xlii
imprisonment, powers of, 1211
king's right to restrict building by proclamation in, 486–90
Magna Carta, confirmation of liberties by, 797–98
plague, xliii, lxii
Recorder of London, Coke elected as, xxxvii
wards determined by ancient wall of, 1052
water supply, xxxv

Long Parliament (1640), lxvi

Lopez, Roderigo, xl, 539

Lord President of the North, li

Lord President of Wales, xlvii, xlviii–xlix, li

Lord President of York, xlvii, xlviii–xlix

Lords. *See* House of Lords; nobility

Lords Lieutenant, 1231–32, 1274–75

lost items, finding by witchcraft, 1045

love, unlawful, witchcraft used to promote, 1046

Lowe, Leonard (Leonard Lowe's Case), 332–33

Lumbard, Octavian, 10, 14

Lumley, Lord (Lord Lumley's Case), 1004

Lusheburgh, 989

Lutrell's Case, 1355

Lycophoron, 66

Lyons' Inn, xxxv, 75, 580

Machiavelli, Nicolo, 1226

MacKalley's (McKalley's) Case, 314–25, 1355

Madison, James, xxxi

Magdalen College, Cambridge Case, 387–88

magistrates, 99–101

Magna Carta, xxvii, xxx, lix, lxiii, lxv, lxix. *See also* Petition of Right
advowsons, 894
amercement of free men, 812–16
arrests, 861–68
bail, 869
barons, 763–75
bibliographical material, 1363–64
bridges and banks, 816–18
case law in *Reports,* cited in, 134, 244, 245, 248, 249, 254, 405, 415, 443–44, 472
castle-guard, knights holding land by, 825–26

This book is set in Adobe Garamond, a modern adaptation by Robert Slimbach of the typeface originally cut around 1540 by the French typographer and printer Claude Garamond. The Garamond face, with its small lowercase height and restrained contrast between thick and thin strokes, is a classic "old-style" face and has long been one of the most influential and widely used typefaces.

Printed on paper that is acid free and meets the requirements of the American National Standard for Permanence of Paper for Printed Library Materials, z39.48-1992. ⊗

Book design by Erin Kirk New, Watkinsville, Georgia
Typography by Impressions Book and Journal Services, Inc., Madison, Wisconsin
Printed and bound by Worzalla Publishing Company, Stevens Point, Wisconsin